THE ELDRITCH EVOLA
…& OTHERS

TRADITIONALIST MEDITATIONS ON LITERATURE, ART, & CULTURE

by

JAMES J. O'MEARA

EDITED BY GREG JOHNSON

Counter-Currents Publishing Ltd.
San Francisco
2014

Cover design by Kevin I. Slaughter

Published in the United States by
COUNTER-CURRENTS PUBLISHING LTD.
P.O. Box 22638
San Francisco, CA 94122
USA
http://www.counter-currents.com/

Hardcover ISBN: 978-1-935965-69-5
Paperback ISBN: 978-1-935965-70-1
E-book ISBN: 978-1-935965-71-8

Library of Congress Cataloging-in-Publication Data

O'Meara, James J., 1956-
  The Eldritch Evola . . . & others : traditionalist meditations on litera-
ture, art & culture / by James J. O'Meara ; edited by Greg Johnson.
     1 online resource.
  Includes bibliographical references and index.
  Summary: "The Eldritch Evola . . . collects a number of essays by
James J. O'Meara in which he applies his Traditionalist, New Right,
and masculinist analysis to such figures as Julius Evola, H. P. Love-
craft, Henry James, Thorstein Veblen, Ralph Adams Cram, Richard
Wagner, Owen Wister, Olaf Stapledon, Harry Partch, Scott Walker,
Andy Nowicki, and Graham Harman" -- Provided by publisher.
  Description based on print version record and CIP data provided by
publisher; resource not viewed.
  ISBN 978-1-935965-71-8 (epub) -- ISBN 978-1-935965-69-5 (hardcover
: alk. paper)
 1. Literature and society. 2. Arts and society. 3. Popular culture. I.
Johnson, Greg, 1971- editor. II. Title. III. Title: Traditionalist medita-
tions on literature, art & culture.

PN51
809'.93358--dc23

                                      2013019932

CONTENTS

For

Ricky Devereaux
1954–?

The Boy Next Door

PREFACE

"Writing was perdifficult for him; and he detested it; but his stars forced him to write; and the overcoming of difficulties was not unpleasant."

> —Fr. Rolfe (Baron Corvo), *Nicolas Crabbe or The One and the Many*

"Well, I'm not going to leave you alone. I want you to get mad!"

> —Howard Beale, "The Mad Prophet of the Airwaves," *Network*

It had to happen.

After the release of my first book, or, more properly, first collection of essays, late last year; after the ecstatic and dismayed reviews, the tumultuous interviews, the viral internet campaigns, the flame wars, and yes, regretfully, the loss of so many brave American boys in the subsequent Marrakech Riots so unfairly, yet understandably, laid at my doorstep, another volume was inevitable.

The People, the People had spoken! And while normally I say The People be damned, ungrateful, ignorant wretches that they are, I was persuaded, or prevailed upon to consider, that this time *vox populi* was indeed *vox dei*.

I clearly recall the night the decision was made, "the die it was cast"; for I beheld on my TV screen the return of the *Gilmore Girls*! Sure, it was a different, even crappier cable network, and there was a young woman actually named "Sutton" pretending to be Lauren Graham, and doing a damn'd fine job of it (I imagine the painful meeting with the network execs shouting "I've got a thousand actresses that can give me that Gilmore Girl feeling!"), and many other actors were missing, and the rest were obstinately pretending to be entirely different people, and above all, what had kept me away so long, the title had been changed to the cringingly awful *Bunheads*, but otherwise it was all there, what really mattered: the smug look of unearned superiority, the knowing yet strangely irrelevant pop culture references, the endless, run-on dialogue that was maddeningly never really *about* what it was supposedly about (the "gap," as Graham Harman will say, in a book reviewed within this collection), it was all *there* again, and so too was the need for another book—to strike another blow!

> Whenever and wherever there is a decline of righteousness, O descendant of Bharata, and a rise of unrighteousness, at that time I descend Myself.
>
> —Bhagavad Gita, 4.7

The wheel had turned! The stars were once more aligned, in that blasphemously suggestive way.

The time had come to brave the creaking service elevator of The Glove Factory and slowly descend to the surface world once more, there to deliver a strangely, damnably *wet* brown paper-wrapped package to the waiting, hooded figured known only as "The Publisher."

It was the book you now hold in your hands.

Constant Readers will notice that this collection, like the first, spans quite a—as the kids say—"gamut." You will find the very first pieces that graced the virtual pages of the Counter-Currents website, as well as some that appeared after the last book, and even, through some rip in the space-time continuum, at least one that hasn't appeared yet—but which will surely appear by the time this collection gets to print. There's something for the whole Family, Mom and Dad, Buddy and Sis, and even Charlie.

Perhaps now is the time, and perhaps this is the place, to say a few words about that vexed and vexing topic, "why I write." Though well intentioned, it is a question that evokes the same wry response "William Lee," the narrator of William Burroughs' *Junkie* and the author's *Doppelgänger*, gives to the inevitable question, "Mr. Lee, why do you take drugs?" I do not write in order to save the world, or change the world, or make anyone better or happier, although that would be nice. I write because, like the character in Fritz Lang's *M*, my head is, from time to time, usually in the too-early morning, full of voices and ideas, and if I am to escape them, then I must . . . write. If, like him, I had to use a stubby pencil on a window sill, rather than the free word processor bundled into Windows (not even Word!) and address myself to the local newspapers rather than the World Wide Web, I'd never have produced all this that follows here; on the other hand, if I lived back then, I might not have as much to write against.

And so, Dear, Constant Reader, it is time for us to part. As a wise man once said, "You go your way, and I'll go mine; and if we meet, it's beautiful." According to a poster on the wall of Ricky Devereaux's basement dope den in 1968, that man's name was . . . Adolf Hitler. Whatever happened to that guy?

James J. O'Meara
Rust Belt, USA
March 3, 2014

ACKNOWLEDGEMENTS

Once again I must thank first Herr Professor Doktor Doktor Greg Johnson, B.A., M.A., PhD., D. Phil. *honoris causis*, *éminence grise*, *miglio fabro*, etc., etc., for suggesting, nay, demanding this new collection. Thanks also to Gwendolyn von Taunton, who was kind enough to select one of these pieces for the first issue of her fine new journal *Aristokratia*.

My numberless intellectual debts should be clear from what follows, but I have especially benefited, to the extent that I could remember them afterwards, from numerous *sake*-driven conversations with Collin Cleary, Jef Costello, and Derek Hawthorne—although Dr. Cleary did insist that my piece on Wagner was "absurd."

And a special thanks to all those Constant Readers, especially to those who, during a recent period of financial instability, made contributions to my blog, bought me books online, and otherwise kept me from taking the long ride on the Night Train to Mundo Fine.

"Black sheep, outcast, misfit, Ishmael
Every stranger each his own tale"

SRC, "Black Sheep"
Detroit, 1968

THE ELDRITCH EVOLA

"And thus, as a closer and still closer intimacy admitted me more unreservedly into the recesses of his spirit, the more bitterly did I perceive the futility of all attempt at cheering *a mind from which darkness, as if an inherent positive quality, poured forth upon all objects of the moral and physical universe, in one unceasing radiation of gloom.*"

— E. A. Poe, "The Fall of the House of Usher"

"Old Castro remembered bits of hideous legend that *paled the speculations of theosophists and made man and the world seem recent and transient indeed.* There had been aeons when other Things ruled on the earth, and They had had great cities. Remains of Them, he said the deathless Chinamen had told him, were still be found as Cyclopean stones on islands in the Pacific. They all died vast epochs of time before men came, but there were arts which could revive Them when the stars had come round again to the right positions in the cycle of eternity."

— H. P. Lovecraft, "The Call of Cthulhu"

"Of such great powers or beings there may be conceivably a survival . . . a survival of a hugely remote period *when . . . consciousness was manifested, perhaps, in shapes and forms long since withdrawn before the tide of advancing humanity . . . forms of which poetry and legend alone have caught a flying memory and called them gods,* monsters, mythical beings of all sorts and kinds."

— Algernon Blackwood

A little while ago, I decided to use up more of my enforced leisure by reading Part Two of Baron Evola's *Revolt Against the Modern World,* or at least the first few chapters, with an eye towards once and for all getting a straight picture of the various "ages" and "races" that constitute his take on Tradition, filtering René Guénon's model through the more historically oriented work of Herman Wirth and Co.[1]

Damned if I didn't start coming all over with fear and dread, and not just in my attic (if I had one), not unlike those that prevented me from reading completely through Guénon's *Reign of Quantity* until several false starts over 25 years.

This time I decided to try and analyze what this dread consisted in, and I think I've got it: By the time one reaches the farthest limits of recorded, or even archeologically validated history, *the worst has already happened*, and there's nothing you can do about it.

And is this not indeed the theme of "horror" fiction?

Now, I've never paid attention to the occasional "smart" comments about Traditionalism as reading like "science fiction," based largely on supposed borrowing from Theosophy. In fact, I agree with this guy, who makes a *modus tollens* out of the mockers' *modus ponens*:

What is one to do then with a writer of foresight, whose literacy and education remain indubitable, who nevertheless *serves up his social and political analysis, however trenchant it is, in the context of an alternate history, the details of which resemble the background of story by Lord Dunsany or Clark Ashton Smith?* I am strongly tempted to answer my own question in this way: That *perhaps we should begin by reassessing Dunsany and Smith*, especially Smith, whose tales of decadent remnant-societies — half-ruined, eroticized, brooding over a shored-up luxuriance, and succumbing to momentary appetite with fatalistic abandon — speak with powerful intuition to our actual circumstances. *I do not mean to say, however, that Evola is only metaphorically true, as though his work, like Smith's, were fiction.* I mean that Evola

---

[1] Julius Evola, *Revolt Against the Modern World*, trans. Guido Stucco (Rochester, Vt.: Inner Traditions, 1995). See also Evola's "My Explorations of Origins and Tradition," *The Path of Cinnabar: The Intellectual Autobiography of Julius Evola*, trans. Sergio Knipe (London: Arktos, 2009).

is truly true, on the order of one of Plato's "True Myths,"
no matter how much his truth disconcerts us.[2]

I'm ashamed to say I've never read more than one Clark Ashton Smith story, and that years ago in some Lovecraft Mythos
anthology, but I'm more inclined anyway to take this back to the
Master himself, Lovecraft. How much does Lovecraft resemble
Evola, and moreover, is this superficial, or is there a reason?

The answer may lie in Lovecraft's essay "Supernatural Horror in Literature": "The oldest and strongest emotion of mankind is fear, and the oldest and strongest kind of fear is fear of
the unknown."

In a 1927 letter to *Weird Tales* editor Farnsworth Wright,
Lovecraft writes: "I consider the touch of *cosmic outsideness—of
dim, shadowy non-terrestrial hints—*to be the characteristic feature
of my writing."

> Theosophists have guessed at the *awesome grandeur of the
> cosmic cycle wherein our world and human race form transient
> incidents.* They have hinted at strange survivals in terms
> which would freeze the blood if not masked by a bland
> optimism. *But it is not from them that there came the single
> glimpse of forbidden eons which chills me when I think of it and
> maddens me when I dream of it.*[3]

Lovecraft takes fear as his theme, and he knows that the
greatest fear is inspired not by ghoulies and gore but by the
dread of nameless eons. Nameless eons are the stock in trade of
Traditionalist cyclical cosmology.

It's no surprise that Michel Houellebecq, today's Prince of
Nihilism, gets it: "The human race will disappear. Other races
will appear and disappear in turn. The sky will become icy and
void, pierced by the feeble light of half-dead stars. Which will

---

[2] Thomas F. Bertonneau, "Against Nihilism: Julius Evola's 'Traditionalist' Critique of Modernity," http://www.counter-currents.com
/2010/12/against-nihilism-julius-evolas-traditionalist-critique-of-
modernity/

[3] H. P. Lovecraft, "The Call of Cthulhu."

also disappear. Everything will disappear."[4]

But surely Evola and Co. are not frivolous entertainers, but serious initiates. If Lovecraft seeks to inspire fear, does Evola, and if so, how is that connected to initiation?

We could try this: if Evola inspires new respect for the Lovecraftians, then what if we read Lovecraft as if he were Evola?

It was Alisdair Clarke who called my attention to *Polaria: The Gift of the White Stone* by W. H. Müller.[5] I've never seen more than a couple other references to it (such as this amused and bemused review by one Julianus[6]) and copies of the barely 200 page paperback seem to have become quite rare, fetching over $200.00 on Amazon.

Müller takes off, with all apparent sincerity, from the preposterous thesis that H. P. Lovecraft "was a Practicing Occultist and that the Lovecraft Circle was a group of High Adepts," despite overwhelming evidence, found in literally dozens of volumes of letters and innumerable personal reminiscences, to say nothing of S. T. Joshi's many works, of being a cast-iron materialist of the village atheist ilk. As Julianus says:

> The book itself is a Vast Muddle of Mystical Verbiage that draws on Sufism, Theosophy, Réne Guénon, Robert Graves, and others to create a bizarre Syncretic Symbolism from "Phonetic Encodings" in Lovecraft's work. The Linguistic Fog is comparable only to the work of Kenneth Grant, and it is truly strange that Herr Müller nowhere acknowledges his debt to the Typhonian Titan.[7]

Actually, in its preposterous thesis defended with po-faced sincerity by means of vast scholarship and word and letter mumbo-jumbo, as well as its overall atmosphere of occult doom,

---

[4] Michel Houellebecq, *H. P. Lovecraft: Against the World, Against Life,* trans. Dorna Khazeni, introduction by Stephen King (London: Gollancz, 2008).

[5] W. H. Müller, *Polaria: The Gift of the White Stone* (Las Vegas: Brotherhood of Life Books, 1997).

[6] http://hermetic.com/bkwyrm/readone.php?recordID=00124.004

[7] http://hermetic.com/bkwyrm/readone.php?recordID=00124.004

I was more put in mind of such works of Ariosophic fascism as Jorg Lanz von Liebenfels' *Theozoology*.

Never the less, there are some good bits, relevant to our theme; if Lovecraft's tales can be given an initiatic spin, then the connection with Evola becomes clearer:

> Lovecraft cloaked his profound esoteric insight in *an imagery of horror. . . . Thus it was given a subtle but clear initiatory nature.* Many feel attracted by Lovecraft's forceful imagery, but only a very few know the reason. Only those with a preparedness and already drawn toward the Threshold would be ready to delve into Lovecraft's work and recover from its depths the eonian Polar message.[8]

> Remember, "The oldest and strongest emotion of mankind is fear." For Fear read "initiation via experiencing the death of the ego and its world."

> Both ego-less animal existence and man's ego, which is but matrical sensory cognition, originate in the same Matrix of Dream. This must be transcended. It is Polar insight, the inward-looking way that leads out of this cyclic Matrix. *However, the man's ego, being the man-god, fears mystical dissolution, because it fears its "death." Only if "death" is realized as illusion by experiencing it mystically in life,* [perhaps by reading some "weird tales"] can essencification and spiritual unity be achieved. The ego fears "death" because it does not know that there is none. "Fear" is the sword the ego wields, yet its iron melts away in the black heat of Wisdom.

> In Lovecraft's stories the elements of decay and death prevail. *These are the emotional patterns of one approaching the seventh plane of the Threshold. The transformative Way across the Bridge of Fog, from animal-man to god-man, is painful.* Everyone claiming the contrary, is speaking with a Minotaurian voice. [Man-animals? Ruh-roh, here comes that Theo-

---

[8] Müller, *Polaria*, p. 113.

zoology again!]

The Way leads *through the Tomb* of the Individual toward the Emergence of the Entity. The same is applicable to humanity. *Saturn is throwing its charnel light toward this planet*. But the Pilgrim must know that Saturn is but the Threshold, not the Destination.[9]

The Minotaurian voice that Müller refers to is the voice that asserts the supremacy of the ego. It is the animal-man trapped in the labyrinth of ordinary, uninspired consciousness.[10]

Both Evola and Lovecraft also drew the same or similar immediate political conclusions, both under the influence of cycles, those of Guénon and Spengler, respectively:

> Lovecraft saw cultural decline as a slow process that spans 500 to 1000 years. He sought a system that could overcome the cyclical laws of decay, which was also the motivation of Fascism. Lovecraft believed it was possible to re-establish a new "equilibrium" over the course of 50 to 100 years, stating: "There is no need of worrying about civilization so long as the language and the general art tradition survives."[11]

(For the Fascist theme of regeneration or palingenesis, see Roger Griffin's *Modernism and Fascism*, reviewed here by Alisdair Clarke.[12])

Continuing that somewhat optimistic note, perhaps even ego death may not be so bad; in "Calling Cthulhu,"[13] Erik Davis de-

---

[9] Müller, *Polaria*, p. 113.

[10] Alisdair Clarke, "Ego Death, Destiny and Serpents in Germanic Mythology," http://aryanfuturism.blogspot.com/2006/11/ego-death-destiny-and-serpents-in.html

[11] Kerry Bolton, "Lovecraft's Politics," http://www.counter-currents.com/2010/08/lovecrafts-politics/

[12] Alisdair Clarke, "Fascism and the Meaning of Life," http://aryanfuturism.blogspot.com/search?q=Fascism+and+the+Meaning+of+Life

[13] Erik Davis, "Calling Cthulhu: H. P. Lovecraft's Magickal Real-

scribed the then-nascent cult of pop-Cthulhu, and noted that Lovecraft's "dread" and "horror" seemed to belong to a 19th century materialist confronting vast new vistas opened up by science, not unlike those opened by drugs; as he describes it in a more recent article on Cthulhu porn:

> In this tangy bon-bon of nihilistic materialism, Lovecraft anticipates a peculiarly modern experience of dread, one conjured not by irrational fears of the dark but rather by the speculative realism of reason itself, staring into the cosmic void. . . . This terror before the empty and ultimately unknowable universe of scientific materialism is what gives the cosmic edge to the cosmic horror that Lovecraft, more than any other writer, injected into the modern imagination (though props must be given up as well to Arthur Machen, William Hope Hodgson, and, in the closing chapters of *The Time Machine* at least, H. G. Wells). While many secular people proclaim an almost childlike wonder at the mind-melting prospect of the incomprehensibly vast universe sketched out by astrophysics and bodied forth by doctored Hubble shots, Lovecraft would say that we have not really swallowed the implication of this inhuman immensity — that we have not, in other words, correlated our contents.[14]

By contrast, we in the 20th (now 21st) century have actually come to welcome such derangement of the senses, like teenagers love glue huffing.

This seems discount the value of the fear and terror aspect itself, but it's more soundly based on the real Lovecraft, cowering in his attic, than the "alchemical master" postulated by Müller.

Counter-Currents/*North American New Right*
January 23, 2011

---

ism," in his *Nomad Codes: Adventures in Modern Esoterica* (Portland, Or.: Yeti, 2010), http://www.levity.com/figment/lovecraft.html

[14] Erik Davis, "Cthulhu is not Cute!," http://www.techgnosis.com/chunkshow-single.php?chunk=chunkfrom-2010-05-03-1521-0.txt

THE LESSON OF THE MONSTER;
OR, THE GREAT, GOOD THING ON THE DOORSTEP

We've been very pleased by the response to our essay "The Eldritch Evola," which was not only picked up by Greg Johnson for his estimable website Counter-Currents, but even managed to lurch upwards and lay a terrible, green claw on the bottom rung of the "Top Ten Most Visited Posts" there in January of 2011.

Coincidentally, we've been delving into the newer Penguin *Portable Henry James*,[1] being a sucker for the Portables in general, and especially those in which a wise editor goes to the trouble of cutting apart a life's work of legendary unreadability and stitching together a coherent, or at least assimilable, narrative, for the convenience of us amateurs, from Malcolm Cowley's first, the legendary *Portable Faulkner* that rescued "Count No-Account," as he was known among his homies,[2] to the recent *Portable Jack Kerouac* epic saga recounted by Ann Charters.[3]

The "new" *Portable Henry James* attempts something of the sort (as opposed to the older one, which was your basic collection) by recognizing the impossibility of even including large excerpts from the "major" works, and instead gives us some of the basic short works (*Daisy Miller*, *Turn of the Screw*, "The Jolly Corner," etc.) and then hundreds of pages of travel pieces, criticism, letters, even parodies and tributes, as well as a list of bizarre names (Cockster? Dickwinter?) and above all, in a section called "Definition and Description," little vignettes, often only a paragraph, exemplifying the Jamesian precision, a sort of anthology of epiphanies, the great memorable moments from "An Absolutely Unmarried Woman" to "An American Corrected on What Constitutes

---

[1] *The Portable Henry James*, ed. John Auchard (New York: Penguin, 2003).

[2] *The Portable Faulkner*, ed. Malcolm Cowley, rev. and expanded ed. (New York: Penguin, 2003).

[3] *The Portable Jack Kerouac*, ed. Ann Charters (New York: Penguin, 2007).

'the Self'" from the novels, and similar nonfiction moments from James' travels, such as "The Individual Jew" to "New York Power" to "American Teeth" and "The Absence of Penetralia."

The latter section in particular is part of a defense which the editor seems to feel needs to be mounted in his Introduction, of the Jamesian "difficult" prose style (as are the collection of tributes, including the surprising, to me at least, Ezra Pound).

I bring these two together because I could not help but think of ol' Lovecraft himself in this context. Is Lovecraft not the corresponding Master of Bad Prose? As Edmund Wilson once quipped, the only horror in Lovecraft's corpus was the author's "bad taste and bad art."

One can only imagine what James would have thought of Lovecraft, although we know, from excerpts here on Baudelaire and Hawthorne, what he thought of Poe, and more importantly, of those who were fans: "to take [Poe] with more than a certain degree of seriousness is to lack seriousness one's self. An enthusiasm for Poe is the mark of a decidedly primitive stage of reflection"; James may even have based the poet in "The Aspern Papers," a meditation on America's cultural wasteland, on Poe. However, his distaste is somewhat ambiguous, as compared with Baudelaire, Poe is "vastly the greater charlatan of the two, as well as the greater genius."

For all his "better" taste and talent for reflection, it's little realized today, as well, that James's reputation went into steep decline after his death, and was only revived in the '50s, as part of a general reconsideration of 19th-century American writers, like Melville, so that even James could be said to have, like Lovecraft, been forgotten after death, except for a small coterie that eventually stage-managed a revival years later.

Are James and Lovecraft as different as all that? One can't help but notice, from the list above, that a surprising amount of James's work, and among it the best, is in the "weird" mode, and in precisely the same "long short story" form, "the dear, the blessed *nouvelle*," in which Lovecraft himself hit his stride for his best and most famous work. (Both "Daisy Miller" and "At the Mountains of Madness" suffered the same fate: rejection by editors solely put off by their 'excessive' length for magazine publication.) The *nouvelle* of course accommodated James' legendary prolixity.

The editor, John Auchard, puts James's prolixity into the context of the 19th century "loss of faith." Art was intended to take the place of religion, principally by replacing the lost "next world" by an increased concentration on the minutia of this one. Experience might be finite, but it could still "burn with a hard, gem-like flame" as Pater famously counseled.

That counsel, of course, took place in the first, then self-suppressed, then retained afterword to his *The Renaissance*. René Guénon has in various places diagnosed this as the essential fraud of the Renaissance, the exchange of a vertical path to transcendence for a horizontal dissipation and dispersal among finite trivialities, usually hoked-up as "man discovered the vast extent of the world and himself," blah blah blah. As Guénon points out, it's a fool's bargain, as the finite, no matter how extensive and intricate, is, compared to the infinite, precisely *nothing*.

Baron Evola, on the other hand, distinguishes several types of Man, and is willing to let some of them find their fulfillment in such worldliness. It is, however, unworthy of one type of Man: Aryan Man. See the chapter "Determination of the Vocations" in his *The Doctrine of Awakening*.[4]

So the *nouvelle*-length accumulation of detail and precision of judgment, in James, is intended to produce some kind of this-worldly ersatz transcendence. Was this perhaps the same intent in Lovecraft, the use of the *nouvelle* length tale to pile up detail until the mind breaks?

Lovecraft of course was also a thoroughgoing post-Renaissance materialist, a Cartesian mechanist with the best of them; when he finally got "The Call of Cthulhu" published, he advised his editor that:

Now all my tales are based on the fundamental premise that common human laws and interests and emotions have no validity or significance in the vast cosmos-at-large. One must forget that such things as organic life, good and evil,

---

[4] Julius Evola, *The Doctrine of Awakening: The Attainment of Self-Mastery According to the Earliest Buddhist Texts*, trans. H. E. Musson (Rochester, Vt.: Inner Traditions, 1995).

love and hate, and all such local attributes of a negligible and temporary race called mankind, have any existence at all.[5]

But as John Miller notes, this is exactly what is needed to produce the Lovecraft Effect: "That's nihilism, of course, and we're free to reject it. But there's nothing creepier or more terrifying than the possibility that our lives are exercises in meaninglessness."[6]

What is there to choose, between the unrealized but metaphysically certain nothingness of the Jamesian finite detail, and the all-too-obvious nothingness of Lovecraft's worldview?

What separates James from Lovecraft and Evola is, along the lines of our previous effort, is precisely what T. S. Eliot, in praise of James (the essay is in the *Portable* too): "He has a mind so fine no idea could penetrate it." Praise, note, and contrasted with the French, "the Home of Ideas," and such Englishmen, or I guess pseudo-Englishmen, as Chesterton, "whose brain swarms with ideas" but cannot *think*, meaning, one gathers, stand apart with skepticism. One notes the Anglican Eliot seeming to flinch back, like a good English gentleman, from those dirty, unruly Frenchmen like Guénon, and such Englishmen who, like Chesterton, went "too far" and went and "turned Catholic" out of their love of "smells and bells."

What Evola and Lovecraft had was precisely an Idea, the idea of Tradition; in Lovecraft's case, a made-up, fictional one, but designed to have the same effect. But that's the issue: when is Tradition only made up? For Evola and Guénon, the mind of Traditional Man is indeed not "fine" enough to evade penetration by the Idea; he is open to the transcendent, vertical dimension, which is realized in Intellectual Intuition.

I've suggested elsewhere[7] that Intellectual Intuition, or what Evola calls his "Traditional Method" is usefully compared with what Spengler called, speaking of his own method, "physiognom-

---

[5] H. P. Lovecraft Letter to Farnsworth Wright (July 27, 1927), in *Selected Letters 1925–1929* (Sauk City, Wis.: Arkham House, 1968), p.150.

[6] http://www.heymiller.com/2010/08/h-p-lovecraft/

[7] http://www.gornahoor.net/?p=624

ic tact." A couple years ago I found a passage in one of the few books on Spengler in English, by H. Stuart Hughes, where it seemed like he was actually giving a good explication of Guénon's metaphysical (vs. systematic philosophy) method. I think it could apply to Evola's method as well. Hughes writes:

> Spengler rejected the whole idea of logical analysis. Such "systematic" practices apply only in the natural sciences. To penetrate below the surface of history, to understand at least partially the mysterious substructure of the past, a new method — that of "physiognomic tact" — is required.
>
> This new method, "which few people can really master," means "instinctively to see through the movement of events. It is what unites the born statesman and the true historian, despite all opposition between theory and practice." [It takes from Goethe and Nietzsche] the injunction to "sense" the reality of human events rather than dissect them. In this new orientation, the historian ceases to be a scientist and becomes a poet. He gives up the fruitless quest for systematic understanding. . . . "The more historically men tried to think, the more they forgot that in this domain they ought *not* to think." They failed to observe the most elementary rule of historical investigation: respect for the *mystery* of human destiny. [8]

So causality/science, destiny/history. Rather than chains of reasoning and "facts" the historian employs his "tact" (really, a kind of Paterian "taste") to "see" the big picture: how facts are composed into a destiny. Rather than compelling assent, the historian's words are used to bring about a shared intuition.

I suppose Guénon and Co. would bristle at being lumped in with "poets" but I think the general point is helpful in understanding the "epistemology" of what Guénon is doing: not objective (but empty) fact-gathering but not merely aesthetic and "subjective" either, since metaphysically "seeing" the deeper connec-

---

[8] H. Stuart Hughes, *Oswald Spengler*, 2nd ed. (New Brunswick, N.J.: Transaction, 1992), p. 71.

tion can be "induced" by words and thus "shared."

What Guénon, Evola, and Spengler seek to do deliberately, what Lovecraft did fictionally or even accidentally, what James's mind was "too fine" to do at all, is to not see mere facts, or see a lot of them, or even see them *very very intently*, but to see *through* them and thus acquire metaphysical insight, and, through the method of obsessive accumulation of detail, share that insight by inducing it in others.

Speaking of "penetration," one does note James's obsession with "penetralia"; also one recalls the remarkable way Schuon brings out how in Christianity the Word is brought by Gabriel to Mary, who in mediaeval paintings is often shown with a stream of words penetrating her ear, thus conceiving virginally, while in Islam, Gabriel brings the Word to Muhammad, who recites (gives birth to) the Koran. Itself a wonderful example of the Traditional Method: moving freely among the material elements of various traditions to weave a pattern that re-creates an Idea in the mind of the listener. Do you see how Christianity and Islam relate? Do you see?

Finally, we should note that Lovecraft, for his own sake, did get in a preemptive shot at James:

> In *The Turn of the Screw*, Henry James triumphs over *his inevitable pomposity and prolixity* sufficiently well to create a truly potent air of sinister menace; depicting the hideous influence of two dead and evil servants, Peter Quint and the governess, Miss Jessel, over a small boy and girl who had been under their care. *James is perhaps too diffuse, too unctuously urbane, and too much addicted to subtleties of speech to realise fully all the wild and devastating horror in his situations*; but for all that there is a rare and mounting tide of fright, culminating in the death of the little boy, which gives the novelette a permanent place in its special class.[9]

Counter-Currents/*North American New Right*
February 21, 2011

---

[9] *Supernatural Horror in Literature*, Chapter VIII.

THE PRINCESS &
THE MAGGOT

Although apparently written back in 2008, long before I began writing about James and Lovecraft, I only recently stumbled across this quote from pioneer Lovecraft scholar S. T. Joshi, which might be said to encapsulate my concern in this series of articles:

> The history of Lovecraft's reputation—his initial rejection by Edmund Wilson and others as a pulp hack; the championing of his work by Derleth, Fritz Leiber, and George T. Wetzel; the revolution in scholarship as a result of the work of such critics as Dirk W. Mosig and Donald R. Burleson; and his final acceptance as a canonical author with the publication of his work in Penguins Classics and the Library of America—would make for an interesting chapter in the evolution of literary taste. Lovecraft remains unique in being simultaneously a figure commanding respect among highbrow critics and a significant figure in popular culture, the source of films, role-playing games, and other media adoptions.[1]

Having just read Maxwell Geismar's admittedly idiosyncratic *Henry James and the Jacobites*,[2] a futile and almost obsessive attempt from the early '60s to "cry stinking fish" and deflate the effete James "fad" in the name of an alternative American tradition of manly Marxists like Twain, Wolfe, and London, it struck me that, allowing for Joshi's justifiable boosterism, there was at least one other author, an America author, an author of (for at least part of) the same 20th century, that could tell the same story: Henry James.

---

[1] S. T. Joshi, "Introduction" to *H. P. Lovecraft: The Complete Fiction* (New York: Barnes & Noble, 2008).

[2] Published in England as *Henry James and His Cult* (London: Chatto and Windus, 1964).

While James certainly never thought of himself as a pulp or other genre writer, his reputation had many more ups and downs over his lifetime than his secure place in the literary Pantheon today would lead you to expect (for example, publishers thought a Collected Edition was called for, but it was a legendary dud). And after his death, he was as forgotten as Lovecraft always was, dismissed as both a hack (his melodramatic plots) and as possessing an unreadable verbose and precious style.

Then, a new generation of critics, led by the partisans of the so-called "New Criticism" discovered James for their own purposes, elevated him into "The Master," and even cobbled together an aesthetic for the novel from his self-serving Prefaces he added to that collected edition. James was part of the Penguin Modern Classics from the beginning, along with the Library of America. One might even compare the mammoth editing and biographical work of Leon Edel to Joshi himself.

As for popular media, James has long become a staple of the Merchant-Ivory film or Masterpiece Theatre TV genres, and my copy of "The Turn of the Screw" has an appendix listing three pages of various adaptations, including operas—although I must grant Joshi that no role-playing games have appeared.

With this parallel in mind, I'd like to explore some additional similarities of their lives and careers as reflected in their writings—admittedly, in a rather chiastic fashion—by taking a look at an early Lovecraft tale, and an early James novel, as James reflects on it years later.

> My coming to New York had been a mistake; for whereas I had looked for poignant wonder and inspiration in the teeming labyrinths of ancient streets that twist endlessly from forgotten courts and squares and waterfronts to courts and squares and waterfronts equally forgotten, and in the Cyclopean modern towers and pinnacles that rise blackly Babylonian under waning moons, I had found instead only a sense of horror and oppression which threatened to master, paralyze, and annihilate me. —"He," 1925

Although permanently associated with New England (his gravestone reads "I am Providence") Lovecraft's life, and work, took a weird turn in 30s, when for reasons still unclear he married one Sonia Greene, a Russian Jewish immigrant, and moved to Brooklyn, New York. She promptly lost her job and left for the Midwest to find work, leaving Lovecraft to shift for himself, unemployed and unemployable, until his return to Providence in 1926.

Surrounded by alien beings — "I'll be shot if three out of every four persons — nay, full nine out of every ten — weren't flabby, pungent, grinning, chattering niggers! Help!"[3] — Lovecraft consoled himself with visits to a handful of simpatico friends, such as Samuel Loveman, and long, sometimes all-night walks among such districts as preserved enough Federal architecture to spur his historical interests. "He" was the result of one such walk, that started in Brooklyn and ended, next morning, in Elizabeth, New Jersey.

During his increasingly desperate stay, he composed a whole series of stories reflecting his traumatic life in New York — recently collected, with photos of the actual locales, as *From the Pest Zone*.[4] These stories, such as "The Horror at Red Hook" and the one we are looking at, "He," were something new for Lovecraft; more, shall we say, "Lovecraftian." As Michel Houellebeq says in his invaluable monograph *H. P. Lovecraft: Against the World, Against Life*:

> New York had marked him definitively. His hatred for the "stinking, amorphous hybridity" of this modern Babel, for the "giant strangers, ill-born and deformed, who gabble and shout vulgarly, destitute of dreams, within its confines" did not cease, during the course of 1925, to exasperate him to the point of delirium. Once might even say that one of the fundamental figures of his work — the idea of a titanic and grandiose city, in the fundaments of which

---

[3] H. P. Lovecraft, *Lord of Visible World: An Autobiography in Letters*, ed. S. T. Joshi and David E. Schultz (Athens, Ohio: Ohio University Press, 2000), p. 179.

[4] H. P. Lovecraft, *From The Pest Zone: Stories From New York*, edited by S. T. Joshi and David E. Schultz (New York: Hippocampus Press, 2003).

swarm repugnant creatures of nightmare—was inspired directly by his experience of New York.[5]

New York helped him. He, who was so polite, so courteous, had discovered hate. Returning to Providence he composed magnificent stories, vibrant like incantations, precise as dissections.[6]

Indeed, it was soon after his return to Providence that he produced . . . "The Call of Cthulhu."

Here we reach the first of our chiastic parallels: Lovecraft left New England for New York; James left New York for (Old) England.

Of course, there are more than few important differences. James, for one, was already an established author, although in the early period we'll be looking at he had had a string of "bombs" and would eventually face utter defeat and even public humiliation (booed from the stage on opening night) when he attempted a new career in drama.

James was fleeing what he judged to be a colonial culture too "thin" to really produce art (see his infamous essay on Hawthorne, where he lists all the things America lacks). Lovecraft would have demurred, but as a dogmatic "materialist," he by no means agreed with his Puritan ancestors' theology; he merely respected them for sternly believing in something. In any event, the "New" England Lovecraft loved was definitely rooted in the 17th-century England he took as his literary and intellectual model. As we shall see, when James returned to New York many years later, he found it as loathsome as Lovecraft did.

Moreover, Geismar emphasizes that James' idea of "England" was largely imaginary, as literature-inspired as the hermetic Lovecraft's ideas of everywhere outside Providence, and so he was just as likely to find the reality, at least at first, to be alien. And he had the artistic skill to be able to imagine what London,

---

[5] Michel Houellebeq, *H. P. Lovecraft: Against the World, Against Life* (New York: McSweeney's, 2005), p. 32.

[6] Houellebeq, p. 37.

or any great metropolis, would be like to someone who lacked the *"entrée"* James had through his money, fame, and family connections—everything Lovecraft lacked.

In short, Lovecraft idolized the "England" of New England, while James left New York, and America, precisely to immerse himself in a similarly unreal Albion of the mind.

While Joshi has covered more than adequately the background of nearly hysterical street wandering out of which "He" emerged, we have in the case of James his own account, in the "Preface" included in the doomed New York Edition, of the circumstances in which *The Princess Casamassima* came to be.

The simplest account of the origin of *The Princess Casamassima* is, I think, that this fiction proceeded quite directly, *during the first year of a long residence in London, from the habit and the interest of walking the streets. I walked a great deal—for exercise, for amusement, for acquisition, and above all I always walked home at the evening's end, when the evening had been spent elsewhere,* as happened more often than not; and as to do this was to receive many impressions, so the impressions worked and sought an issue, so the book after a time was born. It is a fact that, as I look back, the attentive exploration of London, *the assault directly made by the great city upon an imagination quick to react,* fully explains a large part of it. There is a minor element that refers itself to another source, of which I shall presently speak; but *the prime idea was unmistakeably the ripe round fruit of perambulation.* One walked of course with one's eyes greatly open, and I hasten to declare that such a practice, carried on for a long time and over a considerable space, positively provokes, all round, *a mystic solicitation,* the urgent appeal, on the part of everything, to be interpreted and, so far as may be, reproduced. "Subjects" and situations, character and history, the tragedy and comedy of life, are things of which the common air, in such conditions, seems pungently to taste; and to a mind curious, before the human scene, of meanings and *revelations the great grey Babylon* easily becomes, on its face, a garden bristling with an immense illustrative flora. Possible stories, presentable figures, rise from the thick jungle as the observer moves, fluttering up like startled game, and before he knows it indeed *he has fairly to guard himself against the brush of importunate wings.* He goes on as with his head in *a cloud of humming presences* – especially during the younger, *the initiatory time,* the fresh, the sharply-apprehensive months or years, more or less numerous. We use our material up, we use up even the thick tribute of the London streets – if perception and attention but sufficiently light our steps. But I think of them as lasting, for myself, quite sufficiently long; I think of them as even still – dreadfully changed for the worse in respect to any romantic idea as I find them – breaking out on occasion into eloquence, throwing out deep notes from their vast vague murmur.

There was a moment at any rate when they offered me no image more vivid than that of *some individual sensitive nature or fine mind, some small obscure intelligent creature whose education should have been almost wholly derived from them, capable of profiting by all the civilisation, all the accumulations to which they testify, yet condemned to see these things only from outside* – in mere quickened consideration, mere wistfulness and envy and despair. It seemed to me I had only to imagine such a spirit intent enough and troubled enough, and to place it in presence of the comings and goings, the great gregarious company, of the more fortunate than himself – all on the scale on which London could show them – to get possession of an interesting theme. I arrived so at the history of little Hyacinth Robinson – he sprang up for me out of the London pavement. To find his possible adventure interesting I had only to conceive his watching the same public show, the same innumerable appearances, I had watched myself, and of his watching very much as I had watched; save indeed for one little difference. *This difference would be that so far as all the swarming facts should speak of freedom and ease, knowledge and power, money, opportunity and satiety, he should be able to revolve round them but at the most respectful of distances and with eve-*

ry door of approach shut in his face. For one's self, all conveniently, there had been doors that opened—opened into light and warmth and cheer, into good and charming relations; and if the place as a whole lay heavy on one's consciousness there was yet always for relief this implication of one's own lucky share of the freedom and ease, lucky acquaintance with the number of *lurking springs* at light pressure of which particular *vistas would begin to recede, great lighted, furnished, peopled galleries,* sending forth gusts of agreeable sound. . . .

Truly, of course, there are London *mysteries (dense categories of dark arcana)* for every spectator, and it 's in a degree an exclusion and a state of weakness to be without experience of the meaner conditions, the lower manners and types, the general sordid struggle, the weight of the burden of labour, the ignorance, the misery and the vice. *With such matters as those my tormented young man would have had contact — they would have formed, fundamentally, from the first, his natural and immediate London.* But the reward of a romantic curiosity would be the question of what the total assault, that of the world of his work-a-day life and the *world of his divination* and his envy together, *would have made of him, and what in especial he would have made of them.* As tormented, I say, I thought of him, and that would be the point—if one could only see him feel enough to be interesting without his feeling so much as not to be natural.[7]

I've taken the liberty of italicizing the particularly "Lovecraftian" wording. James seems to have verily conjured up in his powerful imagination the near destitute, near starving, near friendless (though technically "married" and with many correspondents) Lovecraft. What James makes of Hyacinth, what he imagines Hyacinth would make of himself in such a position, is an anarchist; his imagination, though powerful, was, as Geismar insists, too snobbish to let him imagine someone like Lovecraft

---

[7] Henry James, *The Art of the Novel: Critical Prefaces* with an introduction by R. P. Blackmur (New York: Scribner's, 1934), pp. 59–61, 61–62.

who could have picked himself up, returned to Providence, and used his experience to make himself a writer; a writer, perhaps, like Henry James.

The other notable thing about "He" is the famous "racism."[8] Lovecraft loathes the buildings and streets, but also, perhaps more so, the people in them. You could say he loathes the mongrel New Yorkers first and last; in that same opening passage:

> [T]he throngs of people that seethed through the flume-like streets were squat, swarthy strangers with hardened faces and narrow eyes, shrewd strangers without dreams and without kinship to the scenes about them, who could never mean aught to a blue-eyed man of the old folk, with the love of fair green lanes and white New England village steeples in his heart.

And in the climactic, terrifying vision of the Babylon of the future from "He":

> I saw the heavens verminous with strange flying things, and beneath them a hellish black city of giant stone terraces with impious pyramids flung savagely to the moon, and devil-lights burning from unnumbered windows. And swarming loathsomely on aërial galleries I saw the yellow, squint-eyed people of that city, robed horribly in orange and red, and dancing insanely to the pounding of fevered kettle-drums, the clatter of obscene crotala, and the maniacal moaning of muted horns whose ceaseless dirges rose and fell undulantly like the waves of an unhallowed ocean of bitumen.

---

[8] See the letters collected by A. Trumbo as "The Racial Worldview of H. P. Lovecraft" in three parts at Counter-Currents:

Part One: http://www.counter-currents.com/2010/09/the-racial-worldview-of-h-p-lovecraft-part-1/

Part Two: http://www.counter-currents.com/2010/09/the-racial-worldview-of-h-p-lovecraft-part-2/

Part Three: http://www.counter-currents.com/2010/09/the-racial-worldview-of-h-p-lovecraft-part-3/

Lovecraft loathed New York's "multicultural tapestry" (and any New Yorker of today will recognize those pounding drums, from subway platforms to parks to "Occupy Wall Street"). "Whenever we found ourselves in the racially mixed crowds which characterize New York, Howard would become livid with rage," Greene later wrote. "He seemed almost to lose his mind."[9]

> When you see my new tale "The Horror at Red Hook," you will see what I make of this idea in connexion with the gangs of young loafers and herds of evil-looking foreigners that one sees everywhere.[10]

> New York is dead, and the brilliancy which so impresses one from the outside is the phosphorescence of a maggoty corpse.[11]

James's London, though the center of a world-wide empire, was still sufficiently White to afford no such horrors; it was still at least if one had, like James, entrée to the right circles. "The Great Good Place" is perhaps the *reductio ad absurdum* of James's idea of Paradise as a well-appointed London club.

But James, near the end of his career, returned to New York, and found that "all had changed, changed utterly," as Yeats might have said. In the relevant chapters of *The American Scene* James records his incomprehension and horror, again in very recognizably Lovecraftian terms which I have italicized:

> One's supreme relation, as one had always put it, was one's relation to one's country—a conception made up so largely of one's countrymen and one's countrywomen. Thus it was as if, all the while, with such a fond tradition of what these products predominantly were, the idea of the country itself underwent something of that profane

---

[9] Lin Carter, *Lovecraft: A Look Behind the Cthulhu Mythos* (New York: Ballantine Books, 1972), p. 45.

[10] Lovecraft, *Lord of Visible World*, p. 176.

[11] Lovecraft, *Lord of Visible World*, p. 198.

overhauling through which it appears to suffer the indignity of change. Is not our instinct in this matter, in general, essentially the safe one—that of keeping the idea simple and strong and continuous, so that it shall be perfectly sound? To touch it overmuch, to pull it about, is to put it in peril of weakening; yet on this free assault upon it, this readjustment of it in *their monstrous, presumptuous interest, the aliens, in New York,* seemed perpetually to insist. The combination there of their quantity and their quality—that *loud primary stage of alienism which New York most offers to sight*—operates, for the native, as *their note of settled possession,* something they have nobody to thank for; so that unsettled possession is what we, on our side, seem reduced to—the implication of which, in its turn, is that, to recover confidence and regain lost ground, *we, not they, must make the surrender and accept the orientation.* . . .

The carful, again and again, is a foreign carful; *a row of faces, up and down, testifying, without exception, to alienism unmistakable, alienism undisguised and unashamed.* You do here, in a manner perhaps, discriminate; the launched condition, as I have called it, is more developed in some types than in others; but I remember observing how, in the Broadway and the Bowery conveyances in especial, *they tended, almost alike, to make the observer gasp with the sense of isolation.* It was not for this that the observer on whose behalf I more particularly write had sought to take up again the sweet sense of the natal air.[12]

And of course, the most alien are the Jews, who call to mind nothing so much as the fish-spawn of Lovecraft's Innsmouth:

The sense of this quality was already strong in my drive, with a companion, through the long, warm June twilight, from a comparatively conventional neighbourhood; it was the sense, after all, of *a great swarming, a*

---

[12] Henry James, *The American Scene* (London, Chapman & Hall, 1907), pp. 85–86, 125.

swarming that had begun to thicken, infinitely, as soon as we had crossed to the East side and long before we had got to Rutgers Street. *There is no swarming like that of Israel when once Israel has got a start, and the scene here bristled, at every step, with the signs and sounds, immitigable, unmistakable, of a Jewry that had burst all bounds.* That it has burst all bounds in New York, almost any combination of figures or of objects taken at hazard sufficiently proclaims; but I remember how *the rising waters, on this summer night, rose, to the imagination, even above the housetops and seemed to sound their murmur to the pale distant stars.* It was as if we had been thus, in the crowded, hustled roadway, where multiplication, multiplication of everything, was the dominant note, *at the bottom of some vast sallow aquarium in which innumerable fish, of over-developed proboscis, were to bump together, for ever, amid heaped spoils of the sea. . . .*

There are small strange animals, known to natural history, *snakes or worms,* I believe, who, when cut into pieces, wriggle away contentedly and live in the snippet as completely as in the whole. So the denizens of the New York Ghetto, heaped as thick as the splinters on the table of a glass-blower, had each, like the fine glass particle, his or her individual share of the whole hard glitter of Israel. This diffused intensity, as I have called it, *causes any array of Jews to resemble (if I may be allowed another image) some long nocturnal street* where every window in every house shows a maintained light. The advanced age of so many of the figures, the ubiquity of the children, carried out in fact this analogy; they were all there for race, and not, as it were, for reason: that *excess of lurid meaning,* in some of the old men's and old women's faces in particular, would have been absurd, in the conditions, as a really directed attention—it could only be the gathered past of Israel mechanically pushing through. The way, at the same time, this chapter of history did, all that evening, seem to push, was a matter that made the "ethnic" apparition again sit *like a skeleton at the feast.* It was fairly as if I could *see the spectre grin* while the talk of the hour gave me, across the board, facts and figures, chapter and verse, for *the extent of the Hebrew conquest of New York. . . .*

Phantasmagoric for me, accordingly, in a high degree, are the interesting hours I here glance at content to remain — setting in this respect, I recognize, an excellent example to all the rest of the New York phantasmagoria. Let me speak of the remainder only as phantasmagoric too, so that I may both the more kindly recall it and the sooner have done with it.[13]

The very "scientific" nature of the change, what others might laud with the cliché of "the march of progress" paradoxically emphasizes the ancient Babylonian aspect, rather like Lang's *Metropolis* recalls Moloch — scientific progress as a genocidal trap:

I remember the evolved fire-proof staircase, a thing of scientific surfaces, impenetrable to the microbe, and above all plated, against side friction, with *white marble* of a goodly grain. The white marble was surely the New Jerusalem note, and we followed that note, up and down the district, the rest of the evening, through more happy changes than I may take time to count. What struck me in the flaring streets (over and beyond *the everywhere insistent, defiant, unhumorous, exotic face*) was the blaze of the shops *addressed to the New Jerusalem* wants and the splendour with which these were taken for granted; the only thing indeed a little ambiguous was just this *look of the trap too brilliantly, too candidly baited for the wary side of Israel itself.* It is not for Israel, in general, that Israel so artfully shines — yet its being moved to do so, at last, in that luxurious style, might be precisely the grand side of the city of redemption. Who can ever tell, moreover, in any conditions and in presence of any apparent anomaly, what the genius of Israel may, or may not, really be "up to"?[14]

The New Jerusalem is the New Babylon enslaving the former masters.

---

13 Henry James, *The American Scene*, pp. 131–32.
14 Henry James, *The American Scene*, p. 135.

So finally, James came to the realization that his New York, revisited after years abroad, had changed as much, become as alienated a maggot-ridden corpse, as Lovecraft's New York of the near and distant Future; returning now to the beginning of Lovecraft's story, do we not hear the Jamesian voice?

So instead of the poems I had hoped for, there came only a shuddering blankness and ineffable loneliness; and I saw at last a fearful truth which no one had ever dared to breathe before — the unwhisperable secret of secrets — *the fact that this city of stone and stridor is not a sentient perpetuation of Old New York as London is of Old London and Paris of Old Paris, but that it is in fact quite dead, its sprawling body imperfectly embalmed and infested with queer animate things which have nothing to do with it as it was in life.* Upon making this discovery I ceased to sleep comfortably; though something of resigned tranquility came back as I gradually formed the habit of keeping off the streets by day and venturing abroad only at night, when darkness calls forth what little of the past still hovers wraith-like about, and old white doorways remember the stalwart forms that once passed through them. With this mode of relief I even wrote a few poems, and still refrained from going home to my people lest I seem to crawl back ignobly in defeat. — "He"

One measure of how the cultural climate has changed — and not to Lovecraft's advantage — is that such passages as the ones in James could be published not by some squalid pulp magazine, but by Harper in 1904, and republished by Scribner in 1944, and today in the Library of America, and reprinted and excerpted in critical works ever since — without any real outrage or even notice (even from Auden, in his introduction to the 1944 reprint) except from the aforementioned Geismar, who sneers at James's unmanly whining about his elite group being shoved aside, rather than joining the New Americans on the right side of History. (Before attacking the effete James "cult" in the '60s, Geismar had been instrumental in returning Jack London to critical favor, in the process needing to provide a similar though more forgiving Freudian interpretation of his "racism" — see *Rebels and Ancestors: The American Novel 1890–1915*.[15])

"Lovecraft's racism," by contrast, is a research theme in itself, constantly condemned or exculpated; Joshi's short note to "He" in the collection cited finds room to warn that it is "disturbingly racist,"[16] and dealing with an earlier story he denigrates Lovecraft's obvious distinction between earlier English and Dutch immigrants, what might be called the Founding Race, and the later "wretched refuse" as a "sophism" that allows him to recast the latter as "maggots."[17]

James' New York experience produced, of course, stories of his own, one of which, "The Jolly Corner," is not only perhaps his last good work, but also one of his "ghost stories," frequently anthologized alongside Lovecraft. In this tale, the narrator does not so bluntly "gasp" at the swarming aliens; in good WASP fashion, he has retreated to his ancestral townhouse, where he directs his loathing inward. By this time, his loathing of what New York had become had extended to a loathing of what — *he* — might have become if New York had claimed him.

But *that* will be the subject of another essay.

Counter-Currents/*North American New Right*
October 17, 2011

---

[15] Maxwell Geismar, *Rebels and Ancestors: The American Novel 1890–1915* (Boston: Houghton Mifflin, 1953).

[16] *H. P. Lovecraft: The Complete Fiction*, p. 332.

[17] S. T. Joshi, *A Dreamer and a Visionary: H. P. Lovecraft in his Time* (Liverpool, UK: Liverpool University Press, 2001) p. 224.

THE CORNER AT THE CENTER OF THE WORLD: TRADITIONAL METAPHYSICS IN A LATE TALE OF HENRY JAMES

"The human individual is, at one and the same time, much more and much less than is ordinarily supposed in the West; he is greater by reason of his possibilities of indefinite extension beyond the corporeal modality, . . . but he is also much less since, far from constituting a complete and sufficient being in himself, he is only an exterior manifestation, a fleeting appearance clothing the true being, which in no way affects the essence of the latter in its immutability."

—René Guénon[1]

"Time, space, and natural law hold for me suggestions of intolerable bondage, and I can form no picture of emotional satisfaction which does not involve their defeat—especially the defeat of time, so that one may merge oneself with the whole historic stream and be wholly emancipated from the transient and the ephemeral."

—H. P. Lovecraft[2]

"There's only one corner of the universe you can be sure of improving, and that's your own self . . . [by] the sacrifice of self-will to make room for knowledge of God."

—Aldous Huxley[3]

When last we looked in on James and Lovecraft, we found

---

[1] "Oriental Metaphysics"

[2] Letter to August Derleth (21 November 1930)

[3] Aldous Huxley, *Time Must Have a Stop* (New York: Harper & Brothers, 1944).

them occupying rather similar positions: wandering the streets of New York, "almost gasp[ing] with a sense of isolation"[4] in a city transformed by immigration from a colony of the Nordic race to some loathsome futuristic Babylon.

Returning to their respective home bases, they were in quite different situations. Lovecraft returned to Providence and was taken in by his aunts, living in an increasingly shabby series of genteel houses, James, however, had not merely the funds of a reasonably successful writer[5] to provide for a comfortable residence; his share in the family real estate was making considerable gains under the surprisingly wise management of his nephew, Harry James (New York attorney and budding money manager, not the big band trumpeter).

After receiving some particularly good investment news ("Very interesting & valuable to me is your news of the new Syracuse arrangement. . . . I feel as if it has placed my declining years *a l'abri* of destitution"[6]) James turned his hand to what would be his last great ghost story — "The Jolly Corner"[7] — that re-imagines his recent homecoming through the egotistical musings and nocturnal wanderings (in his luxurious family mansion on once-fashionable Irving Place, not in the street, like Lovecraft, whose "declining years" would also not escape destitution either) of a character who seems to combine Henry's imagination

---

[4] Henry James, *The American Scene* (London, Chapman & Hall, 1907), p. 86.

[5] And what greater irony than that the real nob, James, could make a living as a writer, while the impoverished Lovecraft sabotaged his career over and over again in order to keep up the pretense of being a "gentleman" amateur; one recalls more recently the uber-WASP John Cheever, who at age eleven "promised his proud Yankee parents never to seek fame or wealth with his literary career;" see Blake Bailey, *Cheever: A life* (New York: Knopf, 2009), p. 596.

[6] Quoted from Michael Anesko, *Monopolizing the Master: Henry James and the Politics of Modern Literary Scholarship* (Stanford: Stanford University Press, 2012), p. 42.

[7] 1908, with countless reprints. I am using the one on pp. 337-70 of *American Fantastic Tales: Terror and the Uncanny from Poe to the Pulps*, edited by Peter Straub (New York: Library of America, 2009).

with Harry's grasping business sense—exactly what Lovecraft lacked in order to make his way in the new, capitalistic world.

Spencer Brydon returns to the city and house of his birth, after years of typically Jamesian vague epicurean wanderings in Europe, in order to look over his property—one building in the middle of the street, suitable for a lucrative remodeling, the other abutting the avenue, which he thinks of as the "Jolly Corner." Finding his fellow Americans boring, he spends his time exploring his properties, occasionally indulging in gossip and assurances of mutual admiration with his chaste confidante, Alice. She it is, however, who sets the weird plot in motion:

Once Alice Silverton's conditional words—"if [you] had but stayed at home"—fix themselves in Brydon's consciousness, he responds to them by imagining that, somewhere within the recesses of the deserted birthplace on the jolly corner, his alter ego, the might have been self, lurks. With his newly discovered business acumen working as a catalyst for curiosity, Brydon yearns to track him down, confront him.[8]

What's going on in this uncanny story? Of course, there have been all the usual interpretations; Freudian (James confronting, or not, the childhood "wound" which kept him out of the army, and perhaps marriage as well), Jungian (an elderly man—56!—seeks wholeness by confronting his shadow), Marxist (James realizes the true face of American capitalism isn't his family's genteel wealth but the grasping robber barons[9]), and so on.

I think that here, once again, we can profit from looking at things from a Traditional point of view. To do so, let's lay out some of the puzzling, or at least noticeable, elements in this tale.

The first thing we need to notice—we can hardly avoid it, it dominates the text of the first part—is Brydon's extraordinary

---

[8] Ibid, p. 43.

[9] There is in fact a curious contemporary photo of J. P. Morgan which James may have seen while consulting over the illustrations in the recent New York Edition of his works, where Morgan seems to be about to gut the viewer with a hand, like that of the spectre in James' tale, that indeed is missing two fingers. See Adeline R. Tinter: *The twentieth-century world of Henry James: changes in his work after 1900* (Baton Rouge: Louisiana State University Press, 2000), pp. 44ff.

egotism. Right from the start, he tells us of how silly everyone is, asking for what he "thinks" about New York—"my thoughts [are] almost altogether about something that concerns only myself." Why is he here at all? "He had come—putting the thing pompously—to look at his "property," sounding a Stirnerite note. And he freely admits to coming home from "a selfish, frivolous, scandalous life. And you see what it has made of me." Indeed, 'me' is what it is all about: "He found all things come back to the question of what he personally might have been, how he might have led his life and "turned out," if he had not so, at the outset, given [a financial career] up."

And fortunately, for such a massive egotist, he has a confidante, Alice, who can assure him, if he had "turned out" differently, even as a "brute, a black stranger," a "monster," even: that he was "good enough," for, sounding like Seinfeld's mother, "How should I not have liked you?" Besides, she notes with approval, "You don't care for anything but yourself."[10]

Armed with such support, Brydon affirms his curious whim as if he were a Grail knight swearing to perform some Quest for his Lady: "But I do want to see him. . . . And I can. And I shall."[11]

But at the last moment, he hits on different, rather more "cunning" plan, as Blackadder's manservant Baldrick might say: rather than confront the spectre, he will one-up the spirit by exercising the supreme upper-class WASP virtue: discretion. No coward ever retreated from the battlefield with more self-respect

---

[10] Again, Lovecraft, unlike the confirmed bachelor Brydon, actually had a wife, the Russian-born Brooklyn Jewess, Sonia Greene, who, unlike Harry James, was unsuccessful in business and left Lovecraft in New York, not with Brydon's choice of buildings, one to remodel, (on Irving Place, not tenements for Syrian immigrants and the impecunious Lovecraft, surely, but for the declining remnants of Old New York) the other to indulge in nocturnal ghost hunts, but with a succession of tenements where Lovecraft would stint and starve while tormented by the "mad piping" not of Elder Gods but of Syrian immigrants.

[11] If not a knight, then the Fisher King, who was punished for his pride in combat with an unmanning wound, like James, or the mutilated fingers of the spectre. See Julius Evola, *The Mystery of the Grail* (Rochester, VT: Inner Traditions, 1996; Chapter 16: "The Test of Pride."

intact, even enhanced:

> . . . though moved and privileged as, I believe, it has never
> been given to man, I retire, I renounce–never, on my hon-
> our, to try again. So rest for ever–and let *me!*

After all, he goal all along was to have "saved his dignity and
kept his name, in such a case, out of the papers. . . ."

Although the spectre won't, as it happens, let him leave without confrontation — resulting in another cowardly act, fainting —
Alice arrives to rest his head in her comforting lap, and assure
him that:

> "You came to yourself" she beautifully smiled.
> "Ah, I've come to myself now — thanks to you, dearest.
> But this brute, with his awful face — this brute's a black
> stranger. He's none of *me,* even as I *might* have been," Bry-
> don sturdily declared . . .
> [W]ell, he must have been, you see, less dreadful to me.
> And it may have pleased him that I pitied him." . . . "He
> has a million a year," he lucidly added. "But he hasn't
> you."
> "And he isn't — no, he isn't — *you!*" she murmured, as he
> drew her to his breast. [All emphases here and in the pre-
> vious quote are James']

End on note of domestic bliss.

Lovecraft's narrators, by contrast, seem to err on the opposite
side, foolhardiness. They may faint, but only after a determined
facing of the truth, no matter how many warnings they may
have gotten, and how much they latter hope for sweet forgetful-
ness or death.

Next, what is the house? The very first impression we are
given of the house, as he begins to make his nocturnal rounds,
evokes the traditional symbolism of Universal Manifestation as a
graph of indefinite points along horizontal and vertical axes, or
as a tapestry woven of warp and woof.

Traditional Metaphysics, as presented by René Guénon in a

series of works that began appearing shortly after James' death,[12] envisions the Totality of Existence, or 'Universal Manifestation,' as, symbolically, a three dimensional grid, formed by the intersection of three planes, representing an indefinite series states of being. The individual being, the human being, for instance, is as it were a line drawn from the center to the periphery, along one possible state of being. But there are, of course, other and higher states, the acquisition of which is the goal of spiritual development. This can be thought of as a return from the periphery to the Center, so that the individual being has manifested all the possibilities of one level, and from which it can ascend to higher levels. In Sufi terms, the being who has actualized these possibilities is Primordial Man, in effect, the New Adam (the old Adam having left the Center, the Garden, and its central axis, or Tree) while the being that has further achieved all the higher states is Universal Man (the Adam Kadmon of the Qabbala).

As Brydon enters the house each night:

He always caught the first effect of the steel point of his stick on the old marble of the hall pavement, *large black-and-white squares* that he remembered as the admiration of his childhood and that had then made in him, as he now saw, for the growth of an early conception of style.

There is an analogy between Universal Manifestation and personal development, though like all analogies it is inverted: physical manifestation entails diversity and a spreading out; personal development a return to simplicity. This is because by returning to the Primordial State, the Garden of Eden, one reaches the Center of the horizontal world, from which the vertical assent to higher possibilities and forms can be made.

---

[12] See, for example, *Introduction to the Study of the Hindu Doctrines* (*Introduction générale à l'étude des doctrines hindoues*, 1921); *Man and His Becoming according to the Vedânta* (*L'homme et son devenir selon le Vêdânta*, 1925); *Symbolism of the Cross* (*Le symbolisme de la croix*, 1931); and *The Multiple States of the Being* (*Les états multiples de l'Être*, 1932), all of which exist in excellent English editions produced and kept in print by the estimable James Wetmore and his press, Sophia Perennis, in Ghent, New York.

This effect was the dim reverberating tinkle as of some far-off bell hung who should say where?—in the depths of the house, of the past, of that mystical other world that might have flourished for him had he not, for weal or woe, abandoned it. On this impression he did ever the same thing; he put his stick noiselessly away in a corner–feeling the place once more in the likeness of some great glass bowl, all precious concave crystal, set delicately humming by the play of a moist finger round its edge. The concave crystal held, as it were, this mystical other world, and the indescribably fine murmur of its rim was the sigh there, the scarce audible pathetic wail to his strained ear, of all the old baffled forsworn possibilities.

The image of a bowl of precious crystal, within which is manifested a pathetic little tone, by the tracing of a finger along its rim, is remarkable, and sounds like it ought to be a Traditional symbol of Universal Manifestation, but I can't really place it anywhere; here, Henry may have made a more original contribution to mysticism than either his father Henry or brother William!

The house itself clearly embodies the horizontal and vertical dimensions of universal manifestation, the three-dimensional unfolding of indefinite possibilities on each of an equally indefinite hierarchy of levels, forming an indefinite multiplicity of stages or stations. Such symbolism is often fairly explicitly manifested in the design of traditional buildings or dwellings, such as the Native American teepee (the hole in the apex of which allows smoke, or the soul, to escape) or the Muslim house built around an courtyard open to the sky.[13]

As Brydon "crapes" about his house (Irish servant dialect humor!) he finds himself confronting his obsession:

that of his opening a door behind which he would have made sure of finding nothing, a door into *a room shuttered*

---

[13] See, for example, Ananda Coomaraswamy, *The Door in the Sky* (Princeton: Princeton University Press, 1997).

and void, and yet so coming, with a great suppressed start, on *some quite erect confronting presence*, something *planted in the middle of the place and facing him* through *the dusk.*

The Center of the Primordial State is indeed associated in the world's traditions with erect presences of one sort or another, especially trees or castles, planted in the center of a Garden—as in Genesis—or an invisible or inaccessible Island—as in the Grail Legend. Dusk, of course, is the preeminent symbol of the liminal state where transformations can take place. And do we not have hear an echo of Lovecraft's "The Shuttered Room"?[14]

Reaching the top floor, where "the light he had set down on the mantel of the next room would have to figure his sword"—again, the ironic Grail note—he finds his goal:

The door between the rooms was open, and from the second another door opened to a third. These rooms, as he remembered, gave all three upon a common corridor as well, but *there was a fourth, beyond them, without issue save through the preceding.*

Here one also recalls the three stages of reality or consciousness, analogous to waking, dreaming and deep sleep, and the fourth, Turya, of primal bliss.[15]

He had come into sight of the door in which the brief chain of communication ended and which he now surveyed from the nearer threshold, the one not directly facing it. Placed at some distance to the left of this point, it would have admitted him to the last room of the four, the room without other approach or egress, had it not, to his intimate conviction, been closed *since* his former visitation, the matter probably of a quarter of an hour before. He stared with all his eyes at the wonder of the fact, arrested again where he stood and again holding his breath while he

---

[14] See Julius Evola, *The Hermetic Tradition*, Chapter 1, "The Tree, The Serpent and the Titans."

[15] See *Man and His Becoming according to the Vedânta.*

sounded his sense. Surely it had been *subsequently closed*—
that is it had been on his previous passage indubitably
open! [James's emphases]

As we have seen, his smug, self-regarding "discretion" allowed him to refuse to open that door, to pass, it would appear,
a test set up for him since he had last seen the open door, and
instead to retreat back to the lobby, only to faint when the spectre does appear, unwanted, and block his exit.

And as we also saw, after his failure and faint, he awakens in
the lap of his motherly confidante:

> on the lowest degree of the staircase, the rest of his long
> person remaining stretched on his old black-and-white
> slabs. They were cold, these marble squares of his youth;
> but *he* somehow was not, in this rich return of conscious-
> ness—the most wonderful hour, little by little, that he had
> ever known, leaving him, as it did, so gratefully, so abys-
> mally passive, and yet as with a treasure of intelligence
> waiting all round him for quiet appropriation; dissolved,
> he might call it, in the air of the place and producing the
> golden glow of a late autumn afternoon. He had come
> back, yes—come back from further away than any man but
> himself had ever travelled; but it was strange how with
> this sense what he had come back *to* seemed really the
> great thing, and as if his prodigious journey had been all
> for the sake of it.

Back on the lowest degree of human development, yet con-
gratulating himself like a Monty Python knight on his remarkable and triumphant journey, and rejoicing in the return of his
egoic, and egotistical, daylight consciousness.

Finally, we must ask the main question: why is the ghost mutilated?

This is just classic misdirection, as in a magician's trick. Why
are the ghost's fingers mutilated has absorbed the critics. But if
the ghost is some representation of the narrator, then the ghost is
like an image in a mirror. If the ghost's fingers are mutilated, ra-

ther than ask "Gee, why are the fingers in the mirror mutilated?" we should ask, "Why are the narrator's fingers mutilated?"

I would suggest that the spectre in the doorway (the "Thing on the Doorstep" or "Lurker on the Threshold") is NOT the thing behind the door. Brydon, having fled the chance of reaching the Center, is confronted rather by its inversion, the paltry ego which, however grand in worldly terms, is a sadly limited sight—a mutilation, in fact—in comparison to the fully developed Primordial Man who reigns at the Center. Brydon is far too proud of his single possibility, and perceives the fullness of the Primordial Man as a mutilation rather than the fulfillment of all possibilities.

Rather than standing erect in the primal darkness on the top floor (like the tree, or ithyphallic god, at the Center of the Garden; the "darkness" of course is another traditional symbol-through-inversion, the overwhelming fullness of Universal Manifestation symbolized by darkness, like a strong light that blinds rather than illuminates) he awakens lying flat on the ground, in the morning sun, on the lap of his motherly confidante.

Brydon has in effect chosen to remain on the level he was born—the squares making up the floor of his childhood home—rather than move forward into the center (Primordial Man), nor, consequently, to rise from there to a higher level, eventually actualizing all possibilities of manifestation (Universal Man).[16] In the words of E. M. Forster (cited with approval by Camille

---

[16] Brydon's egocentrism is to be entirely distinguished from the idea of the Absolute Ego which Evola had developed as a philosophical concept long before encountering Guénon. "In his full possession of power, man reaches absolute indifference, so that it makes no sense for him to act any more" [Evola, quoted by H. T. Hansen in his "Introduction" to *Men Among the Ruins* (Inner Traditions, 2002, p. 30). The latter needs nothing, from a feeling of already having enough, of being, indeed, above both fullness and lack, indifferent to both, while Brydon continually needs the approval of the world—"I am good, aren't I." He is dedicated to "preserve his good name," while as Coomaraswamy observes, "Blessed is the man on whose tomb can be written *Hic jacet nemo*" [Here lies no one]. (A. K. Coomaraswamy, *Hinduism and Buddhism* [New York: Philosophical Library, n.d.], p. 30).

Paglia): "Maimed creatures alone can breathe in Henry James' pages—maimed yet specialized."[17]

Or, as St. Mark asks, "What would it profit a man to gain the whole world [to say nothing of a real estate development, even one on Irving Place] and to lose his [chance of a fully developed] soul?"

Speaking of the New Testament, Brydon may be fruitfully contrasted with an earlier figure from classic American literature: Melville's Bartleby. While H. Bruce Franklin[18] has explored Bartleby's parallels to Christ and to Hindu asceticism— transmitted through Emerson's Transcendentalism—I think we can even more closely identify him with Guénon and Evola's realized being, who embodies

> . . . the style of an impersonal activity; *to prefer* what is essential and real in a higher sense, free from the trappings of sentimentalism and from pseudo-intellectual super-structures—and yet all this must be done by *remaining upright*, feeling the presence in life of that which leads beyond life, drawing from it precise norms of behaviour and action.[19]

Bartleby has gone so far beyond Brydon that he no longer has a house or home at all, living surreptitiously in his employer's office (one can't really say "at his job") and, ultimately, lying in a prison yard and staring at the wall. While Bartleby is famous for his refusal to perform any of his employer's tasks with his "I would prefer not to," he also, at one point, insists that rather than do so he "would prefer to be stationary," making him functionally identical to the Chakravartin, the Realized Man who rules the universe from his unmoving position at the center.[20]

---

[17] In *Sexual Personae: Art and Decadence from Nefertiti to Emily Dickinson* (New Haven: Yale University Press, 1990), p. 616.

[18] The relevant chapter on Bartleby from his out of print monograph, *The Wake of the Gods: Melville's Mythology* can be found along with the story in *Melville's Short Novels* (New York: Norton, 2002).

[19] *Men Among the Ruins*, p. 220.

[20] See Guénon's *King of the World* (Ghent, N.Y.: Sophia Perennis, 2005).

Bartleby's erstwhile employer, who narrates his tale, is clearly a member of what William James would later call the "healthy-minded" and, for all his sympathy and somewhat grudging efforts on Bartleby's behalf, unable to finally understand him.[21] He suggests that Bartleby's melancholy nature must have been amplified unduly by his tenure in the Dead Letter Office; yet it is precisely this daily confrontation with death, that is, the transience of what Salinger's Buddy Glass called "this goddamned phenomenal world" that enables one to rise above it. Unlike James' "discrete" Brydon, Bartleby has confronted death and used that extreme situation to leverage himself into the Center, erect and stationary, at rest as the world revolves around him.[22]

And his famous, sentimental conclusion—"Ah, Bartleby! Ah, humanity!"—would better be directed against such all too human specimens as Brydon. As for Bartleby, he has indeed "remain[ed] upright, feeling the presence in life of that which leads beyond life, drawing from it precise norms of behaviour and action."

Counter-Currents/North American New Right
October 31, 2011

---

[21] As Evola notes, the philistine thinks that the realized man, the Magus, would be rich and exercise all kinds of magic powers, being incapable of understanding either that a disinterest in all such frivolity is a prerequisite for spiritual progress—"I would prefer not to"—as well as the "boomerang" effect of actions in the subtle realm having untoward results in this world; see *Hermetic Tradition*, Chapter 51, "The Invisible Masters"

[22] Readers of William Burroughs will recall that Bartleby's prison was even then known colloquially as "The Tombs." It's true, that our last glimpse of Bartleby is lying in the prison yard, but again, the principle of inversion is at work here; the employer's limited perspective can only grasp Bartleby's position in a distorted way—Guénon, in *Man and His Becoming*, has some curious speculations about how the "delivered man" [the *mukta*] would seem to vanish from out three-dimensional vision—while also paralleling Brydon's opposite movement, from his failed trial to lying on the floor, snugly cradled in Alice's lap.

"A General Outline of the Whole"
Lovecraft as Heideggerian Event

Graham Harman
Weird Realism: Lovecraft and Philosophy
Winchester, UK: Zero Books, 2012

A winter storm in NYC is less the Currier and Ives experience of upstate and more like several days of cold slush, more suggestive — and we'll see that *suggestiveness* will be a very key term — of Dostoyevsky than Dickens.

On a purely personal level, such weather conditions I privately associate[1] with my time — as in "doing time" — at the small Canadian college (fictionalized by fellow inmate Joyce Carol Oates as "Hilberry College"[2]) where a succession of more or less self-pitying exiles from the mainstream — from Wyndham Lewis and Marshall McLuhan to the aforementioned Oates — suffered the academic purgatory of trying to teach, or even interest, the least-achieving students in Canada in such matters as Neoplatonism and archetypal psychology.[3]

One trudged to ancient, wooden classrooms and consumed endless packs of powerful Canadian cigarettes, washed down with endless cups of rancid vending machine coffee. No Starbucks for us, and no whining about second-hand smoke. We were real he-men back then! There was one student, a co-ed of course, who did complain, and the solution imposed was to exile her — exile

---

[1] On such "private associations" see Hesse, *The Glass Bead Game*, (New York: Holt, 1969), pp. 70–71.

[2] Whose biographer, Greg Johnson, is not to be confused with our own Greg Johnson here at Counter Currents — I think. For the fictionalized Hilberry see *The Hungry Ghosts: Seven Allusive Comedies* (Boston: Black Sparrow Press, 1974). *Allusive* — there's that idea again!

[3] Did they succeed? Judge for yourself: Thomas Moore: *Care of the Soul: Guide for Cultivating Depth and Sacredness in Everyday Life* (San Francisco: HarperCollins, 1992).

within exile!—to a chair in the hallway, like a Spanish nun allowed to listen in from behind a grill.

Speaking of Spain, one of the damned souls making his rounds was a little, goateed Marrano from New York, via Toronto's Pontifical Institute of Mediaeval Studies, no less, who was now attempting to explain Husserl and Heidegger, to "unpack" with his tiny hands what he once called, with an incredulous shake of the head, "that incredible language of his," to his sullen and ungrateful students.[4]

I thought of this academic Homunculus, who played Naphta to another's Schleppfuss[5] in my intellectual upbringing, when this book made its appearance in my e-mail box one recent, snowing—or slushy—weekend. For Harman wants to explain Husserl and Heidegger as well, or rather, his own take on them, which I gather he and a bunch of colleagues have expanded into their own field of Object Oriented Ontology (OOO) or Speculative Realism. And to do so, he has appropriated the work of H. P. Lovecraft, suggesting that Lovecraft play the same role of philosophical exemplar in his philosophy, as Hölderlin does in Heidegger's.

"That incredible language of his" indeed!

Part One tries to explain this Object Oriented business, but only after he tries to justify or excuse dealing with someone still often regarded as a glorified pulp hack on the same level with the great Hölderlin. He tries to short-circuit the attacks of highbrow critics, still exemplified by Edmund Wilson's, by denouncing their rhetorical strategy of *paraphrase*.

Paraphrase? What's wrong with that? Perfectly innocent, what? Well, no. Drawing on Slavoj Žižek's notion of the "stupidity of content"—the equal plausibility of any proverb, say, and its opposite—Harman insists that nothing can be paraphrased into something else—reality is not itself a sentence, and so it is "is too real to be *translated without remainder* into sentences" (p. 16, my italics). Language can only *allude* to reality.

---

[4] Eventually he would sink so low as to teach "everyday reasoning" to freshman lunkheads.

[5] See Thomas Mann's *The Magic Mountain* and *Doktor Faustus*, respectively.

What remains left over, resistant to paraphrase, is the background or context that gave the statement its meaning.[6] Paraphrase, far from harmless or obvious, is packed with metaphysical baggage—such as the assumption that reality itself is just like a sentence—that enables the skilled dialectician to reduce anything to nonsensical drivel.

Harman gives many, mostly hilarious, examples of "great" literature reduced to mere "pulp" through getting the Wilson treatment. (Perhaps too many—the book does tend to bog down from time to time as Harman indulges in his real talent for giving a half dozen or so increasing "stupid" paraphrases of passages of "great" literature.)[7]

---

[6] The hero of this vindication of Rhetoric over Dialectic turns out to be . . . McLuhan! The medium is the message—don't be hypnotized by the content, take a look at the all-important effects of the context. I've suggested before that my own work be seen, like McLuhan's, less as dogmatic theses to be defended or refuted (dogmatism is for Harman the great sin of worshipping mere content) but rather as a series of probes for revealing new contexts for old ideas.

See my Counter-Currents Interview in *The Homo and the Negro* as well as my earlier "You Mean My Whole Fallacy Is Wrong!" (http://jamesjomeara.blogspot.com/2011/03/youve-misunderstood-my-whole-fallacy-i.html). Once more, we find that education at a Catholic college in the Canadian boondocks is the best preparation for grasping post-modernism, no doubt because it reproduces the background of Brentano and Heidegger. It was Canadian before it was cool!

[7] The Wilson treatment is on display whenever some Judeo-con or Evangelical quotes passages from some alien religious work—usually the Koran these days—to show how stupid or bloodthirsty the natives are, while ignoring similar or identical passages in his own Holy Book. So-called "scholars" play the same game, questioning the authenticity of some newly discovered Gnostic work like the *Gospel of Judas* for containing, "absurdities" and "silliness" while finding nothing odd about the reanimated corpses—reminiscent of Lovecraft's genuinely pulp hackwork *Herbert West, Reaminator*—of the "orthodox" writings. Indeed, some have suggested that Lovecraft's *Necronomicon* is itself a parody of The Bible, its supposed Arab authorship a mere screen. This typically Semitic strategy of deliberately ignoring the allusive context of your opponent's words while retaining your own was diagnosed by the Aryan Christ, in such well-known fulminations against the Phari-

Genre or "pulp" writing is itself the epitome of taking the background for granted and just fiddling with the content, and deserves Edmund Wilson's famous condemnation of both its horror and mystery genres. But Lovecraft, contra Wilson, is quite conscious, and bitingly critical, of the background conditions of pulp—both in his famous essays on horror and, unmentioned by Harman, his voluminous correspondence and ghost-writing—and thus ideally equipped to manipulate it for higher, or at least more interesting, purposes.

The pulp writer takes the context for granted (the genre "conventions") and concentrates on content—sending someone to a new planet, putting a woman in charge of a space ship, etc.[8] If Lovecraft did this, or only this, he would indeed be worthy of Wilson's periphrastic contempt. But Lovecraft is interested in doing something else: "No other writer is so perplexed *by the gap between objects and the power of language to describe them, or between objects and the qualities they possess*" (p.3, my italics).

Since philosophy is the science of the background, Lovecraft himself is to this extent himself a philosopher, and useful to Harman as more than just a source of fancy illustrations: "Lovecraft,

---

sees as Matthew 23:24 : "You strain at a gnat, and swallow a camel" or Matthew 7:3: "And why beholdest thou the mote that is in thy brother's eye, but considerest not the beam that is in thine own eye?"

[8] Bad sci/fi hits rock bottom in the content-oriented department with the ubiquitous employment of the "space" prefix: space-food, space-pirates, space-justice, etc., frequently mocked on MST3K. David Bowie's space-rock ode "Moonage Daydream" contains the cringeworthy "Press your space face close to mine" but this is arguably a deliberate parody, while the rest of the song brilliantly exploits the Lovecraftian allusive/contextual mode of horror, moving from its straightfaced opening—"I'm an alligator"—through a series of Cthulhuian composites—"Squawking like a pink monkey bird"—ultimately veering into Harman's weird porn mode—"I'm a momma-poppa coming for you." Deviant sex and cut-up lyrics—another context-shredding technique—clearly points to the influence of William Burroughs, who created subversive texts based on various genres of boys' books ranging from sci/fi (*Nova Express*) to detective (*Cities of Red Night*: "The name is Clyde Williamson Snide. I am a private asshole.") to his alt-Western masterpiece *The Western Lands* trilogy.

when viewed as a writer of gaps between objects and their qualities, is of great relevance for my model of object oriented ontology" (p. 4).

Back, then to Harman's philosophy or his "ontography" as he
calls it. I call it Kantianism, but I'm a simple man. The world presents us with objects, both real (Harman is no idealist) and sensuous (objects of thought, say), which bear various properties, both
real (weight, for example) and sensuous (color, for example).
Thus, we have real and sensuous objects, as well as the real and
sensuous qualities that belong to them ... usually.

All philosophers, Harman suggests, have been concerned with
one or another of the *gaps* that occur when the ordinary relations
between these four items fail. Some philosophers promote or delight in some gap or other, while others work to deny or explain it
away. Plato introduced a gap between ordinary objects and their
more real essences, while Hume delighted in denying such a gap
and reducing them to agglomerations of sensual qualities.

Harman, in explicitly Kantian fashion this time, derives four
possible failures (Kant would call them antinomies). Gaps can occur between a real object and its sensuous qualities, a real object
and its real qualities, a sensuous object and its sensuous qualities,
and a sensuous object and its real qualities. Or, for simplicity,
RO/SQ, RO/RQ, SQ/SO, and SO/RQ.

Take SQ/SO. This gap, where the object's sensuous qualities,
though listed, Cubist-like, *ad nauseam*, fail, contra Hume, to suggest any kind of objective unity, even of a phenomenal kind—the
object is withdrawn from us, as Heidegger would say. It occurs in
a passage such as the description of the Antarctic city of the Elder
Race:

> The effect was that of a Cyclopean city of no architecture
> known to man or to human imagination, with *vast aggrega-
> tions* of night-black masonry embodying monstrous perver-
> sions of geometrical laws. There were truncated cones,
> sometimes terraced or fluted, surmounted by tall cylindrical
> shafts here and there bulbously enlarged and often capped
> with tiers of thinnish scalloped disks; and strange beetling,
> table-like constructions suggesting piles of multitudinous

rectangular slabs or circular plates or five-pointed stars with each one overlapping the one beneath. There were composite cones and pyramids either alone or surmounting cylinders or cubes or flatter truncated cones and pyramids, and occasional needle-like spires in curious clusters of five. *All of these febrile structures seemed knit together* by tubular bridges crossing from one to the other at various dizzy heights, and *the implied scale of the whole* was terrifying and oppressive in its sheer gigantism. (*At the Mountains of Madness,* my italics)

SQ/RO? This Kantian split between an object's sensuous properties and what its essence is implied to be, occurs in the classic description of the idol of Cthulhu:

If I say that my somewhat extravagant imagination yielded *simultaneous pictures* of an octopus, a dragon, and a human caricature, I shall not be unfaithful to *the spirit of the thing.* A pulpy, tentacled head surmounted a grotesque and scaly body with rudimentary wings; but it was the *general outline* of the whole which made it most shockingly frightful. ("The Call of Cthulhu," my italics)

SO/RQ? Harman admits it's rare in Lovecraft, (and elsewhere, though he finds hints of it in Leibniz) but he finds a few examples where scientific investigation reveals new, unheard of properties in some eldritch or trans-Plutonian object.

In every quarter, however, interest was intense; for the utter alienage of the thing was a tremendous challenge to scientific curiosity. One of the small radiating arms was broken off and subjected to chemical analysis. Professor Ellery found platinum, iron and tellurium in the strange alloy; but mixed with these were at least three other apparent elements of high atomic weight which chemistry was absolutely powerless to classify. Not only did they fail to correspond with any known element, but they did not even fit the vacant places reserved for probable elements in the periodic system. ("Dreams in the Witch House")

And RO/RQ? You don't want to know, as Lovecraft's protagonists usually discover too late. It's the inconceivable object whose surface properties only hint at yet further levels of inconceivable monstrosity within. Usually, Lovecraft relies on just slapping a weird name on something and hinting at the rest, as in

> [O]utside the ordered universe [is] that amorphous blight of nethermost confusion which blasphemes and bubbles at the center of all infinity—the boundless daemon sultan Azathoth, whose name no lips dare speak aloud, and who gnaws hungrily in inconceivable, unlighted chambers beyond time and space amidst the muffled, maddening beating of vile drums and the thin monotonous whine of accursed flutes. (*Dream Quest of Unknown Kaddath*)

You can see, in each case, how the horrific effect, and the usability for Harman's ontography, would entirely disappear if given a Wilsonian "paraphrase": It was a squid with wings! The object, when analyzed, revealed new, hitherto unknown elements!

Confused yet? Bored? Don't worry. The whole point of Harman's book, to which he devotes the vast portion of the text, is analyzing passages from Lovecraft that provide vivid illustrations of one or more of these gaps. In this way Harman's ontography acquires its Hölderlin, and Lovecraft is rescued from pulp purgatory.

While there is considerable interest in Heidegger on alt-Right sites such as this one,[9] I'm sure there is considerably more general interest in Lovecraft. But Harman's whole book is clearly and engagingly written, avoiding both oracular obscurity and overly-chummy vulgarity; since Harman is admirably clear even when

---

[9] Harman does a better job explaining Husserl and Heidegger than my little Marrano, but then he has had another three decades to work on it. He does, however, focus mainly on Heidegger's tool analysis, and his own, somewhat broader formulation.

For a wider focused, more objective, if you will, presentation of Heidegger, see Collin Cleary's "Heidegger: An Introduction for Anti-Modernists," starting here: http://www.counter-currents.com/2012/06/heidegger-an-introduction-for-anti-modernists-part-1/

discussing himself or Husserl, no one should feel unqualified to take on this unique—Lovecraftian?—conglomeration of philosophy and literary criticism.

The central Part Two is almost 200 pages of close readings of exactly 100 passages from Lovecraft. As such, it exhibits a good deal of diminishing returns through repetition, and the reader may be forgiven for skipping around, perhaps to their own favorite parts. And there's certainly no point in offering my own paraphrases!

Nevertheless, over and above the discussion of individual passages as illustrations of Speculative Realism, Harman has a number of interesting insights into Lovecraft's work generally. It's also here that Harman starts to reveal some of his assumptions, or biases, or shall we say, *context*.

"RACISM"

Harman, who, word on the blogs seems to be, is a run-of-the-mill liberal rather than a po-mo freak like his fellow "European philosophers,"[10] tips his hand early by referring dismissively to criticism of Lovecraft as pulp being "merely a social judgment, no different in kind from not wanting one's daughter to marry the chimney sweep" ("Preliminary Note"). And we know how silly that would be! So needless to say, Lovecraft's forthright, unmitigated, non-evolutionary (as in Obama's "My position on gay marriage has evolved") views on race need to be disinfected if Harman is to be comfortable marrying his philosophy to Lovecraft's writing.

His solution is clever, but too clever. Discussing the passage from "Call of Cthulhu" where the narrator—foolishly as it hap-

---

[10] Needless to say, he never notices that his liberalism is rooted in the ultimate dogma-affirming, context-ignoring movement, Luther's "sola scriptura." His liberalism is such as to allow him to tell a pretty amusing one-liner about Richard Rorty, but only by attributing it to "a colleague." On the one hand, he cringes for Heidegger for daring to refer to a "Senegal Negro" (p. 59) but dismisses Emmanuel Faye's "Heidegger is a Nazi" screed as a "work of propaganda" (p. 259). See Michael O'Meara's, "Heidegger the 'Nazi,'" his review of Faye, here: http://www.counter-currents.com/2010/07/heidegger-the-nazi/

pens—dismisses a warning as coming from "an excitable Span-iard" Harman suggests that the racism of Lovecraft's protago-nists[11] adds an interesting layer of—of course!—irony to them. As so often, we the reader are "smarter" than the smug protagonist, who will soon be taken down a few pegs.

But this really won't do. Lovecraft's protagonists are not stupid or uninformed, but rather too well-informed, hence prone to self-satisfaction that leads them where more credulous laymen might balk. "They's ghosts in there, Mister Benny!"

Unfortunately for Harman, Lovecraft was above all else a Sci-entist, or simply a well-educated man, and the Science of his day was firmly on the side of what today would be called Human Bi-odiversity or HBD.[12] Harman may, like most "liberals" find that distasteful, something not to be mentioned, like Victorians and sex—a kind of "liberal creationism" as it's been called—but that's his problem.

It would be more interesting to adopt a truly Lovecraftian theme and take his view, or settled belief, that Science, or too much Science, was bad for us; just as Copernicus etc. had de-throned man for the privileged center of the God's universe, the "truth" about Cthulhu and the other Elder Gods—first, there very existence, then the implication that they are the reality behind everyday religions—has a deflationary, perhaps madness induc-ing, effect.

Consider this famous quotation from the opening of "The Call of Cthulhu" as quoted by Harman himself in Part Two:

The sciences, each straining in its own direction, have hitherto harmed us little; but someday the piecing together of dissociated knowledge will open up such terrifying vistas of reality, and our frightful position therein, that we shall either go mad from the revelation or flee from the deadly light into the peace and safety of a new dark age.

---

[11] "Not even Poe [another embarrassing "racist", well what do you know?] has such indistinguishable protagonists" (p. 10).

[12] Indeed, "racism" is one of those principles Baron Evola evoked in his *Autodefesa* as being "those that before the French Revolution every well-born person considered sane and normal."

Thus Harman could argue that HBD may be true but bad for us to know — something very like the actual position of such liberal Comstocks as Richard Lewontin.

Consider, to switch genres, *Dr. No*. Quarrel, the ignorant, superstitious but loyal native retainer, is afraid to land on Crab Key, due to the presence of a dragon. Bond and his American buddy Leiter mock his fear (Leiter: "Hey Quarrel, if you see a dragon, you get in first and breathe on him. With all that rum in you, he'll die happy.") But of course the dragon — which turns out to be a flame-throwing armored tractor — incinerates Quarrel whilst Bond and the equally superstitious but much more toothsome Honey Ryder are taken prisoner. While in this genre we know that Bond is the heroic knight who will ultimately slay the dragon, for now he does seem to be what Dr. No calls him, "just another stupid policeman" who would have done well to listen to the native — not unlike any number of Lovecraft's educated protagonists.[13]

This smug assumption that knowledge leaves us safe, and indeed safer, is what Lovecraft is satirizing when the narrator of "Call of Cthulhu" dismisses the warnings of the "excitable Spaniard," not, as Harman would have it, lampooning "racism" on some meta-level.[14]

Also, Michel Houllebeq, an author Harman otherwise praises, has emphasized that Lovecraft is anything but self-assured, either

---

[13] Kingsley Amis has cogently argued that the key to Bond's appeal is that he's just like us, only a little better trained, able to read up on poker or *chemin de fer*, has excellent shooting instructors, etc. But if we had the chance . . . See Amis, Kingsley *The James Bond Dossier* (London: Jonathan Cape, 1965).

[14] It might be interesting to apply Harman's OOO to a film like Carpenter's *They Live*. In "He Writes, You Read, *They Live*," my review of Lethem's book on the movie, reprinted in *The Homo and the Negro*, I mentioned liking another point, also from Slavoj Žižek: contrary to the smug assumptions of the Left, knowledge is not necessarily something people want, or which is pleasant — hence the protagonist has to literally beat his friend into putting on the reality-revealing sunglasses. Here we have both Lovecraft's gaps and notion that knowledge is more likely something you'll regret: Lovecraft and Žižek, together again!

as a White man, or for the White race itself.[15] If "racism" is able to play the self-debunking role Harman wants it to, this is only because of Lovecraft's self-doubts, based on his horrific experiences in the already multi-culti New York City of the 1920s, that the White race would be able to survive the onslaught of the inferior but strong and numerous under-men. As Houellebecq says, Lovecraft learned to take "racism back to its essential and most profound core: fear."

"FASCISTIC SOCIALISM"

On a related point, Harman puts this phrase, from Lovecraft's last major work, *The Shadow out of Time* (which he generally dislikes, for reasons we'll dispute later), in italics with a question mark, and leaves it at that, as if just throwing his hands up and saying "well, I just don't know!" Alas, this is one of Lovecraft's most interesting ideas. Like several American men of letters, such as Ralph Adams Cram, Lovecraft concluded that Roosevelt's New Deal was an American version of Fascism, but, unlike the Chamber of Commerce types who made the same identification, he approved of it for precisely that reason!

More generally, "fascistic socialism" was essentially what Spengler and others of the Conservative Revolution movement in German advocated; for example:

Hans Freyer studied the problem of the failure of radical Leftist socialist movements to overcome bourgeois society in the West, most notably in his *Revolution von Rechts* ("Revolution from the Right"). He observed that because of compromises on the part of capitalist governments, which introduced welfare policies to appease the workers, many revolutionary socialists had come to merely accommodate the system; that is, they no longer aimed to overcome it by revolution because it provided more or less satisfactory wel-

---

[15] Michel Houellebecq, *H. P. Lovecraft: Against the World, Against Life* (London: Gollancz, 2008). See more generally, and from the same period, Lothrop Stoddard, *The Revolt Against Civilization: The Menace of the Under Man*, ed. Alex Kurtagić, introduction by Kevin MacDonald (Shamley Green: The Palingenesis Project, 2011).

fare policies. Furthermore, these same policies were basically defusing revolutionary charges among the workers. Freyer concluded that capitalist bourgeois society could only be overcome by a revolution from the Right, by Right-wing socialists whose guiding purpose would not be class warfare but the restoration of collective meaning in a strong *Völkisch* ("Folkish" or "ethnic") state.[16]

But then, Harman would have to discuss, or even acknowledge, ideas that give liberals nose-bleeds.

WEIRD PORN

Harman makes the important distinction that Lovecraft is a writer of gaps, who chooses to apply his talents of literary allusion to the content of horror; but gaps do not exclusively involve horror, and we can imagine writers applying the same skills to other genres, such as detective stories, mysteries, and westerns.[17] In fact,

> A literary "weird porn" might be conceivable, in which the naked bodies of the characters would display bizarre anomalies subverting all human descriptive capacity, but without being so strange that the erotic dimension would collapse into a grotesque sort of eros-killing horror. (p. 4)

Harman just throws this out, but if it seem implausible, I would offer Michael Manning's graphic novels as example of weird porn: geishas, hermaphrodites, lizards and horses—or rather, vaguely humanoid species that suggest snakes and horses, rather like Harman's discussion of Max Black's puzzle over the gap produced by the proposition "Men are wolves"—create a kind of steam punk/pre-Raphaelist sexual utopia.[18]

---

[16] Lucian Tudor, "Hans Freyer and the Quest for Collective Meaning," here: http://www.counter-currents.com/2013/02/hans-freyer-the-quest-for-collective-meaning/#more-36698

[17] Again, just as Burroughs applied his cut-up technique to various pulp genres.

[18] See my discussion of Manning in "The Hermetic Environment and Hermetic Incest: The True Androgyne and the 'Ambiguous Wis-

PROLIXITY

Speaking of Lovecraftian allusiveness not being anchored to horror or any particular genre or content, brings us to my chief interest, and chief disagreement, with Harman's discussion of Lovecraft's literary technique.

I knew we would have a problem when right from the start Harman adduces *The Shadow out of Time* as one of Lovecraft's worst, since this is actually one of my favorites, and the one that first convinced me of his ability to create cosmic horror through the invocation of hideous eons of cosmic vistas. Harman first notes, in dealing with the preceding novella, *At the Mountains of Madness*, that while the first half would rank as Lovecraft's greatest work if he had only stopped there, the second half is a huge letdown: Lovecraft seems to descend to the level of pulp content, as he has his scientists go on a long, tedious journey through the long abandoned subterranean home of the Elder Race, reading endless hieroglyphs and giving all kinds of tedious details of their "everyday" life.[19]

For Harman, "Lovecraft's decline as a stylist becomes almost alarming here" (p. 225) and will continue—with a brief return to form with "Dreams in the Witch House," where Harman makes the interesting observation that Lovecraft seems to be weaving in every kind of Lovecraftian technique and content into one grand synthesis— until it ruins the second half as well of *Shadow*.

In a series of articles here on Counter Currents—soon to be reprinted as part of my next book, *The Eldritch Evola . . . & Others*—I suggested that not only should Lovecraft's infamous verbosity no more be a barrier to elite appreciation than the equally deplored but critically lauded "Late Style" of Henry James, but also, and more interestingly, that conversely, we could see James developing that same style as part of an attempt to produce the same effect as Lovecraft's, which fans call "cosmicism" but which I would rather call cosmic horror (akin to the "sublime" of Burke or

---

dom of the Female,'" http://jamesjomeara.blogspot.com/2010/12/hermetic-environment-and-hermetic.html

[19] Everyday life of pre-Cambrian radiata with wings, of course.

Kant).[20] Or perhaps: Weird Realism.

While Harman has greatly contributed to a certain micro-analysis of Lovecraft's style, he seems, like the critics of the Late James, to miss the big picture. Although useful for rescuing Lovecraft from pulp oblivion, he still limits Lovecraft's significance to either mere literature, or illustrations of Harman's ontography. I suggest this still diminishes Lovecraft's achievement.

The work of Lovecraft, like James, has the not inconsiderable extra value, over and above any "literary" pleasure, of stilling the mind by its very *longeurs*, leaving us open and available to the arising of some other, deeper level of consciousness when the gaps arise.[21]

But this is not on the table here, because Harman, like all good empiricists (and we are all empiricists today, are we not?) rejects, or misconstrues, the very idea of our having access to a super-sensible grasp of reality that would leap beyond, or between, the

---

[20] My suggestion was based on some remarks of John Auchard in Penguin's new edition of the *Portable Henry James*, that James's work could be seen as part of the attempt to substitute art for religion, by using the endless accumulation of detail—James's "prolixity" as Lovecraft himself chides him for—to "saturate" everyday experience with meaning.

[21] Colin Wilson's second Lovecraftian novel, *The Philosopher's Stone* (Los Angeles: Tarcher, 1971)—originally published in 1969, republished in a mass market edition in 1971 at the request of, and with a Foreword by, Joyce Carol Oates, bringing us back to Hilberry—introduced me to the idea of length, and even boredom, as spiritual disciplines. One of the main characters "seemed to enjoy very long works for their own sake. I think he simply enjoyed the intellectual discipline of concentrating for hours at a time. If a work was long, it automatically recommended itself to him. So we have spent whole evenings listening to the complete *Contest Between Harmony and Invention* of Vivaldi, the complete *Well Tempered Clavier*, whole operas of Wagner, the last five quartets of Beethoven, symphonies of Bruckner and Mahler, the first fourteen Haydn symphonies. . . . He even had a strange preference for a sprawling, meandering symphony by Furtwängler [presumably the *Second*], simply because it ran on for two hours or so." The book is available online here: http://lucite.org/lucite/archive/fiction_-_lovecraft/14047169-the-philosophers-stone-by-colin-wilson.pdf

gaps; what in the East, and the West until the rise of secularism, would be called intellectual intuition.[22]

> Reality itself is weird because reality itself is incommensurable with any attempt to represent or measure it. Lovecraft is aware of this difficulty to an exemplary degree, and through his assistance we may be able to learn about how *to say something without saying it* – or in philosophical terms, *how to love wisdom without having it. When it comes to grasping reality, illusion and innuendo are the best we can do.* (p. 51, my italics)

As usual in the modern West, we are to shoulder on as best we can, in an empty, meaningless world, comforted only by patting ourselves on the back for being too grown up, too "smart," to believe we can not only pursue wisdom, but reach it. As René Guénon put it, it is one of the peculiarities of the modern Westerner to substitute a theory of knowledge for the acquisition of knowledge.[23]

Counter-Currents/*North American New Right*
February 28, 2013

---

[22] With the inconsistency typical of a Modern trying to conduct thought after cutting off the roots of thought, Harman advises us that "It takes a careful historical judge to weigh which [contextual] aspects of a given thing are assimilated by it, and which can be excluded" (p. 245). What makes a "careful" judge is, of course, intuition. Cf. my remarks on Spengler's "physiognomic tact" and Guénon's intellectual intuition in "The Lesson of the Monster; or, The Great, Good Thing on the Doorstep," above.

[23] How one can transcend the limits of secular science and philosophy, without abandoning empirical experience as the Christian does with his blind "faith", is the teaching found in Evola's *Introduction to Magic*, especially the essay "The Nature of Initiatic Knowledge." "Having long been trapped in a kind of magic circle, modern man knows nothing of such horizons. . . . Those who are called "scientists" today [as well as, even more so, "philosophers"] have hatched a real conspiracy; they have made science their monopoly, and absolutely do not want anyone to know *more* than they do, or in a *different* manner than they do."

MIKE HAMMER, OCCULT DICK:
KISS ME DEADLY AS LOVECRAFTIAN TALE

Kiss Me Deadly (1955; 106 minutes; Black and White)
Director: Robert Aldrich[1]
Writers: Mickey Spillane (novel), A. I. Bezzerides (screenplay)
Stars: Ralph Meeker, Albert Dekker, Paul Stewart , Gaby Rodgers, Jack Elam, Wesley Addy, Strother Martin, Percy Helton, and introducing Cloris Leachman.

"A crack formed and enlarged, and the whole door gave way—but from the other side; whence poured a howling tumult of ice-cold wind with all the stenches of the bottomless pit, and whence reached a sucking force not of earth or heaven, which, coiling sentiently about the paralysed detective, dragged him through the aperture and down unmeasured spaces filled with whispers and wails, and gusts of mocking laughter."—H. P. Lovecraft, "The Horror at Red Hook" (*Weird Tales*, 1927)

"Soberin and Gabrielle are vying for the contents of the box. Gabrielle shoots Soberin, believing that she can keep the mysterious contents for herself. As she slyly opens the case, it is ultimately revealed to be stolen radionuclide material, which in the final scene apparently reaches explosive criticality when the box is fully opened. Horrifying sounds emit from the nuclear material as Gabrielle and the house burst into flames."—Wikipedia, *Kiss Me Deadly*[2]

"The key Mike found led him to something of which he had no comprehension and which will very possibly kill him, and maybe destroy the Earth. He and Gabrielle are caught in a world of meanings that preexist them—culture, science, religion and myth. They proceed as they do in

---

[1] "Eldritch"?

[2] http://en.wikipedia.org/wiki/Kiss_Me_Deadly%20/%20Plot

pursuit of something they don't understand—but think they understand the value others place on it. They are fatally wrong."[3]

While recently reading Barton St. Armond's classic article "H. P. Lovecraft: New England Decadent,"[4] I came to the Lovecraft quote above and had an odd thought: I've seen this before![5] Then it hit me: the finest screen adaptation of H. P. Lovecraft occurred already in 1955, and quite unconsciously at that. I suppose that's the best way, the way it had to be; no bothering with Lovecraft's purple prose or mythos monsters; just the pure essence of Lovecraftian terror, mixed with a lot of sleaze to keep the marks happy and then sloshed up on the screen. It's called *Kiss Me Deadly*.

Here's a synopsis courtesy of DVD Savant:

Sleazy, cynical detective Mike Hammer (Ralph Meeker) makes his living with divorce cases, often unleashing his sexy secretary Velda (Maxine Cooper) as an agent provocatrix on straying adulterers. When he picks up naked-under-a-trench coat hitchhiker Christina Bailey (Cloris Leachman, in her first movie) and she's later tortured to death, Hammer decides to ditch the bedroom work and pursue the secret behind the brutality, purely for profit. His government agent friend Pat Chambers (Wesley Addy) warns him off, but Mike slowly pulls the case apart by threatening witnesses and putting Velda and his best buddy Nick (Nick Dennis) in harm's way. When the secret turns out to be a mysterious box stolen from a government science lab, Hammer finds out too late that he's latched onto something far too big, and too hot, to handle.[6]

---

[3] William Luhr, *Film Noir* (Malden, Mass: Wiley, 2012), p. 141.

[4] Barton St. Armond, *H. P. Lovecraft: New England Decadent* (Providence, R. I.: WaterFire Providence, 2013), includes plates of the works discussed, from Goya to Clark Ashton Smith.

[5] "You've seen these films! Haven't you, my man?"—Will Graham, *Manhunter*.

[6] http://www.dvdtalk.com/dvdsavant/s286kiss.html

This is a Lovecraft tale? Sound absurd? Can you prove it isn't?[7] Consider this from the screenwriter: "I wrote it fast because I had contempt for it. It was automatic writing. Things were in the air and I put them in it."[8]

Not your usual *auteur*'s claim of authorship. It's the usual note of contempt of well-paid Hollywood commie hacks[9] for two-fisted American pulp writers, here Mickey Spillane rather than Lovecraft,[10] and with the interesting additional note of surrealist writing techniques. As happens in many a horror tale, you don't have to believe in the Ouija board to conjure up something ugly "in the air" when you play with it.

Although opening to indifferent business, the film has become a legendary *noir*, ultimately getting a Criterion Collection release a couple years back. Reading all the commentary and fanboy buzz on the net you can't get far without hearing about how Aldrich and Bezzerides not only had contempt for the material, but wanted to take down the whole Mike Hammer phenomenon, which they seemed to think spelled either the coming of Fascism or the return of the Stone Age.[11] The message they

---

[7] "Can you prove you didn't? You certainly can't prove I did." Ray Milland, *Dial 'M' for Murder*, 1954.

[8] Quoted in Luhr, p. 138.

[9] "Although a leftist at the time of the Hollywood blacklist, Bezzerides denied any conscious intention for this meaning in his script," http://en.wikipedia.org/wiki/Kiss_Me_Deadly%20/%20Critical_resp onse.

[10] Although earlier pulp detective writers had been up-marketed and used to make some well-regarded films, the Hollywood Elite drew the line at Spillane, who was far too popular, too "fascist" (unlike a good party member like Dashiell Hammett) and had even started off in the lowest depth, comic books (Luhr, p. 129). Oddly enough, *KMD* itself was singled out by the Kefauver Commission as 1955's number one menace to American Youth. Chandler and Hammett preceded Lovecraft in the canonical Library of America, followed by P. K. Dick; can you imagine Spillane there?

[11] Later, there would be a similar panic among the "respectable" culturati over James Bond; Kingsley Amis easily shows the absurdity of Bond as a Hammer-style "sadist" in his The *James Bond Dossier* (Lon-

seemed to want to deliver—best expressed by Fed pal Pat near the beginning—is surprisingly up-to-date: don't take the law into your own hands, give up your guns, stop listening to conspiracy theories, and trust—but above all, don't question—the Feds.

But as I've said before, the writer who lets his imagination free is not likely to produce something pleasing to the PC crowd.[12]

In the case of this film, by portraying Hammer not as Spillane intended—a somewhat more violent, lower-class but still Marlowe-style knight errant—but rather as a psychopathically violent moron, they produced an astounding sleazy and ultra-violent film that barely escaped the box office poison of a "C for condemned" rating from the Catholic Legion of Decency and was cited as a threat to America at the very same Congressional hearings investigating those damned comic books![13]

---

don: Jonathan Cape, 1965).

[12] See especially the conclusion of "A Light Unto the Nations: Reflections on Olaf Stapledon's *The Flames*," below. The problem is especially tricky with fascism; one doesn't "know" anyone of such a type—Pauline Kael famously said she "didn't know anyone who voted for [Nixon]"—so one all too easily draws on oneself and produces an accidental and revealing portrait of liberal totalitarianism; see my "The Fraud of Miss Jean Brodie," http://www.counter-currents.com/tag/muriel-spark/. For contrast, consider Henry James' *The Bostonians*; as F. R. Leavis says, "James understands the finer civilization of New England, and is the more effective as an ironic critic of it because he is not merely an ironic critic; he understands it because he both knows it from inside and sees it from outside with the eye of a professional student of civilization who has had much experience of non-Puritan cultures."—F. R. Leavis, *The Great Tradition* (New York: G. W. Stewart, 1948), p. 134. He later refers to this as "insight . . . utterly unaccompanied by animus" (p. 135).

[13] J. Hoberman, *The Magic Hour: Film at Fin de Siècle* (Philadelphia: Temple University Press, 2003), p. 23. Spillane was so infuriated by the portrayal that he made sure the next time Hammer was filmed to not only write and finance the movie but play Hammer his own damn self. The result, *The Girl Hunters* (filmed in England other than some shots of Spillane swanning around Midtown Manhattan in a white trench coat—"Just like a cop to wear a white trench coat" Burroughs had noted in the opening chapter of *Naked Lunch*—and featuring the pre-Bond

But Hammer is brutish and stubborn, keeping the cops and the feds in the dark even though they keep trying to impress upon him the importance of this case; he doesn't seem to realize just how far in over his head he is. . . . Hammer's no hero, and the film's staggering climax represents his complete failure: his realization of the horrible forces he's been toying with, followed by a nuclear meltdown from which he barely escapes. And then the film simply ends, with abrupt finality, leaving Hammer as a broken, irrelevant archetype, an out-of-date relic whose time has passed with the relative innocence of the pre-atomic age.[14]

Once compared with what Aldrich & Co. produced, Spillane's Hammer did indeed seem more like Marlowe or the Thin Man; the self-sabotage is rather like Tarantino's *Inglourious Basterds*, where the Jewish and American sadism makes the audience sympathize with the Nazi "villains."[15] It's no surprise to recall how Tarantino already ripped off (or "paid homage to") *KMD*'s "glowing what's-it in the suitcase" McGuffin for *Pulp Fiction*.[16]

Still, I need to answer a number of objections you undoubtedly have. First, you might point out that Lovecraft liked to make his protagonists scholars, however oddball, or professors, scientific explorers, or even just wealthy slackers ("The Hound," "Pickman's Model"), not thugs like Hammer. Even the "detec-

---

Shirley Eaton) is . . . interesting.

[14] Only the Cinema: "Films I Love, #22: *Kiss Me Deadly*," http://seul-le-cinema.blogspot.com/2009/03/films-i-love-22-kiss-me-deadly-robert.html.

[15] See Trevor Lynch's review in *Trevor Lynch's White Nationalist Guide to the Movies*, ed. Greg Johnson, Foreword by Kevin MacDonald (San Francisco: Counter-Currents, 2012).

[16] As did Steven Spielberg ("Marion, don't look in the box!") and Alex Cox (*Repo Man*); Brian Wall adds Bunuel (*Belle du Jour*) and David Lynch (*Mulholland Drive*); see Brian Wall, *Theodor Adorno and Film Theory: The Fingerprint of Spirit* (New York: Palgrave Macmillan, 2013), p. 67. Hoberman (*The Magic Hour*) adds Truffaut's *Shoot the Piano Player*.

tive" in the quote above is, rather implausibly, a dandy from Trinity College, Dublin who returns to New York to join the police force and investigate occult matters.[17]

Well, the film picks Hammer up "out of the gutter [he] came from" as the mob boss says (even the mob loathes him; the feds want someone "to open a window" after interrogating him) and tidies him up into "more of a Playboy-inspired dream guy, a proto-James Bond who has to fend off dishy dames with a club."[18] Not that Mike himself is now an effete snob. As the *New York Times* says: "Mike himself is a sort of cultural caveman, whom Aldrich pointedly *surrounds with* high art: modern paintings, 19th-century poetry, radios that invariably pour forth classical music whenever Mike switches one on."[19]

Like a good post-war consumer, Mike has read all about the "Playboy Philosophy" and has bought all the right toys, from his mid-century modern bachelor pad—complete with wall-mounted, reel-to-reel answering machine[20]—to his brand-new Corvette; the rest of the surrounding, the "culchah" items, are provided by his clients and informants.[21]

---

[17] Hence St. Armand's interest, as one of several stores where Lovecraft reveals and works out his Decadent and Symbolist influences.

[18] "Spillane also seems to have invented the sadistic quip during killings—but Bezzerides gives this role to the deadly female instead." http://www.dvdtalk.com/dvdsavant/s286kiss.html

[19] "But there's also "a new kind of art in the world," as one character explains to Mike, and its embodiment turns out to be the object of his search, a leather-bound steel box." http://www.nytimes.com/2011/07/03/movies/robert-aldrichs-vera-cruz-and-kiss-me-deadly-on-dvd.html.

[20] "*KMD* may have one of the best '50s images of consumer iconography. On Hammer's wall is a reel-to-reel answering machine. These devices actually existed in that era, and the make is Code-A-Phone." — http://www.freepresshouston.com/film/thoughts-on-kiss-me-deadly/.

[21] "The detective, played by Ralph Meeker (the actor who replaced Marlon Brando in *A Streetcar Named Desire*), drives a Jaguar, has a futuristic telephone answering machine built into his bachelor pad's wall, and, a bag of golf clubs in the corner, lives a version of what was not yet called the Playboy philosophy. The faux Calder mobile and checkerboard floor pattern add to the crazy, clashing expressionism." —

After meeting the Rossetti-spouting Christina, he searches her book-lined apartment—casually stealing the book he needs, of course—and finds out that she "always seemed have [the radio] tuned to that station"—the all-Schubert station, apparently—so the next time Mike's at home needing to do some hard thinking, sure enough he turns on a radio set to the same station, as if Mike usually listens to string quartets rather than bachelor pad exotica (Brooklyn hipsters from the '90s would kill for that so-ironic pad, man). During another "think, damn it" session he asks Velda to read out the poem Christina has marked, presumably to allow him to concentrate on this difficult "thinking" business, but it sure seems as if he could be functionally illiterate.

The final clue falls into his hands at a "modern art" gallery, where, archetypically, he gives away his entrance by walking, caveman that he is, right into and smashing a glass end-table. (I'd love to hear that was a goof Aldrich decided to keep in.)

So while Mike isn't himself an egghead, he is surrounded by cultural references, which actually is what gives the Lovecraft touch.

> Like one of *Mad*'s parodies, the movie unfolds in a deranged cubist space, amid the debris of Western civilization—shards of opera, deserted museums, molls who paraphrase Shakespeare, mad references to Greek mythology and the Old Testament. A nineteenth-century poem furnishes the movie's major clue.[22]

The movie is filled with cultural references, from Rossetti at the beginning[23] to the pompous, soon to be shut up with a bullet Dr. Soberin at the end.

"*Kiss Me Deadly*: The Thriller of Tomorrow," by J. Hoberman, online at: http://www.criterion.com/current/posts/1896-kiss-me-deadly-the-thriller-of-tomorrow

[22] Hoberman, op. cit.

[23] Luhr: "The use of the Rossetti sonnet to uncover a major clue underscores the film's repeated references to past culture" (p. 140).

Dr. Soberin: As the world becomes more primitive, its treasures become more fabulous.

The latter sequence is particularly choice, as Soberin rattles off his culture markers and Lilly, doubling Mike (a point we shall return to), childishly, or barbarically, stubbornly (another key point) ignores his insinuations and insists on *knowing* — not literary or mythical references, but *what's in the box*.

Dr. Soberin: Curiosity killed a cat and it certainly would have you if you'd followed your impulse to open it. You did very well to call me when you did.

Lily: Yes, I know. But what's in it?

Dr. Soberin: You have been misnamed, Gabrielle [Lily's real name, also the actress's name, misnames her?]. You should have been called Pandora. She had a curiosity about a box and opened it and let loose all the evil in the world.

Lily: Never mind about the evil. What's in it?

Dr. Soberin: Did you ever hear of Lot's wife?

Lily: No. [WTF never heard of Lot's wife?]

Dr. Soberin: No. Well, she was told not to look back. But she disobeyed and she was changed into a pillar of salt.

Lily: Well, I just want to know what it is.

Dr. Soberin: The head of Medusa. That's what's in the box, and who looks on her will be changed not into stone but into brimstone and ashes. But of course you wouldn't believe me; you'd have to see for yourself, wouldn't you?

Perhaps it's her Damian meets Lolita eroticism, but the

filmmakers are again subverted, as the audience is definitely on Lily's side as she shuts up Soberin—poimanently, ya see?—and opens the damned box.[24] Though not before Soberin delivers his peroration:

> **Dr. Soberin**: Listen to me, as if I were Cerberus barking with all his heads at the gates of hell. [What, she didn't get Lot's wife and she'll get this?] I will tell you where to take it, but don't . . . don't open the box![25]

Even the film's Voice of Reason[26] is equally pompous and fragmented—decadent, if you will. When Pat finally tells Mike what's up, he speaks slowly, as if talking to a dense child, but still can't really put it together himself, and mumbling discon-

---

[24] Talk about subverting the filmmakers' intent, some have even discovered a "liberal subtext" that makes Mike a sort of Alan Alda: "As much as anything else, it's the positive images of women, immigrants, African-Americans, and poor people, along with Hammer's getting on with them so well, especially the folks at the jazz club, boxing gym, and auto repair shop, that gives the film much of its leftist edge." —Café Noir, http://mexnoir.blogspot.com/2011/10/kiss-me-deadly.html. This "common touch" angle is especially worked in the aforementioned *Girl Hunters*, where a good third of the film is Hammer/Spillane collecting favors and plaudits from all the little people who are so grateful to owe him—even his landlord won't take his back rent: "Take, take; remember when you gave?" That Hammer is played by Spillane himself and many of the little people are real friends of his gives it a rather odd tone. I leave it to the reader to reflect on what the praise of "getting on with" the poor tells us about the liberal's rather feudal idea of his role in society.

[25] "The force of Soberin's mythical invocations is the reverse of what he desires; the free-floating prestige of his examples only seems to add to the glamour of the box" (Martin Harries, *Forgetting Lot's Wife: On Destructive Spectatorship* [New York: Fordham University Press, 2007], p. 74).

[26] The film can't strictly have a "hero" since the message is "obey the (Liberal) government." Heroism and individualism are only good when bad fascists are in charge; then it's "question (non-Liberal) authority."

nected words he hopes will ring a bell with no further effort on his world-weary part:

Lt. Pat Murphy: Now listen, Mike. Listen carefully. I'm going to pronounce a few words. They're harmless words. *Just a bunch of letters scrambled together.*[27] But their meaning is very important. Try to understand what they mean. "Manhattan Project, Los Alamos, Trinity."[28]

But anyway, rather than a cultured protagonist, the Lovecraftian note here is carried by the presentation of a cultural wasteland, where culture exists only a scattering of dying embers, tossed around without much or any understanding by the Last Men (perhaps, given what happens when the box is opened, literally Last Men).[29] It's the world Lovecraft believed himself to be condemned to live in, not his (imaginary) Regency past.

That landscape, physically, in terms of shooting locations, is Los Angeles, today (as of 1955). Surely *that* can't be Lovecraftian? Just so, precisely its absence of human culture makes LA the perfect Lovecraftian location. The nighttime scenes are all polished chrome glaring like boiling acid under blinding neon and fluorescent lights (like the box's contents) while the daytime scenes seem to be filled with grey dust under a pitiless sun that just went nova (foreshadowing the effects of the box's light).[30]

More importantly, perhaps, many of the exteriors were shot in the Bunker Hill section (an appropriately New English name, don't you think?) and thus have a more typically Lovecraftian touch of old, ruined neighborhoods. Indeed, shortly after the film was made the whole area was flattened for an "urban re-

---

[27] Like Lovecraft's occult gobble-de-gook.

[28] Of course, we also recall Lovecraft's incantations and cosmic mumbo-jumbo; even, perhaps, the Trinity that Red Hook's detective hales from?

[29] This, of course, is the note that interests St. Armond, Lovecraft's self-image as a Decadent, an 18th-century gentleman exiled in a philistine future.

[30] The first look like the digitally over-restored print of Ed Wood's *Night of the Ghouls,* the second like a lost work of Coleman Francis. Actually, the later kinds of scenes are perhaps more Clark Ashton Smith than Lovecraft, but just go with me on this.

newal" project, making the film, ironically, something of an archeological record of a now long-vanished, once "modern" area.[31]

And even more importantly, Aldrich, perhaps to show that Mike is "crooked" or "screwed up," decided to use a number of odd camera angles, not only, say, on the stairs of Lily's flophouse but even the presumably modern and normal hospital Mike awakens in early in the film.

As St. Armand notes:

So many of these skewed structures which we find in Lovecraft . . . with their gambrel roofs and rotten timbers and *rooms tilted at crazy or obtuse angles*, are, of course, psychic allegories of decadent and tumbled-down minds, twisted to exquisite and picturesque degrees of insanity. . . . Here the dreamland which . . . *populates modern Boston* with ghouls and living gargoyles is *no longer an antiquarian fancy but rather immediately beneath the cellar door or around the nearest corner.*[32]

Then, there's the violence; sure that's un-Lovecraft? No one in

---

[31] "The Bunker Hill area underwent a controversial total redevelopment which destroyed and displaced a community of almost 22,000 working-class families renting rooms in architecturally significant but run-down buildings, to a modern mixed-use district of high-rise commercial buildings and modern apartment and condominium complexes" (http://en.wikipedia.org/wiki/Angels_Flight#Dismantling). "In 1955, Los Angeles city planners decided that Bunker Hill required a massive slum-clearance project. The top of Bunker Hill was cleared of its houses and then flattened as the first stage of the Bunker Hill Redevelopment Project to populate Bunker Hill with modern plazas and buildings. When the height limit of buildings for Los Angeles was finally raised (previously buildings were limited to 150 feet), developers built some of the tallest skyscrapers in the region to take advantage of the area's existing dense zoning. In approving such projects, the city sought to project a modern, sophisticated image" (http://en.wikipedia. org/wiki/Bunker_Hill,_Los_Angeles#Bunker_Hill_Redevelopment_Pr oject).

[32] Op. cit., loc. 732.

Lovecraft's world goes about gathering information like Mike does. He has two methods: if he sees you as a member of the white collar class, a coroner or health club concierge, he'll peel off some cash to offer what he considers a fair price; should you refuse, or hold out for more, that's when the finger-breaking starts.

Otherwise, he just jumps right in like a skinhead at a mosh pit, and you're lucky if he finds it more amusing to snap your rare Caruso 78 in half rather than your spine.[33]

Admittedly, this thuggish kind of violence is quite out of Lovecraft's line—breaking fingers in drawers, dropping a jacked-up car on a hapless sidekick and the like—although remember, he did like Robert Howard's Conan. More to the point, however, is that the filmmakers have taken a page from the horror genre and realized that it's often more effective—and less likely to get you into trouble with the censors—and even perhaps more cinematically fun to imply, not show.[34]

Thus, when Christina is tortured to death with some kind of metal-crimping device, we only see her legs squirming as we hear her shrieks. Actually, the shrieks continue after they stop spasming, which is perhaps a mistake but certainly emphasizes the illusory, make-believe nature what we're seeing;[35] it also

---

[33] Even before Miranda, movie audiences preferred not to see such methods used by "good guys." Mike treats every suspect and informant the way Batman does the Joker in *The Dark Knight*, rendering the Joker's attempt to taunt him acting like the Joker himself nugatory. Mike is already a combination of Batman and Joker, giving his big, smarmy smile a psychotic resonance. Hoberman: "The movie stops in its tracks to focus on his excited grin as he snaps a collector's priceless 78 record." Presumably this is how the filmmakers—and good liberals today—think vigilantes are or would be, rather than concerned citizens performing a distasteful but needful duty. Interestingly, Mike does all his violence *after* Pat the Fed takes his gun away; so much for "guns cause violence." He pries a key, not a gun, from the coroner's "cold dead fingers" after smashing them in a desk drawer.

[34] I'm reminded of *The Black Cat*, where the vengeful Lugosi flays Karloff alive . . . off screen.

[35] Luhr, p. 129. Similar claims, of course, are made by the advocates of the Ed Wood or Coleman Francis *oeuvres*. It's been claimed online

suggests the kind of torturous results of the warping of the space/time continuum Lovecraft's protagonists tend to fall into. Again, we don't see Nick *being* crushed beneath the car, nor anything but his arm afterwards.

And in a famous sequence, Mike dispatches a goon by some kind of movie-land "martial arts" trick; it's shot from below, so we don't see what he does (Vulcan deathgrip?) and the camera then lingers on Jack Elam's wonderfully creepy face as he emotes sheer terror/confusion over what he's seen. Later, his boss is compelled to wonderingly ask Mike "What'd you do to him, anyway? You scared Charlie half to death," rather like any number of doomed Lovecraftian protagonists.

As the movie nears the end, we see more and more—perhaps the need to keep the pace accelerating prevented Aldrich from using any tricky shots?—such as breaking the coroner's fingers and bitch-slapping the health club concierge, and, of course, Lily's iconic immolation, which we'll devote some space to soon. This is consistent with the notion of the horror tale revealing more and more as the climax approaches. And of course, you can't blame them for not showing the local, or possibly global, effects of the suitcase; ten years later even *Dr. Strangelove* only used stock footage of mushroom clouds.

But—but—but—What about the sex? Surely *that's* not in Lovecraft. Well, indeed, women are pretty hard to find in Lovecraft, and the only sexual congress seems to be with extra-dimensional monsters (e.g., "The Dunwich Horror").[36] In the same way, the only sex we find in *KMD* is implied by the blackmail set-ups Mike sends Velda on. For a supposed swinging bachelor, Mike gets laid about as much as *SNL*'s Czechoslovakian Brothers. Like the violence, it's all in the implications.

The Feds *tell* us he's a "bedroom dick" (he settles divorce cas-

---

that Christina's dubbed screams are the same ones used for Gaby at the end (or vice versa) which also nicely bookends the film and emphasizes the make-believe, but also amps up the Gaby/Lily/Christina doubling we'll explore later.

[36] For a complete accounting, see Ben P. Indick, "Lovecraft's Ladies" in *Discovering H. P. Lovecraft*, ed. Darrell Schweitzer, 2nd ed. (Holicong, Penn.: Wildside Press, 1995).

es through blackmail) and that while Velda handles the men, he handles the women, but we never see or hear of any, and that's just business anyway. Christina starts off on his bad side by making him wreck his sports car, and she's soon dead anyway; the mob boss's sister, a drunk nympho, throws herself on him, but he only uses her to get into the house, then dumps her ("Here's to friendship" is as far as she gets), while he recognizes Lily is a crazy nymphet not to be touched.

Altogether, Mike, like Lovecraft, is a he-man woman-hater that probably agrees with one of the goons: "Women are worse than flies."

Speaking of Lily: played with Satanic, screen-melting intensity by Gaby Rogers,[37] she's a sort of multi-*Doppelgänger*. The doomed Christina, nekkid and running barefoot, is the classic movie woman in distress, yet is nevertheless rather masculine, with her short hair and trench coat, the first of many sexually antipathetic roles that Cloris "Frau Blucher" Leachman would play. Lily easily takes over her role (*Lily* to Christina's *Rossetti* obsession)—while pretending to be Christina's roommate—as Mike's guide to the underworld (in both senses); when they meet she's also (presumably) nekkid, under a robe this time, and barefoot; when next they meet she's be running and screaming like Christina as well. Eventually, Velda will supply her with the nifty black/white Chanel suit that neatly emphasizes her duplicitous nature.[38]

---

[37] "Rodgers, born Gabrielle Rosenberg in Germany in 1928, was the niece of the founder of phenomenology, Edmund Husserl, and grew up in Amsterdam, where she remembered playing with Anne Frank as a child; she appeared on the cover of *Cosmopolitan* in 1957, representing "The New Face of Broadway," and married songwriter Jerry Leiber, author of "Jailhouse Rock," "Hound Dog," "Love Potion No. 9," and numerous others" (http://www.criterion.com/current/posts/1902-the-great-whozits).

[38] Many critics have discussed the checkerboard and "x" symbols found throughout the film; I of course would liken them to the Traditional symbolism of Universal Manifestation as a weaving pattern of warp and woof. See "The Corner at the Center of the World: Traditional Metaphysics in a Late Tale of Henry James," above.

Her trench coat makes her a double for the standard private dick.[39] Her fatal colloquy with Soberin shows her fully in the private dick mode, demanding to *know* and *see*.

This girl/boy/woman is not an easy person to live with, as Dr. Soberin and Mike discover. She is, as played by ex-European Gaby Rogers, *née* Rosenberg (another atomic caper resulting in death by fire), the ultimate Jamesian American Girl:

Daisy Miller's freedom in the face of European social conventions is of a kind that would make her insufferable in any civilized society. . . . She is utterly uneducated, and no intelligent man could stand her for long since there could be no possible exchange of speech with her; she has nothing to recommend her but looks, money, confidence and clothes.[40]

Gaby has looks and confidence, and clothes courtesy of Velda; when Soberin threatens to cut her out on the money, she responds by pulling out something Leavis and James — and Soberin — didn't count on: the private dick's best friend, a roscoe,[41] with predicable — and unpredictable — results.

The mythical elements here are pretty deep or widespread. When, near the beginning of the film, the thug with the pliers asks the jerkass we will come to know near the end as Dr. Soberin whether the now-dead Christina should be tortured some more, Soberin makes some typically pompous and leadenly "amusing" remarks about "that would be resurrection from the dead." When Mike, who should have died in the car with Christina, is somehow rescued and wakes up in the hospital, he is said to be "back from the dead." Lily Carver comes back from the dead in the person of Gaby, Mike not knowing till the end that

---

[39] "So plainspoken as to be a parody of the hardboiled detective she imitates in her inexorable and inexpressive search for knowledge" — Martin Harries, *Forgetting Lot's Wife*, p. 74.

[40] Leavis, op. cit., p. 143.

[41] "Old ('30s–'40s) term for a handgun: same vintage as gat, heater, cannon, etc. 'He pulled a roscoe and ventilated the gorilla'" — Urban Dictionary, http://www.urbandictionary.com/define.php?term=roscoe.

the Feds fished the real Lily out of the river days ago.

Lily/Gaby, Christina's roommate, thus resurrects both Lily by pretense and Christina by becoming Mike's new naked in a trench coat partner. Confronting his double, Lily/Gaby at the end is like the confrontation of Lovecraft's "Outsider"[42] with his mirror image in the eponymous story — Hoberman calls him "a walking corpse"[43] while Pat the Fed already dismissed him in the third person with "Let him go to hell" — and Mike falls dead (with some help from Gaby's roscoe, of course).

This is Gaby's final resurrection, the true resurrection — not the ridiculous reanimated corpse (as Alan Watts called it) of the exoteric Christian (Mike, the "walking corpse" brought "back from the dead") but St. Paul's Gnostic idea of the Body of Light, with all its parallels in every esoteric tradition.[44]

The pedantic Soberin — too sober to grasp such super-subtle ideas, unlike the "feline" intuition of Gaby — has been doubly routed. Gaby has answered his question from the beginning of the film — "How do you bring back the dead?" — and proven that she is indeed not "misnamed," for she has revealed herself not as subhuman — "feline"[45] — but superhuman, a being of light, an angel — Gabriel.[46]

"Hip" film critics love to talk about how Gaby "subverts" the

---

[42] Darren McGavin, who would star in "Mickey Spillane's Mike Hammer" (1957–'59) later starred in a short-lived 1968 series, *The Outsider*.

[43] "The Thriller of Tomorrow"; a similar confrontation occurs in "The Jolly Corner," the James ghost story I analyze in the work cited in Note 35 above.

[44] See Evola's *Hermetic Tradition*, Part Two, where he discusses how the Realized Man creates for himself a new, indestructible body — the Tantric Diamond Body — by reconstructing himself from the atomic level on up — the film's atomic chain reaction is an inverted symbol of this.

[45] Ironically, after being shot by Gaby, Soberin transforms himself into the dog, Cerberus.

[46] Prominently featured in the Bunker Hill locations is the "Angel's Flight," a rather Lovecraftian funicular railway, featuring two cars, Sinai — pillar of fire? — and Olivet.

detective genre, and especially the Mike Hammer character—this time, girl shoots boy.[47] Despite the filmmakers, I think what's actually happening here is that Gaby is redeeming the Mike character. While even the Feds grudgingly admit Mike "can sniff out information like nobody I ever saw" his search for what Velda mocks as "the Great Whatzit" is really motivated by greed, when he suspects the box must be valuable to someone. Gaby's insistence on knowing what's in the box, by contrast, is childish but sincere—she only kills Soberin when he reneges on sharing the proceeds, *after* the long back and forth about Medusa and Co.[48]

But how can Mike be redeemed? The filmmakers, as I've noted, want to push the Good Liberal notion of "shut up and trust the government" and so portray Mike as "stubborn" and Gaby as subhuman (Soberin condescends with "You have the feline perceptions that all women have") rather than inquisitive.

Wesley Addy as Pat the Fed delivers the filmmakers' contemptuous epitaph – "You're sooo smaaaart"—with his trademark WASP condescension. He's kind of a wimpy Al Gore, dealing with a "climate denier" or Ross Perot or George W.; Hoberman say it's "as though addressing a dumb animal" (as Soberin does Gaby).

But is it fair? Noted Lovecraftian Darrell Schweitzer has come to the defense of the "imbecility of [the typical Lovecraft] protagonist":

The critic has probably read ["Dreams in the Witch House"] either in a fantasy magazine or a collection of Lovecraft stories. . . . Walter Gilman, on the other hand, is supposed to be living in the "real" world where things like [anthropomorphic rat familiars] are beyond the range of normal experience. Gilman *knows* that they are impossible.

---

[47] It's as if Brigid O'Shaughnessy shot Sam Spade and took off with the Maltese Falcon. Usually, it's Mike who does the gut-shooting. In Spillane's own film, *The Girl Hunters*, he tricks Shirley Eaton into blowing her own head off with a shotgun.

[48] Soberin's enigmatic remark that the Whatzit "can't be divided" suggests the extra-dimensionality of one of Lovecraft's Elder Gods.

The human mind is *a stubborn thing* [like Mike!], and when it is convinced of something, it isn't always dissuaded by mere proof. . . . He does what any normal, sane person would do. . . . *Unless all heroes are occult detectives* we cannot expect them to readily accept the fact that the laws of existence have been violated.[49]

Mike isn't "stupid" so much as he's in over his head. As I've pointed out before, Lovecraft's protagonists aren't stupid or gullible, but almost always all-too educated, like Dr. Soberin, thus inclined to know, as Schweitzer says, what is and isn't the case, which is exactly what leads them to their doom.[50]

Thus Lovecraft's protagonists are unlike the "occult detectives" once popular in the Victorian age—such as Algernon Blackwood's John Silence or William Hope Hodgson's Carnaki, or most famously, Stoker's Van Helsing.[51] They are not calm, wise experts easily unmasking fake mediums or calling upon some handy bit of mystical folklore to save the day.[52]

However learned conventionally or mystically, they quickly find themselves in too far, asking one question too many.[53] As Lovecraft famously said:

The most merciful thing in the world, I think, is the inability of the human mind to correlate all its contents. We live on a placid island of ignorance in the midst of black seas of

---

[49] "Character Gullibility in Weird Fiction; or, isn't Yuggoth Somewhere in Upstate New York?" in *Discovering Lovecraft*, loc. 1003.

[50] See my review of Graham Harman's *Weird Realism*, "'A General Outline of the Whole': Lovecraft as Heideggerian Event," above.

[51] Blackwood was an initiate of the Golden Dawn; Evola even deigns to quote John Silence on some occult self-defense techniques in his *Introduction to Magic*.

[52] Anomalously, the folklorists from Arkham know just the right formula to dispatch the Dunwich horror and dismiss the revenant Charles Dexter Ward.

[53] ". . . he gradually discovers layers of power and danger that surround him of which he knows nothing and with which he is unprepared to cope" (Luhr, p. 134).

infinity, and *it was not meant that we should voyage far*. The sciences, each straining in its own direction, have hitherto harmed us little; but *some day the piecing together of dissociated knowledge will open up such terrifying vistas of reality, and of our frightful position therein, that we shall* either go mad from the revelation or *flee from the light into the peace and safety of a new dark age.* — "The Call of Cthulhu"

Kiss Me Deadly has been described as the ultimate *noir* film, summarizing the conventions of the genre and then breaking new ground.[54] Hoberman sees this as happening all through the '50s, as if some kind of atomic mutation had taken place:

Genres collide in the great Hollywood movies of the mid-fifties cold-war thaw. . . . The western goes south in *The Searchers;* the cartoon merges with the musical in *The Girl Can't Help It.* Science fiction becomes pop sociology in *Invasion of the Body Snatchers.* And *noir veers into apocalyptic sci-fi* in Robert Aldrich's 1955 masterpiece *Kiss Me Deadly,* which, briefly described, tracks one of the sleaziest, stupidest, most brutal detectives in American movies through a *nocturnal, inexplicably* violent *labyrinth* to *a white-hot vision of cosmic annihilation.* — "The Thriller of Tomorrow"

Note the Lovecraftian language uses. "Veering into apocalyptic sci-fi" would be a perfect description of Lovecraft's own evolution in the thirties, from horror in the *Weird Tales* style to long, "scientifictional" novellas. Perhaps Lovecraft's achievement could be described as taking the three original genres bequeathed to him by his master, Poe — detective, science fiction, and post-Gothic horror — and creating a kind of mash-up more suitable for modern circumstances. To do so, he had to down-

---

[54] "*Kiss Me Deadly* looks back both to canonical *film noir*, whose era was winding down, and ahead to neo-*noir*, or *resurrected noir*, which would not emerge for more than a decade. *Death and resurrection are central themes* [as we saw with Gaby] . . . embodying the baroque endpoint of an exhausted genre, pushing that genre's tropes to and beyond their limits" (Luhr, p. 144).

play the detective's infallible and cool logic (as Poe's Dupin or Conan Doyle's Sherlock), so as to trigger the horrific end, while using science — or "science" — to provide a comforting illusion of normality, against which the horror stands our more "inexplicably."

Kiss Me Deadly strikes the Lovecraftian note because, inadvertently, it arises from the same post-war cultural chaos that would retrospectively root itself in Lovecraft's Synthesis, producing such characteristically modern *noir*-horror-sci-fi works as *Alien*, *Blade Runner*, and *The Matrix*.

It's no surprise that the French loved it; as Hoberman notes:

> In France, *Kiss Me Deadly* was admired mainly by the young critics at *Cahiers du cinéma*, where it was considered "the thriller of tomorrow" and Aldrich, dubbed *Le gros Bob*, was hailed as "the first director of the atomic age."

Claude Chabrol praised the film in rather Poe-esque terms:

> *Kiss Me Deadly*, Claude Chabrol wrote in his passionate review, "has chosen to create itself out of the worst material to be found, the most deplorable, the most nauseous product of *a genre in a state of putrefaction*: a Mickey Spillane story." Aldrich and Bezzerides "have taken this threadbare and lackluster fabric and splendidly rewoven it into rich patterns of the most enigmatic *arabesques*."[55]

At last, let's deal with the famous ending, or rather, the famous endings.[56] This will require a certain amount of exposition. First, the set-up:

> The movie ends at a stylish beach house in Malibu. Carver fells Mike with one shot from a .38, after [inviting him to]

---

[55] Hoberman, "Thriller of Tomorrow."

[56] Conveniently summarized in "The Restoration of *Kiss Me Deadly*" by Glenn Erickson, http://www.dvdtalk.com/dvdsavant/s2356kiss.html, from which I take the following summary of the endings.

"Kiss me Mike. Kiss me. The liar's kiss that says 'I Love You,' but means something else. You're good at giving such kisses." She then opens the box and turns into a pillar of fire . . .

Now the mystery starts.

In the version most often seen from roughly 1960 to 1997, Hammer regains consciousness while Carver burns. He rescues his secretary Velda (Maxine Cooper) from a locked room, and they limp arm-in-arm toward the exit. At that point we cut to a disconnected string of exterior shots. Light and smoke belch from the beach house. Several awkward jump cuts add super-imposed explosions, as a miniature of the house breaks apart. A nondescript "The End" title appears, and the film fades abrupt-ly — not to black, but to gray leader. The music score and roaring sound effects overlap the ragged cut and then end with a poorly-timed fade.

But according to Francois Truffaut's original 1955 review of *Kiss Me Deadly* in *Cahiers du Cinema,* "As the hero and his mis-tress [he means Velda] take refuge in the sea, THE END appears on the screen." The original trailer shows similar shots.

Someone, identity long since lost, thought this worked better, and cut the negative thusly soon after release. Unknown to MGM, Aldrich, or anyone else, a pristine original negative was sitting around in the Aldrich archives.

At the point where standard prints cut to the ragged short ending, this copy continued into a completely new se-quence. The couple *descended some stairs and then took off across the beach.* The shots of the burning house were now separated by four new angles with Velda and Mike *throw-ing long shadows* down the beach. Rear-projected views showed the pair in front of the *exploding beach house.* They watched from the surf until an authentic end title ("The End, A Parklane Picture") appeared. The mystery box growled and howled throughout at full volume, like the monster of a 50s Science Fiction film. [Or the box in *Raiders of the Lost Ark*] The beautiful ending had more production value than anything else in the movie. Although it was disturbing, it was conventionally edited, and resembled nothing that would inspire the French New Wave.

Quite unusually, it is the original ending that provides something of a "happy ending," making it clear that Mike and Velda escape the house. The difference vanishes when you consider that Mike has been shot at close range, already burned by radiation before arriving, and is about 50 feet from a nuclear explosion.[57] For that matter, we don't know if the Whatzit is some kind of Strangelovian doomsday device that will destroy the Earth or trigger WWIII, so "living happily ever after" seems unlike in any event.

Since we are aware of the doubling of Mike and Gaby, as well as the mythical themes running throughout, we can see something else going on in the original, long ending: paradoxically, it is Gaby whose fate is more secure.

We've already called attention to Gaby's checkerboard clothing, and her purer pursuit of knowledge. We can say that this Pure Fool has reached the end of the quest. As we've noted many times, hideous apocalyptic endings are merely a genre convention. What is important here is that Gaby has achieved a state of pure light, becoming a vertical pillar of fire, combining both the Hermetic symbol of light and verticality and the Judaic YHVH. Again, we recall the homage to the scene in *Raiders of the Lost Ark*, which presents the negative, inverted Judaic version, in which the search for knowledge and transcendence fails and is punished as sin.[58]

We cut to Mike, who, having been shot by Gaby, has fallen, in an oddly stiff way, *like a tree falling*, and now lies sprawled at length on the floor. This is the fall into horizontality, the material

---

[57] It's a bit like the end of *Bride of the Monster*, and any number of other '50s movies where atomic blasts happen right and left, with only a small danger of mutating into a 50-foot giant or something, as long as you wear your "protective goggles."

[58] See, as always, Baron Evola's *The Hermetic Tradition*, especially Chapter One on the symbolism of the Tree.

world of space and time.[59] He and Velda then *descend* the stairs and flee *horizontally across* the beach.

As Lovecraft suggested in the quote above, Mike and Velda are seen to *flee from the light into the peace and safety of a new dark age*. They return to the oceans, like the protagonist of "The Shadow over Innsmouth."[60] These are, of course, the Waters of material existence that the Realized Man (or Woman) must cross or walk over.[61]

While behind them, the house, another symbol of the warp and woof of material manifestation, no longer needed, disintegrates, as Gaby's soul, presumably, escapes vertically into the higher dimensions.[62] Of course, this also connects us back to Lovecraft, and most importantly, his master, Poe, and his iconic "Fall of the House of Usher."

Clearly, anyone who wants to create a work of pure, PC agitprop needs to be a little more careful than to simply put yourself on autopilot while dealing with that *infra dig* pulp stuff; it may be smarter than you think — or than you are.[63]

Counter-Currents/*North American New Right*
February 7, 2014

---

[59] In the James tale we analyze in "The Corner," this is how the protagonist ends up, sprawled out on a checkerboard patterned floor; while there's none here, there is one in Mike's apartment.

[60] Remember those "long shadows" they "throw down the beach"?

[61] See René Guénon, *The Multiples States of the Being*, trans. S. D. Fohr (Ghent, N.Y.: Sophia Perennis, 2001), ch. 12, "The Two Chaoses."

[62] See Guénon, *Multiple States*, but especially Ananda K. Coomaraswamy, *The Door in the Sky: Coomaraswamy on Myth and Meaning*, ed. Rama P. Coomaraswamy (Princeton: Princeton University Press, 1997) that exhaustively documents the symbolism of, for example, the hole in the roof of a teepee or another traditional structure, which smoke outlet serves as a symbol of the path of the soul.

[63] "This opus has become a cult film . . . I cannot say why — I never completely understood our screenplay, and my confusion was still there when we ran the completed film" — producer Victor Saville, quoted in Max Allan Collins and James L. Traylor, *Mickey Spillane on Screen: A Complete Study of the Television and Film Adaptations* (Jefferson, N.C.: McFarland, 2012), p. 61.

A Light Unto the Nations:
Reflections on
Olaf Stapledon's *The Flames*

"At various points in our lives we all feel like the one who's watching the flames; at other times, we feel like the one burning."

—Clive Barker[1]

Sometimes, when you finally get around to reading a long-recommended author, you are rewarded by finding something quite unexpected. This recently happened to me with Olaf Stapledon, one of those "grand old men" of pre-'50s science fiction.

In fact, with chronological convenience, Stapledon died right there in 1950, which has also eventually put all his books in the public domain; thus, they've been endlessly reprinted by one publisher after another, in multiple editions, themselves making for nice history of sci-fi covers, from the vaguely Victorian creepiness of Dover, to various Penguin examples of '60s surrealism,[2] to the '80s "New Age" tackiness of one or another California publishers. The more recent ones usually came with "Introductions" by sci-fi gurus like Brian Aldiss or literary fiction big-shots like Doris Lessing or some human potential luminary, depending on the target market, claiming his enormous influence and suggesting you take and read. Needless to say, I, with typical mulishness, failed to take the bait.

Well, actually, I did eventually push myself through *Last and First Men* (1930), his first but not last novel, about which more

---

[1] "Private Legends: An Introduction" in *The Essential Clive Barker: Selected Fiction* (San Francisco: HarperCollins, 1999).

[2] Stapledon's 1930 *Last and First Men* was, weirdly, the third title in Penguin's Pelican series in 1937; "Why the book was not published as a Penguin is a mystery, made curiouser by the almost palindromic fact that *Last and First Men* was the first and last novel to be published as a Pelican." For a chronological collection of Penguin's Stapledon covers: http://www.penguinsciencefiction.org/covers.html#1875.

anon, but more to our present purpose, just recently some enterprising Kindle publisher put the whole kit and caboodle together and, for $3.80 and no space at all, I just had to snap it up.[3]

Stapledon's prose could best be described as "workmanlike"; if you like that sort of thing, it's "reminiscent of H. G. Wells" or some such, if not, it's "sludgy" and "pedestrian." I would call him the C. P. Snow of sci-fi, with F. R. Leavis' devastating dismissal of his fiction in mind.[4]

You might say that he is the anti-Lovecraft, whose prose was certainly non-pedestrian, only to go to the opposite extreme of purple prolixity, to equal critical disdain.[5]

Which is interesting, since I think one reads Stapledon, like Lovecraft, not for their "deathless prose" (Stapledon's is stillborn, Lovecraft's glows with a luminous putrescence) but for imparting the impression that has come to be called "cosmicism." As Robert Anton Wilson described it:

> Basically, I like Lovecraft and Olaf Stapledon better than any other writers in the areas of fantasy, science-fiction and "speculative fiction." This is because I think HPL and Stapledon succeeded more thoroughly than anyone else in creating truly "inhuman" perspectives, artistically sustained and emotionally convincing. That HPL makes the

---

[3] Olaf Stapledon: *Anthology* (*Last And First Men, Odd John, The Flames, Sirius, Last Men in London, Death into Life, Darkness and the Light, A Man Divided, Star Maker* and *Collected Stories*); no publisher given, October 24, 2013.

[4] "Snow is, of course, a—no, I can't say that; he isn't; Snow thinks of himself as a novelist. . . . as a novelist he doesn't exist; he doesn't begin to exist. He can't be said to know what a novel is." See Stefan Collini, "Leavis vs. Snow: The Two-Cultures Bust-Up 50 Years On," *The Guardian*, Friday, August 16, 2013 and "The Two Cultures Today" by Roger Kimball, *The New Criterion*, February 1994.

[5] Most famously, Edmund Wilson's "the only horror is the horror of bad taste and bad art." See "Edmund Wilson, H. P. Lovecraft's Best and Worst Critic" in *Grim Reviews*, November 30, 2007, http://grimreviews.blogspot.com/2007/11/edmund-wilson-hp-lovecrafts-best-and.html

"inhuman" or the "cosmic" a frightening and depressing thing to encounter, while Stapledon makes it a source of mystic awe and artfully combined tragedy-and-triumph, registers merely that they had different temperaments.[6]

Actually, the early Lovecraft was not ashamed to write about ghosts and ghoulies and things that go bump in the night; this "cosmicism" is the position he eventually evolved into, in the process of becoming more of what we would now call a sci-fi writer than a writer of horror. This move, around the late '20s and early '30s, was coincident with his move to the longer novella format, to his publishers' indignation.

With that in mind, *Last and First Men*, Stapledon's first novel, put me in mind of Lovecraft's last major work, his "single greatest achievement,"[7] "The Shadow out of Time."[8] Both works labor to convey a sense of what Lovecraft called cosmic awe, a kind of celestial terror that took the place of the old machinery of ghosts and tombs.[9] In each tale, an alien but in some sense terres-

---

[6] "My Debt to H. P. Lovecraft" (http://www.rawilsonfans.com/ articles/debtHPL.htm). Wilson's conclusion deserves note as well: "Ultimately, I think the value of a writer can be measured by how much he is merely expressing his own idiosyncratic moods of joy or misery and how much he is expressing something that is common to all humanity. I feel that HPL and Stapledon expressed very powerfully a species-wide problem — our disorientation in space and time, consequent upon the Copernican and post-Copernican discoveries which revealed that the human race is not the center of the universe and not the special darling of the gods. Few "mainstream" writers have tackled that intellectual and emotional shock as unflinchingly as did HPL and Stapledon. For that reason, I think many, perhaps most, 'mainstream' writers are not ultimately serious. HPL, in his terrified way, and Stapledon, in his (guardedly) optimistic way, were serious."

[7] Lin Carter, *Lovecraft: A Look Behind the Cthulhu Mythos* (New York: Ballantine Books, 1972), p. 106.

[8] First published in *Astounding Stories* in 1936; the definitive "restored" text is in S. T. Joshi and David E. Schultz, eds., *The Shadow Out of Time: The Corrected Text*, 2nd ed. (New York: Hippocampus Press, 2003).

[9] http://en.wikipedia.org/wiki/Cosmicism%20/%20cite_ref-1

trial intelligence takes over the mind of a contemporary human, revealing in the process the unfathomable extent of time and space—either awesome or terrifying, in each case—and the infinitesimal place of man therein. While both men seem to have been hard-core materialists, Lovecraft was rather more pessimistic and antiquarian than Stapledon,[10] characteristically setting his "advanced" race in the distant past, while Stapledon writes more in the H. G. Wells mode of rugged but inevitable "progress"—at least, until *The Flames*.[11]

Stapledon's last work reminds me more of a slightly earlier work of Lovecraft's, his penultimate masterpiece, "The Whisperer in Darkness."[12] In this novella, Wilmarth, a Professor of Folklore at Miskatonic University (of course) is a typical Lovecraftian smug wise-ass. After pooh-poohing newspaper accounts of sensationalistic tales of alien bodies found after a Vermont flood, he receives a letter from one Henry Aiken, taciturn Vermonter, disputing him, and hinting at unspeakable facts he has witnessed. After an extensive correspondence, he invites Wilmarth to visit, *bringing all the evidence with him*, so as to learn Aiken's ultimate verdict on these Fortean occurrences. Upon arrival, Wilmarth is disturbed not only by Aiken's weird appearance—the chairbound, heavily bundled-up "whisperer" of the title—but his tale: the aliens are real, but he has now learned they are friendly and only want to help us. Needless to say, the climax reveals this to be a horrible—and horrifying—deception.

In "The Flames" we find a very similar plot. The action, such as it is, is easily summarized. A couple pages of "Introductory Note" gives us our frame: what follows will be one of those long

---

[10] Although Wikipedia, *op. cit.*, says "H. P. Lovecraft thought of himself as neither a pessimist nor an optimist but rather an 'indifferentist,'" but without any cited proof.

[11] Olaf Stapledon, *The Flames—A Fantasy* (London: Secker and Warburg, 1947).

[12] First published in 1931, the definitive text appears in S. T. Joshi, ed. *The Dunwich Horror and Others*, 9th corrected ed. (Sauk City, Wis.: Arkham House). Graham Harman, in his *Weird Realism: Lovecraft and Philosophy* (Zero Books, 2012), disagrees with my designation "masterpiece," finding it an interestingly flawed work.

letters people (like Lovecraft) used to write all the time, instead
of blogging or Face Booking, which conveniently provided Victorian authors just enough material for a two or three part magazine story or one of what James called "the dear, the blessed
nouvelle." And we know right away that the genre is the weird
tale, ("a strange document") since our narrator winds things up
with, "The head of the following bulky letter bears the address
of a well-known mental home."

Which bulky letter immediately follows, with the point driv-
en home by this opening: "My present address is bound to prejudice you against me, but do please reserve judgment until you
have read this letter."

We also learn that the writer is known as "Cass," for Cassan-
dra, among his friends from the old Oxbridge days, before the
Great War, doncha know, one of whom is our narrator, who
modestly goes by the corresponding nickname of "Thos" signifying "Doubting Thomas."[13] So we are eavesdropping on the correspondence of some of those literal Old School Boys that used
to run the largest empire the world has ever known, while never
quite leaving the nursery—calling each other silly nicknames,
eating bland, comfortingly over-cooked swill, and perhaps carry-
ing teddy bears. Think Charles and Sebastian, if you take them
seriously,[14] or perhaps Jeeves and Bertie, if not so much.[15]

----

[13] "Thos" of course is the common abbreviation of Thomas, at least
on tea box labels and shop signs in Old Blighty, but we are not given
any clue as to whether it is pronounced "those" or "thoz" or indeed
just rather pointlessly "Thomas." If we had to read it more than a few
times this would be quite irritating to those of us that enjoy listening to
our own inner voice.

[14] "Now, that summer term with Sebastian, it seemed as though I
was being given a brief spell of what I had never known, a happy
childhood, and though its toys were silk shirts and liqueurs and cigars
and its naughtiness high in the catalogue of grave sins, there was something of nursery freshness about us that fell little short of the joy of innocence."—Evelyn Waugh, *Brideshead Revisited, The Sacred & Profane
Memories of Captain Charles Ryder* (1945). See "It's all on account of the
War" by Christopher Hitchens (*The Guardian*, Friday, September 26,
2008), which itself reminds us nostalgically of viewing the Granada TV

Anywho, we plunge ahead into Cass's crazy letter. This has been nicely summarized for us by David Auerbach:

> [T]he sensitive narrator [that is, a clairvoyant with an interest in psychical research, like Stapledon himself] talks to a "flame" in a burning stone who tells of life on the sun and subsequent exile when the planets were formed, with a polite dispassion not so far from that of Hal Clement. [It is then revealed] that the flames are hell-bent on manipu-

---

series on PBS in the '80s, where William F. Buckley, their tame "conservative" was pressed into service to explain why normal people didn't just punch affected twats like Sebastian, to say nothing of Anthony B-b-blanche. Today, of course, Buckley would have some 'splaining to do himself; looking back on his famous dust-up with Gore Vidal, over a decade before, it's remarkable how Buckley has so absorbed the Anglophile as to look like he has his own teddy bear under the chair, while the home-grown, proudly American Vidal seems to affect the same taciturn amusement John Wayne might greet an assault by Wally Cox. Buckley's "I'll sock you in the goddamn face and you'll stay plastered" is straight out of the boy-manliness world of *Stalky & Co.* On the non-Negroid manliness of the real Right, see my *The Homo and the Negro.*

[15] One thing that keeps amusing me about Bertie is his umbrage-taking when, as frequently happens, some more conventional character, an aunt or fiancée's father, starts spreading around their opinion that he's balmy. See, for instance, *Thank You, Jeeves* (1934), which also includes some wonderful references throughout to "nigger minstrels" and blackface—which Bertie of course winds up sporting—for outrage at which on Amazon I am still awaiting. Anyway, 1934 is an interesting date for this kind of foolishness, as it has been said that Hitler underestimated the Brits due to having formed his impression of them from Wodehouse books. No wonder the Nazis thought Wodehouse would make an excellent propagandist. Stephen Fry, himself a big old poofter, deals with the Wodehouse "collaborationist" nonsense in his introduction to *What Ho!: The Best of P. G.* Wodehouse (New York: Penguin, 1981); Fry of course played Jeeves on the BBC series, with Bertie essayed by Hugh Laurie, best known to Americans as quite balmy Dr. House—*viz,* Holmes, as in Sherlock, another Victorian bachelor living with a nanny and an old chum, Dr. Watson, who has old school friends with names like "Stinky."

lating humanity to help them thrive and pursue their spiritual aims, through mind control if necessary. To this end the flame reveals that he and his comrades caused the narrator's wife to commit suicide, so the narrator could devote himself fully to his studies and establish contact with the flames.

[Later] Stapledon plays down the mind-control aspect and the particulars of the flames' existence to focus on their religious history, which is a rewrite of the tail end of *Star Maker*: advanced beings, including the flames, join into a single cosmic mind that then searches the total vision of reality. This time, though, the revelation of the total indifference of the Maker (who, while not quite absent, is not as personified as it is in *Star Maker*) is catastrophic and the cosmic mind collapses. *Star Maker* ended with a little homily on the significance of humanity's efforts; "The Flames" ends with the flames deciding that a Loving God is such a great idea that He must exist, and stupidly start the whole process up again, killing the narrator in the process for questioning them.[16]

The novellas seem quite similar.[17] The lengthy correspond-

---

[16] http://www.waggish.org/2003/the-flames-olaf-stapledon/

[17] I can find no evidence that Stapledon had ever read or even heard of Lovecraft; he even claimed that he had never read any of Wells other than *The Time Machine*. As for Lovecraft, "H. P. Lovecraft held the book in very high regard (though he did not say whether it influenced any of his own stories), saying in a 1936 letter to Fritz Leiber 'no one ought to miss reading W. Olaf Stapledon's *Last and First Men*. . . . Probably you *have* read it. If not, make a bee line for library or bookstall!,'" and in another 1936 letter to Leiber "I'm glad to hear of your perusal of *Last and First Men* — a volume which to my mind forms the greatest of all achievements in the field that Master Ackerman would denominate 'scientifiction.' Its scope is dizzying — and despite a somewhat disproportionate acceleration of the tempo toward the end, and a few scientific inferences which might legitimately be challenged, it remains a thing of unparalleled power. As you say, it has the truly basic quality of a myth, and some of the episodes are of matchless poignancy and

ence between the skeptic and the reluctant believer, the alien be-ings—far more indescribably strange than any Lovecraftian enti-ty—living among us, their plans for us, at first benevolent but then revealed as malevolent, the increasing control over the hap-less believer who is first taken over (in the process, a loved one is killed), then after delivering his "I welcome our new alien over-lords" message is ruthlessly eliminated, etc.

Reading this brief work, an odd feeling gradually came over me; no, not "cosmic awe" but the feeling something was going on here beneath the surface. It didn't read like the usual run of post-War literature.

The first clue was the curiously even-handed noting of German suffering during and after the War. "I had recently done a job in Germany, writing up conditions, and things had got on my nerves; both the physical misery and also certain terrifying psychical reverberations which will sooner or later react on us all."

And a bit later:

I had felt the same terrifying presence in Germany too, but in a different mood. There, it was the presence not of the outer cold and darkness but of the inner spirit of madness and meanness that is always lying in wait to make non-sense of all our actions. Everything that any of the Allies did in that partitioned and tragic country seemed fated to go awry. And then, the food shortage. The children wiz-ened and pinched; and fighting over our refuse bins! And in England one finds people grumbling about their quite adequate rations, and calmly saying that the fate of Ger-mans doesn't matter.

---

dramatic intensity." Finally, in a 1937 letter to Arthur Widner he said "I don't care for science fiction of the sort published in cheap magazines. There's no vitality in it—merely dry theories tacked on to shallow, un-real, insincere juvenile adventure stories. But I do like the few real mas-terpieces in the field—certain of H. G. Wells's novels, S. Fowler Wright's *The World Below,* & that marvelous piece of imagination by W. Olaf Stapledon, *Last & First Men*" (http://en.wikipedia.org/wiki/Last_and_First_Men#Influences_on_other_writers).

Rather unusual for someone who had spent the War in Britain; unlike the expected "filthy Jerry got just what he deserved." Notice that even the "madness and meanness" doesn't seem to refer to the tired old "Nazi madness" but rather the cruelty of the occupying Allies. Was this simply the "cosmic" or "inhuman" perspective? Since Stapledon seems to have been a typical British academic parlour pink,[18] perhaps a holdover from the days of the Hitler-Stalin pact, or even the post-War Trotskyite anti-Stalinism that eventually became neo-conservatism, which in a non-Jew like Stapledon could take the form of sympathy for the German struggle?

But there was more going on here, and as I used Kindle's handy highlight feature to bring together one passage after another, a pattern began to emerge.

The flames originated in the photosphere of the sun. Ironically, the cosmic processes that created the planets had a cataclysmic effect on them, resulting in their dispersal throughout the solar system in various stages of sleep or hibernation, due to their need for enormously high temperatures to live.[19]

"For you, the golden age is in the future; for us, in the past. It is impossible to exaggerate the difference that this makes to all our thought and feeling. . . . With us, save for the few young, the golden age is a circumstantial personal memory

---

[18] Reviewing Leslie A. Fiedler's *Olaf Stapledon: A Man Divided* (Oxford, 1983), Robert Philmus says that "As Fiedler demonstrates, Stapledon was very much a product of the 1930s, embracing a set of leftist attitudes that were common to many other 'Oxbridge-educated sons of the English upper classes'" (http://www.depauw.edu/sfs/ review_essays/philm32.htm). According to Gregory Benford, "[Stapledon's] Marxism, which remained his only irrational faith throughout his life, told him that surely the United States could never be a positive influence," in Olaf Stapledon, *Last and First Men* (London: Gollancz Books, 1999), p. x.

[19] Stapledon's description of the flames awakening in the bitter cold of some planet reminds one of Lovecraft's sympathy for the members of the Ancient Race awakening in the howling Arctic winds when thawed out in "At the Mountains of Madness."

of an incomparably fuller life in the glorious sun."

Wherever they live, the flames have overcome all ethnic or racial differences, and compose a single mind.

> [S]eparate peoples evolved, or perhaps I should say "species." These distinct populations were physically isolated from each other, and each developed its characteristic way of life according to its location. But from a very early time all the solar peoples were to some extent in telepathic communication. *Always,* so far as our elders can remember, the members of each people were in telepathic contact at least with members of their own nation, or rather race; but international, or inter-racial communication was at first hindered by the psychological differences of the peoples. There came at last a time when the whole sun was occupied by a vast motley of peoples in geographical contact with one another, and indeed interpenetrating one another.

Consequently, "We all lived a curiously double life, an individual life and a racial life."

Frozen into a coma on our frigid world, the recent war was a great boon to them:

> He paused, and seemed to sigh. "Those days of the great air-raids," he said, "those were the great days; great at least in comparison with our present reduced circumstances. Thousands upon thousands of us, nay many millions, now lie frozen in sleep among the charred remains of your buildings, *particularly in Germany, where the fires were most extensive and most lasting. The concentration of our spore* in the atmosphere must now be many times greater than it was in pre-war days."

At the risk of showing my hand, I must point out: their spore were *concentrated in Germany, due to the fires.*

Having achieved some degree (ha!) of re-awakening, the

flames offer a deal. While acknowledging a vast difference in physiology and history, and thus totally alien mentalities, perhaps we and they can work together,

"We shall also be so *diverse in our racial idiosyncrasies* that each partner will be thoroughly remolded and revitalized by intercourse with the other" and achieve "a true symbiotic organism."

"What we offer you is *permanent spiritual guidance* and fortification, so that, as individuals and as a race, you may at last overcome your inveterate short-sightedness and meanness. With our help, but not without it, you will wake to a new level of awareness; and in the light of that experience you will be able to organize our common world for the happiness of our two kinds, and for the glory of the spirit."

"You, on your side of the partnership, will use all your astounding intellectual and *practical powers (which we so envy and admire)* to transform the whole planet."

"Your gift is for practical thought and action. . . . . Together, with *your practical cunning, married to our ancient wisdom and spiritual insight*, we should indeed become a creative world organism"

"There will be neither wars nor class-wars, but only generous rivalry in the common venture of our two races, in equal partnership."

"The whole human race will become a race of aristocrats . . . no longer guilt-ridden by living on the labour of enslaved classes . . . *those aristocrats will not be idle...*"

". . . with us you can become . . . true vessels of the spirit."

"What a glorious world-community we shall together form!"

Or, cutting right to the chase:

"What we intend is that you shall use some of your new power and your practical ingenuity *to provide us with a permanent and reasonably large area of very high temperature,* say in Central Africa or South America."

How about Madagascar?

Again, faced with this inspiring vision of hard-working, practical "aristocrats" laboring away without dissent to improve the world, under the wise guidance of the flames, I can't help but feel like giving out an exultant shout: "*Tikkun olam!*"

Cass, however, feels a vague disquiet. Sensing, perhaps, "where have I heard this before?" he asks: "They will regard co-operation with you as sheer slavery. . . . If they are forced to reconcile your superiority in some ways they will regard you as *brilliant perverts, in fact, as satanic.*"

But the flames have already thought of that, smart little buggers that they are: "In order to make your free acceptance of our plan easier for you, we may have to use our special psychic powers to incline your minds toward it."

In fact, they've already started work on Cass, who is "A human being of quite exceptional *detachment from the prejudices of your kind* [and able] to look at this whole matter *without human prejudice* and simply out of love for the spirit."

The method of mind control seems similar to a well-known pseudo-science: "If I had no respect for your individuality I could break in forcibly and lay bare your most secret feelings in spite of all your resistance."

And like many victims of this pseudo-science, the first casualty was Cass's marriage. But then, free from human prejudice as he is, "I think you yourself will agree that our need for you was more important even than your marriage."

With humanity at large, the technique is slightly different: "We might, for instance, undertake the very easy task of stirring up war-scares and forcing your research workers to produce even more destructive atomic weapons."

Alas, the flame seems to have talked too much, perhaps due to its long hibernation. [20] Cass bethinks himself thus:

How could I be sure that my affection for the flame and

---

[20] Kasper Gutman: "Talking's something you can't do judiciously, unless you keep in practice." — *The Maltese Falcon.*

my admiration for his race were spontaneous acts of my own personality? Might they not have been cunningly implanted in me by the flame himself? The more I thought about it the more likely this seemed. And *did not the flame race intend to exercise this hypnotic power over the whole race of men, so as to compel them, yes, compel them, to subject themselves for ever to the will of the flames?* Men would believe they were acting freely, but, in fact, they would be mere robots acting under an inner compulsion. Mankind, hitherto master of its own destiny, would henceforth *be a subject race exploited by a subtler kind, a new Herrenvolk.* Of course I agreed that the only final consideration must be "the glory of the spirit," not the triumph of any one race, human or non-human; but how did I know that these cunning flames would really work for the spirit and *not for racial power and aggrandisement?* How did I know that they were not *at heart, diabolic?* Yes, diabolic! Under a cloak of friendliness and generosity the creature in the fire was scheming to capture my very soul for an inhuman end. Was he not subtly tempting me to commit treason against my own kind? But even, as I thought thus, I was torn by conflict. The behaviour of the flame had throughout been so civilized, so considerate and friendly. How could I reject these amiable advances? Yet, as my feelings warmed toward him, I reminded myself that my very feelings were perhaps not my own, but the outcome of his prompting. Anger and fear seized me again. No! A thousand times better that man should retain his sovereign independence, and go down with colours flying, than that he should surrender his human dignity, his human self-sufficiency, his human freedom.

So, an alien race, possessed of group consciousness, abstractly brilliant but incapable of practical physical work, dispersed against its will throughout the universe, lives in secret, and influences mankind to abandon all racial, national or even species loyalty, so as to unite with the alien race, or rather, submit to its wise leadership, so as to perfect a peaceful, class-less, world society devoted to The Spirit. Oh, and some real estate near Miami Beach.

Stapledon has done something truly remarkable. He has taken the very symbol of the Judaic post-War propaganda—the so-called Holocaust, the Shoah, the fires, the furnaces, blah blah blah—and turned it around, into a powerful new symbol of Judaic conspiracy.

It is they who are the flames—an alien race, dedicated to an abstract, inhuman religion, living among us, in our factories, our very homes, seeking increasing control over our minds, to further their literally alien agenda.

> Presently a surge of remorse and shame and compassion flooded in on me. But I told myself that this was not *my* feeling; it was being forced on me by *the outraged race of flames* in all the hearthfires and furnaces of the world.

Needless to say, none of this was anywhere near Stapledon's intentions, parlour pink and conventional academic Bolshie that he was. I think, that for whatever reason—the War, age, disease—Stapledon here lays aside his "progressive" ideology and relaxes into the imagination, like his narrator, lost in contemplation of a paltry post-War British fireplace. As a result, he has composed a true, as the subtitle has it, fantasy. And fantasy, the imagination, is controlled by a different kind of "inhumanism."

As Jonathan Bowden said about Sarban's fascist-fascinated fantasy novella *The Sound of his Horn:*

> Yet what this novella really exemplifies is a fascination with the dark side, with everything "politically incorrect" long before this terminology entered common usage. Without the thrill of transgression or "inhumanism," much of liberal fiction and art would be completely flaccid and without any depth of characterization. It is the presence of the right/wrong side which makes it all worthwhile in the long-term. For, as Wall/Sarban gets more and more excited, amid a world of female birds and predatory cats, rampaging boar-hounds, and human prey, under the flood-

lights and next to the barbed wire—as the forces of the Reichs forester gets closer . . . one realizes a salient truth. And this is the fact that in a liberal order, the Right appears to be everywhere powerless—except in one's dreams. For the societies created out of Enlightenment nostrums have surrendered their entire unconscious *to the other side.*[21]

And that of course is the rationale for the mind-control technique known as PC. You can't let people just relax and let their thoughts meander. Who knows where they might stray? They might even start to see the flames.

Counter-Currents/*North American New Right,*
November 12, 2013

---

[21] Jonathan Bowden, "Sarban's *The Sound of his Horn,*" in his *Pulp Fascism: Right-Wing Themes in Comics, Graphic Novels, and Popular Literature,* ed. Greg Johnson (Counter-Currents, 2013).

My Wagner Problem — & Ours

"Your themes—they almost always consist of even values, of half, quarter, eighth notes; they are syncopated and tied, to be sure, but nonetheless persevere in what is often a machinelike, stamping, hammering inflexibility and inelegance. *C'est 'boche' dans un degre fascinant.* But don't think I am finding fault!

"As for von Riedesel, he had fallen prey to utter confusion. 'Beg pardon' he said, 'if you please . . . Bach, Palestrina . . .' For him those names possessed the nimbus of conservative authority, and now they had been assigned to the realm of modernistic disintegration. . . . According to [Breisacher], decline, stultification, and the loss of all feeling for what was old and genuine had begun early on and in a place so respectable that no one would ever have dreamt it."

—Thomas Mann, *Doktor Faustus*[1]

"Yes, it is. It is very strange, but with our race and in our latitude, rhythmic control is the most difficult thing for a musician to achieve. There is hardly a musician among us who can play the same note five times without minor variations. Part of the fault is that rhythm is never taught correctly to young musicians. For the Negro or African, it comes naturally—this sense of rhythm. As for myself, I can tolerate wrong notes, but I cannot stand unstable rhythm. Perhaps I was born in Africa in another existence. Once in Vienna after we had finished a recording session, I sur-

---

[1] Thomas Mann, *Doctor Faustus: The Life of the German Composer Adrian Leverkühn, as Told by a Friend,* trans. John E. Woods (New York: Knopf, 1997), Chapters 28 and 37. Both remarks are put in the impudent mouths of Judaics, one a concert promoter, the other a private scholar of hyperconservative views, based perhaps on Leo Strauss. Mann apologizes in both cases for presenting such unflattering portraits of a people he professes to otherwise find admirable. *Le pauvre Mann!* He taught us, *malgre lui,* that the Judaic is always on both sides of every issue!

prised everyone by telling them I was going to hear a Louis Armstrong concert. When they asked why? I told them
that to go to a concert and know that for two hours the
music would not get faster or slower was a great joy to
me."

— Herbert von Karajan[2]

What is it about with the fascination on the Right—even the
alt-Right—with the music of Wagner? Surely no one—even on
the Right—is crazy enough to think that Wagner is *sufficient* to
overthrow the Liberal Hegemony and re-establish Dharma—
sweeping in like the Air Cav in *Apocalypse Now*, blasting out the
"Ride of the Valkyries" because "it scares the hell out of the
slopes."[3] Nor is Wagner necessary for such a task.

Nietzsche, of course, can be cited either way regarding what
he called *The Case of Wagner*. But there is stronger and more orthodox Traditionalist support for the anti-Wagner Case; or rather, for the case against the whole of "Western" music, of which
Wagner is the epitome.

Take Baron Evola. So-called "classical" music, from Palestrina
on, was for him no more than another part of the rotting frame-
work of bourgeois culture, an impediment to be discarded, not
mummified and worshipped.[4] It had, by the early 20th Century,

---

[2] "Karajan on the music of today," interview, *Stereo Review*, 1963,
http://www.overgrownpath.com/2008/09/karajan-on-boulez-
stockhausen-and.html. Karajan falls victim here to the myth of "natural
rhythm." Actually, "swing" doesn't involve metronomic rigidity but rather a kind of syncopation; Armstrong invented it himself, and later had
to teach it to Fletcher Henderson's orchestra, which was reputed to be
the finest in Harlem. Later, Detroit techno legend Carl Craig returned
Karajan's compliment: "Kraftwerk were so stiff, they were funky."

[3] To anticipate, is it not interesting that Wagner fits right in with glob-
alist imperialism, the destruction of a traditional society, and ultimate
ignominious defeat? And that the Colonel's antics are greeting with big
grins by the Negroes riding along?

[4] Julius Evola: *Ride the Tiger: A Survival Manual for the Aristocrats of the
Soul* (Rochester, Vt.: Inner Traditions, 2003), Chapter 23, "Modern Music
and Jazz."

split off into its component parts; the chromatic and harmonic "developments" of which Wagner was an exemplar gave rise to increasingly outré experiments, culminating in the arid academicism of Berg, Webern, Schoenberg and other Judaics who were only too glad to lose the *goyishe* public. The latter, demanding a healthy, danceable, popular music—as Nietzsche did as well—gravitated to jazz. So, the upshot of Western music was a musical culture dominated by Judaics and Negroes.

Alain Daniélou, who had an even better claim to be an authoritative Traditionalist,[5] also had the musical training to make essentially the same case.[6] For Daniélou, the mess starts with the Greeks, who, in their typically intellectualizing and number-obsessed way, misunderstood the system of intervals, creating a 12 tone system that combined the incompatible 5 tone (Chinese) and 7 tone (Hindu) systems. Since Western intervals were from then on inherently inaccurate, the possibilities of expression are defective, no longer matching the states of the world and the moods of the human soul. Bigger and bigger orchestras, then new instruments, like Wagner's special tubas and Adolphe Sax's various horns, a favorite of the Negro long before the vuvuzela invaded Europe's soccer fields. Good Wagnerians like Strauss were finally reduced to hauling actual machinery such as aeoliphones onstage to supplement their increasingly threadbare reserves. Meanwhile, as Daniélou tends us, mediaeval Indian musicians could not just "imitate" nature but summon up actual rain storms!

The history of Western music is the history of various such *ad hoc* attempts to mend things without any understanding of what the problem was; a history which Westerners, in typical fashion,

---

[5] Daniélou was the only first generation Traditionalist to actually live for decades in an actual Traditional setting—rural India, far from the Raj or Gandhi. When he encountered the works of his fellow Frenchman Guénon, he gave them his approval, on the basis of the fearsome amount of traditional Hindu sciences he had learned, by memorization, from authentic *pandits*, not, as with every later Traditionalist, vice versa.

[6] See his *Music and the Power of Sound: The Influence of Tuning and Interval on Consciousness* (Rochester, Vt.: Inner Traditions, 1995), first published in India in 1943.

have labeled as "progress" and demanded the whole world adopt, like their "free markets" and "democracy."

Unlike Evola, Daniélou sees the popularity of Negro music to lie not so much in its vaunted rhythm as in its "blue" or "bent" notes that seek to coax expression from the Massa's oddly rigid scales. Though praising African music *faute de mieux*, the well-propagandized won't like his sensible suggestion that slavery and Jim Crow kept African music vibrant, through forced separation, preventing homogenization via the "melting pot." No tears for Bessie Smith denied access to a White hospital here.

So far from idolizing Wagner, the Traditionalist should hold him in deep suspicion. Of course, this does not mean one should join or cheer the post-modern wreckers, with their "relevant" productions set in dockside whorehouses, or the academic Grundies tut-tutting about sexism, racism, anti-Semitism, and whatever other minority gripe is fashionable. Wagner is a monument of Western Culture, like the cathedrals, probably the closest predecessor to his achievement of the *Gesamtkunstwerk*, which one appreciates and defends however one may generally and ideologically regret the encroachment of the Semitic superstition on Europe. You play the hand you are dealt, you chose your enemies wisely. To live, Burroughs says, is to collaborate.[7] And, as he (or rather, Inspector Lee) goes on to emphasize, there are degrees of collaboration.

And I am not entirely immune to the charms of Wagner myself. Nothing is easier than to just sit back and let Wagner wash over one.[8] But it is, or should be, a guilty pleasure. As John Si-

---

[7] *Nova Express* (New York: Grove Press, 1992), p. 7.

[8] This is the advantage of the *Gesamtkunstwerk* or, as we would say today, the full multi-media experience. Tolkien has recently acquired the similar benefit of having his books, which I confess to having never found readable, turned into easily digestible films, the *Gesamtkunstwerke* of our age. On the LOTR films, and movies as the *Gesamtkunstwerke* of our age generally, see *Trevor Lynch's White Nationalist Guide to the Movies*; ed. Greg Johnson (San Francisco: Counter-Currents, 2012). If my confession of Tolkien's unreadability sounds blasphemous, I can adduce C. S. Lewis as a parallel—on hearing a colleague describe a new book called *The Castle* by this Kafka chap, he concluded it was a new, great Myth for

mon said, when he was upbraided by a reader for giving a bad review to a play at which he had been spotted laughing or crying as the case may be, of course I responded to the manipulation, that's what angers me.[9] But unlike Simon, and like Beckett's Malone, I prefer to remain calm; "I am content, necessarily, but not to the point of clapping my hands."[10]

So Wagner and Western music is a *fait accompli*, part of the thrownness of our *Dasein*. Two cheers! What matters is the future. If not Wagner, what?

The future of Aryan music should be, well, Aryan and Futuristic. I've suggested elsewhere[11] that rather than classical or metal, to say nothing of "classically influenced metal" or whatever, we should set our sights on what's called New Age music. It's technical sophistication and relative lack of interest in rhythm perfectly suits the Aryan Soul. Interestingly, it shares, with metal, the same contempt on the part of the both the *soi disant* "hip" and the middlebrow mainstream media alike.

Whereas, of course, our enemies are only too glad to see us hang ourselves on the cross of Wagner — at best, interpreted for us by the "finest" artists — Judaics, or course;[12] or at worst, another excuse to tar us with the "Nazi" brush. Meanwhile, our

---

our time and eagerly sought out a copy of the book, only to find the actual text to be quite a letdown.

[9] Wagner famously made the same charge of "unearned effects" against Meyerbeer in Part One of his *Opera and Drama* of 1851.

[10] *Malone Dies* in *Three Novels* (NY: Grove Press, 1991), p. 174.

[11] See "I'll Have a White Rock, Please: Implicit Whiteness, Aryan Futurism, and the Godlike Genius of Scott Walker" in *The Homo and the Negro* and "Light Entertainment: The (Implicitly) White Music of Scott Walker," chapter 12, below.

[12] Another early Traditionalist, Marco Pallis, though also not averse to the charms of classical music — see his essay "The Metaphysics of Musical Counterpoint" in *Studies in Comparative Religion*, Vol. 10, No. 2. (Spring, 1976) — was a pioneer in the movement to promote authentic or historically accurate performances of the classical and pre-Bach repertoire, the effect of which was to free us from over a century of romantic — i.e., Judaic — nonsense about sweaty mystical conductors and swooning fiddle virtuosos, filling every performance with enough *portamento* for a klezmer band.

youth's search for expression in music has exhausted even the domestic Negro's wares and now seeks "world" music — anywhere but Europe.

Counter-Currents/*North American New Right*
May 17, 2013

OUR WAGNER, ONLY BETTER:
HARRY PARTCH, WILD BOY
OF AMERICAN MUSIC

"In a healthy culture differing musical philosophies would be coexistent, not mutually exclusive; and they would build from Archean granite, and not, as our one musical system of today builds, from the frame of an inherited keyboard, and from the inherited forms and instruments of Europe's eighteenth century. And yet anyone who even toys with the idea of looking beyond these legacies for materials and insight is generally considered foolhardy if not actually a publicity-seeking mountebank."

—Harry Partch, *Genesis of a Music*

"The 19th century must have been an enormously comfortable place; no one seems to want to leave it."

—Thomas Mann, *Doctor Faustus*

"Do not be afraid to be out of tune with the piano. It is the piano that is out of tune. The piano with its tempered scale is a compromise in intonation."

—Pablo Casals

PART ONE:
A CODA ON WAGNER

I undertook my previous look at Wagner, appropriately enough, in the Nietzschean spirit I have always tried to maintain,[1] reserving my critical work only for those cultural idols of sufficient importance that their take-down would serve a greater cultural good—rather than, for example, the typical internet

---

[1] See Greg Johnson's interview with me, reprinted in *The Homo and the Negro.*

"flame-war."

The results were all I could have hoped for! Cascades of evidence that Wagner was, indeed, an unquestioned, unquestionable idol for the Right, the alt-Right, White Nationalists, whatever.[2] A veritable religious cult, with all the Judaic characteristics Kevin MacDonald has discerned in such thought-negating outfits.[3]

All the memes were there. "How dare you counsel our Youth to desert our European Heritage!" As if "youth" had not been fleeing from classical music for well over a century, the process, in fact, more or less complete, to judge by the collapse of the classical record industry.[4] As if it was I responsible for this killing of the younglings. Again, how appropriate; my arguments were derived from Evola, after all, so why not put me on trial for corrupting the young as well?[5]

And all the other tactics beloved by Cardinals and Witchfinders down through the ages, such as *ignoratio elenchi*: after detailing the flaws in the Western system of intonation, the response: "He hasn't given us any reason to think so." And the *argumentum ad*

---

[2] And how appropriate, that my critics should be exactly the sort that, misinterpreting Nietzsche's advice to "philosophize with a hammer," by which he meant "the sounding out of idols . . . , which are here touched with a hammer *as with a tuning fork*: there are no idols that are older, more assured, more puffed-up—and none more hollow [than Wagner]"—proceed, basing themselves on an understanding of Norse mythology provided by Judaic comic books, to come to his defense, by dreaming of growing great beards and hurling Thor's hammer at me . . . from their parents' basements.

[3] See, for example, Kevin MacDonald, *The Culture of Critique: An Evolutionary Analysis of Jewish Involvement in Twentieth Century Intellectual and Political Movements* (Westport, Conn.: Praeger, 1998), ch. 2, regarding Boasian anthropology as a cult.

[4] See Norman Lebrecht's *The Life and Death of Classical Music* (New York: Doubleday, 2007).

[5] Like Socrates, Evola was charged for "corrupting the youth," and like Socrates in the *Apology*, Evola issued an *Autodifesa* (self-defense statement). For his part, Harry Partch observed that "the deliberate beguiling of youth into the academic 'modern idiom' is worse than an assault on the street. Both are malevolent, but the second is honest" (Gilmore, p. 259).

auctoritatem: "All culture is inherently elitist, who cares what people want to listen to?" (Note the contradiction to the younglings argument, but hey, any tool to hit a heretic.) Or again, after noting that by reducing the modes to only two, major and minor, considerable amount of expressiveness are lost, which is why jazz resorts to "bent" or "blue" notes to recover the modes, an argument, basically, that two is less than twenty, the flat assertion "No one familiar with Western music would think so."

In the words of that great Aryan comedian, Rik Mayall, "I despair, I mean, I really do."[6]

But then, does he not also say, "*Nil desperandum*, we're English, and there's a way out of everything"? And so I will try a different tack, explaining a little more of what's wrong with Wagner, but then offering a positive, Aryan role model that can guide us out of the morass.

1. WHAT'S WRONG WITH WAGNER, OR WESTERN MUSIC?

Harry Partch explained that his musical heresy was due to the fact that most musicians treated equal temperament as if it were "handed out of the clouds of Mount Sinai." Therefore any important music created with it was sacrosanct.[7]

The Western system of ET is neither natural nor inevitable nor optimal, nor even, as composers as early as Wagner himself realized, particularly rich or useful.[8]

---

[6] "You have to be black, homosexual and a woman to work at the BBC," http://keighleyreality.proboards.com/index.cgi?board=genb &action=display&thread=418.

[7] Brian Timothy Harlan, *One Voice: A Reconciliation of Harry Partch's Disparate Theories* (USC PhD. Dissertation, 2007), p. 37. Harlan notes on p. 33 that in the 16th century "Pope Gregory XIII proposed a calendar reform that would immediately eliminate ten days from the year 1582. For many, the reaction to this temperament of time was similar to the reaction to the temperament of tone. In both cases it was viewed as being against the natural order, or against God's plan."

[8] To behold all the wonders of sound otherwise available, consult, if you can find it, Daniélou 's *Tableau Comparatif des Intervalles Musicaux* (Publications de l'Institut français d'indologie, No. 8, 1958), which is "simply a massive table of musical intervals, nothing more. It has 3-limit,

According to Kyle Gann:

Music schools teach that this Big Mac tuning has been around
for centuries and represents an immutable endpoint of progress. It's a lie. . . . There is nothing that musicians take more
for granted than the fact that there are twelve pitches to an
octave, and that these pitches divide the octave into twelve
equal steps. Apparently few musicians question this arrangement, and only a tiny minority can explain whence it arose,
why, and from what principles its authority derives. This 12-
pitch assumption, however, is far from innocent. Twelve-
tone equal temperament, as this common tuning is called, is
a 20th-century phenomenon, a blandly homogenous tuning
increasingly imposed on all the world's musics in the name
of scientific progress. In short, twelve-tone equal temperament is to tuning what the McDonald's hamburger is to
food.[9]

As the little red-haired girl on *The Kids in the Hall* would say, "It's
a *fact*."

The problem with Western music is quite simple, and can be

5-limit, 7-limit, and possibly 11-limit ratios. It has ten times as many intervals as Partch's and Helmholtz's lists combined, including all 17 fifths
of the Arabic system" (http://launch.groups. yahoo.com/group/tun-
ing/message/43210).

One thinks of the flat-footed way "natural" is invoked when human
sexuality is discussed on the Right, even the so-called "alt-Right," as if
the customs of Judaic Bedouin imposed on the West were still regarded
as self-evidently God-given. See James Neill, *The Origins and Role of
Same-Sex Relations in Human Societies* (Jefferson, N.C.: McFarland, 2009)
or Louis Crompton, *Homosexuality and Civilization* (Cambridge: Harvard
University Press, 2003). As Daniélou points out in a different context, to
posit opposing principles, including Male and Female, *ipso facto* evokes
indefinite degrees in between, which Hindu mythology acknowledges
with its pantheon of sexually various gods. See my discussion of this in
"Homosexuality, 'Traditionalism,' and Really-Existing Tradition" in *The
Homo and the Negro*.

[9] http://www.kylegann.com/

expressed with some quite simple mathematics, since music consists of sounds, sounds are vibrations, and vibrations can be expressed as numbers.[10]

> Sound = vibration, thus = frequency. Intervals can be expressed by math. Our perception of pitch is the result of a rapid, and rhythmic, displacement of matter. When an object vibrates it pushes on the surrounding air periodically, resulting in a pulsating pattern of first condensed, then stretched, packets of air. Because the pattern is periodic, if it occurs very slowly it will be perceived as rhythm, but if it occurs faster than about twenty times every second it will be perceived as a tone. The pitch of a vibrating object, consequently, can be traced back to the rate at which it is moving, and in turn, how frequently it is pushing on the air around it. Put more plainly, pitch is measured by vibration speed. (Harlan, p. 26)

Now, if we are to have music, there must, contrary to Pete Townsend, be more than one note, so the question arises, which? Well, sounds are pleasing, or harmonious, when they express a ratio of whole numbers. The simplest of these, of course, would be 1:1, two voices or instruments, perhaps single strings, vibrating at the same rate, called a unison. Next, one might imagine the sounds vibrating in a 2:1 ratio, one twice as fast as the other, the so called octave.[11] To illustrate the octave, and show that such

---

[10] Here, however, an immediate problem arises. Musicians, and especially so called "musicologists," are apt to deny exactly this point, insisting on some mystical essence to their art. It's as if painters insisted that colors had nothing to do with the spectrum. This kind of bourgeois romanticism is what led Partch to abandon musical "training" in favor of self-education via the public library, where happily he ran across Helmholtz's *On the Sensations of Tone as a Physiological Basis for the Theory of Music* (New York: Longmans, Green, 1912) (downloadable from Google Books), a pioneering work that explains all this quite scientifically.

[11] Whether the sounds are simultaneous or in sequence is irrelevant; in the first we have a chord, the method of choice in the West, in the

simple modes can be expressive, consider the goosepimply first two notes—Some . . . where—of "Somewhere over the Rainbow," which is nothing but an octave leap.

OK, so we have two notes, defining a scale; so what notes go in between? Pythagoras, who devised all this for the Greeks, reasoned that the next simplest ratio was 3:2, the so-called perfect fifth, so a system of fifths seems reasonable. Here, however, a problem arises.

Now again, this is not just me talking. Get out your calculator.[12] Let's take 27.5, the vibration of A, and multiply it 2, and do that 7 times. Now, do it again, but this time multiply it by 1.5—that is, 3:2—7 times, and the answer, you will note, is different, yes?

So, how's all that science and abstract reasoning working out for you, Western Man? As the Bubble Boy would say, "Not . . . too . . . good, eh?"

In fact, the history of Western Music plays out rather like the climax of the Bubble Boy episode of *Seinfeld*, with George, the music "theorist" and Grand Poobah, insisting that "the Moops" invaded Spain, because that's what the Trivial Pursuit card says, while the Bubble Boy, representing the human ear, insists that everyone knows it's the Moors, and the card must be misprinted. In short, a whole bunch of attempts to deal with the "extra" vibrations, the so-called "Pythagorean Comma."

Pythagoras himself suggested—well, with guys like Pythagoras, it was more like "God and Reason command"—that we just gather up all the vibrations in a bunch at the back of the scale's neck and snip off the excess, like a rich old lady getting a facelift.[13] In practice, this meant rendering one of the intervals deliberately out of tune, but hoping it was obscure enough not to be noticed.

---

other a mode, and the ear is required to make the mathematical connection by memory. Thus the seemingly endless melodies of Arab, Indian, or basically almost any "non-Western" music.

[12] Or, just read Christopher Small's *Musicking: The Meanings of Performing and Listening* (Middletown, Conn.: Wesleyan University Press, 1998), p. 128, where he kindly lays it all out for you.

[13] As Patsy's doctor suggests: "Just grab her by the scalp, shake her up and down a bit, and chop off the slack." *AbFab*, Season One, "Hospital."

Thus did Western Music receive its ritual circumcision, a theme which we will meet up with again. Perhaps that's why, as Partch suggested in the quote above, musicians think the ET system was handed down on Mount Sinai.

This kind of adjustment happened again and again, for Faustian Man knows only one direction, Onward![14] Re-examining premises, that's for sissies! — essentially, the argument of the critics of my Wagner piece.

Now, as Gurdjieff tells us, no change is possible unless a new, Third Force, enters in. This involved Faustian Man's other obsession, technological development. Now, you might think that technological development would help make the system more accurate, but you'd be wrong, Digital Boy. Western composers were besotted with "modulation" between keys, and also with keyboards. Trouble is, it's hard to re-tune string instruments and nearly impossible to re-tune keyboards. And even without that hassle, think of all those keys for sharps and flats (yes, Bach had a keyboard with separate keys for each).[15]

Thus was born so-called Equal Temperament, in which — wait for it — *every note is out of tune*, and thus every note is equal to every other note.

So, every note is forced to be equal, and interchangeable, so

---

[14] As we will see, the ET System will swamp authentic white folk music, but during the so-called Folk Revival Pete Seeger hit the nail squarely on the head: "We were waist deep in the Big Muddy / And the big fool said to push on" (http://en.wikipedia.org/wiki/Waist_Deep_in_the_Big_Muddy).

[15] "In order to be able to play music that used complex chord progressions, the musicians of the time needed either to build keyboards with lots of split keys [to allow them to play either a G-sharp or an A-flat, for example, since those two notes did not have the same pitch] (which would have been impractical to play) or to have instruments built with compromise tuning systems that would sound good no matter what chord they played. That is, the tuning system would have to fudge a little here and there. One of the pitches would be raised slightly, another lowered slightly. In such a system, some of the chords would sound a little less pure than they had before, but none of them would sound too bad" (http://www.musicwords.net /musictech/justtutor/justtutor3.htm).

that technology can be accommodated, and musicians can have absolute "freedom" from any restrictions imposed by mere nature. Does this sound familiar? Like anything else going on in the 18th century? In France, maybe? And this, my pro-Wagnerians, is of the Right, how exactly?

Thus were all of the dozens of modes, each with its own expressive possibilities, junked in favor of just two, so-called Major and Minor, vaguely signifying some kind of "happy" and "sad."[16] I bet you were taught that Major and Minor were like Black and White, Zero and One, Left and Right, and other *obvious* dualities that *just are*, right? Well, they lied to you again, Bubba.

2A. WHO CARES WHAT'S WRONG WITH WAGNER OR WESTERN MUSIC?

"It is both fascinating and telling that a core principle of Western music theory, the circle of fifths, and a related tuning technique that predominated in ecclesiastical music until the Renaissance, were both predicated on a kind of numerological mysticism." (Harlan, p. 26)

At this point, if my life were an episode of *Mad Men*, I would be Pete Campbell, rushing into Bert Cooper's office to reveal Don Draper's hidden past, and Bert, putting down his copy of *The Fountainhead*, would give me a pitying look and wearily sigh:

Cooper: Mr. Campbell, who cares?

Campbell: Mr. Cooper, he's a fraud and a liar, a criminal even!

Cooper: Even if this were true, who cares? This country was built and run by men with worse stories than whatever

---

[16] "A melody written in the key of C sounds the same as a melody written in the key of D, and so on. By the same token, every key sounds more or less the same, and the distinct characters of different modes are lost, along with their expressive potential" (http://musicmavericks. publicradio.org/features/essay_justintonation.html).

you've imagined here.[17]

---

[17] From the Season One's episode 12, to be followed by one entitled, interestingly, "The Wheel." I'll accept the role of weaselly Campbell for the greater good, but although Bert professes not to care, there are interesting parallels between him and Partch. Men of roughly the same generation, both share the same eccentric personality, alternatively endearingly weird and infuriatingly rude, as well as a penchant for goatees. Above all, both are Japanophiles, without betraying the slightest "spiritual" interests. Bert concludes with "The Japanese have a saying. A man is whatever room he is in."

Having just compared the removal of the comma with circumcision, we can even note Bert's own secret, known only to Roger and later Don, namely his "botched orchiectomy," a point that we will also learn links him with Partch.

Even more importantly, Bert's predilection for Ayn Rand will also link him to Partch. The parallels between Partch and that icon of the Right, Howard Roark, are I think striking. While Partch quit music school rather than being expelled like Roark, both clearly felt contempt for the triviality and irrelevance of their courses and instructors. Partch's "kind of adolescent *auto da fé*" of his earlier, conventional works in a potbelly stove recalls the similar scene where Roark burns all the remaining work of his mentor, Henry Cameron. Both Roark and Partch then drop out of respectable society, supporting themselves with manual labor and even, in Partch's case, riding the rails as a hobo. (A *Mad Men* episode earlier in Season One explored "The Hobo Code.") Roark, however, is more like Wagner in his ability to combine individualism and idiosyncrasy with successfully seeking patronage. While Partch was fairly openly homosexual, Roark, though officially straight, has sometimes struck his readers as far more deeply and significantly involved with Gayle [!] Wynand than with Dominique. And while it's quite easy to imagine Partch delivering the expelled Roark's speech about standing at the front of no tradition, and with more justification—Roark's work, at least as seen in the film, seems to easily fit the real-life International Style that goes so well with globalized Equal Temperament—Partch in fact realized, like the Traditionalists in religion, that what was needed was not an impossible, Promethean independence but rather a synoptic grasp of all available traditions, from the Greeks to the Plains Indians, so as to reach the principles behind them and then find a way to express them anew.

Without drifting too far off the subject, one could also imagine Partch

Yet, true to my Faustian Spirit, I must push on! This is all wrong!

First, the "circle" of fifths is metaphysically absurd.[18]

> The fifths form a spiral whose sounds, coiled around themselves, can never meet. For us, this *limitless spiral* can be *the joint in the center of the world*, the narrow gate that will allow us to escape from the appearance of a closed universe, to travel in other worlds and explore their secrets.[19]
>
> Nature is expansive and open, while *human logic strives toward standardized metrics and closed loops.* In this sense one could state that just intonation is a more natural system, while equal temperament is a more human system. (Harlan, p. 33)

The closed loop of human logic replaces the limitless spiral of reality. The doors of the Black Iron Prison slam shut.

Let's go back to Pythagoras. Restated, his problem arose because the "cycle of fifths" does not yield a circle or cycle, but a spiral. This offended his sense of propriety. Yes, that's right, Western music is based on Pythagoras' obsession with circles.

The circumcision of the Pythagorean Comma was referred to by the composer Dane Rudhyar as "The Great Mutation": the gradual replacement of Mysticism with Rationalism,[20] the beginning of Western man's privileging of the "rational" notions of his little mind over transcendental truth.[21]

---

as a musical John Galt—Rand's actual composer character is a recognizable pedestrian Romantic of the sort Partch would have despised, reflecting Rand's own middlebrow tastes—who drops out of the system and wanders around, hobo-like, seeking converts to create a new musical utopia.

[18] "That's metaphysically absurd. How can I know what you hear?," Firesign Theatre, *Don't Crush That Dwarf, Hand Me the Pliers.*

[19] Daniélou, *Music and the Power of Sound*, p. 8.

[20] "Harry Partch: America's first Microtonal Composer" by Marcus Wolf, http://marcjwolf.com/articles/harry-partch-america-s-first-microtonal-composer/.

[21] "You see? YOU SEE?? Your stupid minds! Stupid! STUPID!!!"—

Pythagoras substituted his little mind for metaphysical truth. Reality, as René Guénon documents the brief but intense *Symbolism of the Cross*, is a spiral, not a circle. It is a screw that spirals upward as it turns at a certain . . . pitch.[22]

Western music was now set adrift, a menace to navigation, cut off from the music of other cultures, such as India and China, whose music was still metaphysically sound[23]; as well as from what should have been its sister sciences — as we have seen, Western musicians eschew acoustics and pretend that their scales are arbitrary combinations of sound miraculously "discovered" when somebody blew into a reed.

2B: "BUT REALLY, WHO CARES?"

Away with all this metaphysical rigmarole! What about the music? It's really purdy! (The sum and substance of most of the objections to my previous article; just like Bert Cooper insisting that lots of great Americans started out as crooks, so what?)

It cannot be denied that ET led to an explosion of creativity, of which Wagner is the ultimate example. But ultimate also means final. This creativity was limited to one kind: modulation between keys — and everything else was sacrificed, such as the expressivity of the numerous modes. Wagner was a "Master" of modulation

------

Plan Nine from Outer Space.

[22] I discuss James and Guénon elsewhere in this volume in "The Corner at the Center of the World," This was also Guénon's fundamental objection to the New Agey notions of "reincarnation," an argument accepted by Evola, Coomaraswamy, and others. The being, as he traverses the possibilities of manifestation at any particular degree, eventually exhausts them all and reaches the center *but at the next higher degree*, there being no reason for a repetition, within Infinite Possibilities, of possibilities that have already been realized. It should come as no surprise that reincarnation was a favorite doctrine of . . . Pythagoras. Thus do we see that not only are music and mathematics related, but all three, music, math, and metaphysics, are, as the Mediaevals would say, convertible.

[23] Like spoken language before Babel, the music of different cultures was once mutually understandable, at least in principle; today, Westerners gape in incomprehension at funny "Oriental" sounding music; as we shall see, even Partch's work would be called "Oriental-sounding."

above all else,[24] but it depends above all on surprise, as more and more discordant intervals are forced into use, and like drug addiction, leads to the inevitable question, "what next?' Thus the "crisis of tonality" after Wagner, leading to the numerous experiments of the 20th century.

> The "crisis of tonality" at the end of the 19th and beginning of the 20th centuries was primarily a crisis of materials. Composers such as Mahler and Wagner had exhausted the rhetorical abilities that the 12 building blocks of tonality would provide. Atonality and 12-tone technique were a means of recycling a new language out of the remnants of a diatonic system. Because of the impossibility for exotic and liberating influences to have any effect on *sound* (the instruments and tuning are still the same) composers used a high degree of abstraction isomorphic manipulation of these arbitrary materials to convey *rhetorically* a new kind of music. (The best examples of this are Cage and Xenakis.)[25]

The Pythagorean Scale, having become an all-encompassing system—scales, instruments, notation, schools, concert and opera halls—known as Equal Temperament, had finally revealed itself as a Chinese Finger Trap. We had abandoned all our supplies and equipment to go up this one tunnel, gone as far as we could, and were now solidly wedged in. As Small says, unconsciously and ominously echoing Evola, "Those who ride the tiger can never dismount."[26]

2C: OH WHO CARES ABOUT MUSIC ANYWAY?

Small "t" traditionalists have non-metaphysical reasons to beef

---

[24] Such as the famous Tristan Chord that Bryan Magee's book takes its name from.

[25] Wolf, "Harry Partch: America's first Microtonal Composer." As we'll see, Partch will eschew abstraction in favor what he'll call "corporeality," and indeed devise his own intonation and instruments.

[26] *Musicking*, p. 129; the allusion, of course, is to Baron Evola's *Ride the Tiger*.

as well. The shiny, new, "modern" Western system, bereft of expressive possibilities but with all the persuasive force of the White Man's Gatling guns behind it, is one of the chief agents of cultural globalization, as young, with-it types turn away from granddad's old music, newly urbanized Third World workers demand up-to-date music like they hear in the Western movies and TV shows, and local oligarchies compete with each other in promoting Western symphonies, opera houses, and conservatories. Sure, we practice rural infanticide or female circumcision (there it is again, and not for the last time!), but just listen to Ying Yang or Abu Simsim play that Chopin *étude*!

The same thing happened Stateside first. After German immigrants established the dominance of their own system of *Kultur*, native White American traditions of music were wiped out.

Sam Francis described this phenomenon in a column on the National Endowment of the Arts (one of the chief life-support systems for the moribund classical culture) compiled in *Shots Fired*. He notes,

There used to be a real popular culture in America, not only in Maine and Montana but even in metropolitan areas like New York and Boston. In that veiled and lost epoch, *many Americans played musical instruments they were raised to play instead of buying recordings produced by European musicians and Japanese corporations*, wrote poetry for themselves instead of puzzling over thin volumes and crippled and bitter verse cranked out by whatever lesbian poetess-in-residence New York publishing houses have decided to make a celebrity for a week, and acted in and sometimes even wrote plays that they produced themselves in local theaters instead of packing the house to gibber over Madonna, Michael Jackson, *Wayne's World*, and *Nightmare on Elm Street, Part 70.*[27]

It's no surprise that before the German Judaics could take over

---

[27] Quoted in http://alternativeright.com/altright-archive/main/the-magazine/superpowers.

the mass cultural enterprise, it had first to be thoroughly regimented by those very industrious and hardworking *Kultur* Germans, determining our tuning system, orchestras, music schools, repertoire (plenty of Wagner!) etc.[28] In the same way, the German Reich earlier had to be set up as a going concern before the Judaics could be bothered to take it over. As usual, the *goyim* do the hard work, the Judaics then move in and take over.[29]

---

[28] See *Understanding Toscanini: How He Became an American Culture-God and Helped Create a New Audience for Old Music* by Joseph Horowitz (New York: Knopf, 1987) and Sam Lipman's hostile review in *The New Criterion* for May 1989. One might even draw a parallel to sports, where, as Steve Sailer has speculated, European Right-wing populism has survived by its roots in local football clubs, while American sport has been a top-down affair of national universities and big corporations; see "The Real Threat to British Elites," http://takimag.com/article/the_real_threat_to_british_elites_steve_sailer%20/%20axzz2VLoEHu6Z.

[29] This 19th-century Germanic migration is to be distinguished from the earlier migration of dissident Protestants such as the Amish and Mennonites, who not only isolated themselves from American (*Englisher*) culture, but also had already seceded from the degeneration of their own culture in the post-Buxtehude *dégringolade*, preserving earlier, truly Aryan folk musical systems. There is more Traditional Aryan spirit in an Amish harvest song than in the entire Ring Cycle. Or consider the music lovingly collected by Harry Smith and published as the multi-record set *Anthology of American Folk Music*, which kicked off the "folk revival" ("folk," now there's a word the Right should like!) by reintroducing recordings of popular musical styles that had disappeared when, due to the Depression, small record companies went bankrupt and only money-making urban "big bands" (broadcasting from atop swank hotels) or opera houses subsidized by robber barons could survive. One could say that the spirit of Bill Kauffman's *Ain't My America. The Long, Noble History of Antiwar Conservatism and Middle-American Anti-Imperialism* (New York: Metropolitan Books, 2008) at least chimes with Greil Marcus's history of Dylan's "invisible republic," *The Old, Weird America* (revised paperback edition under that title) (New York: Picador, 2011). Indeed, the rule of the ET system over what used to be the people's music is rather similar to the New Liberalism in which the PRISM system of surveillance is deemed A-OK because it's been identified with . . . America, the country itself. Once more we see how ET/globalization/ Neo-con-Neo-Liberalism forms a nice tight circle.

2D: Alain and René Told You So

"One half of this music, the melody, was all pomade and sugar and sentimentality. The other half was savage, temperamental and vigorous. . . . It was the music of decline. There must have been such music in Rome under the later emperors. Compared with . . . real music it was, naturally, a miserable affair; but so was all our art, all our thought, all our makeshift culture in comparison with real culture."

—Hermann Hesse, Steppenwolf

"The Atreides House is building a secret army, using a technique unknown to us; a technique involving *sound*."

—Padishah Emperor Shaddam IV
in Frank Herbert's Dune

This spreading global catastrophe spirals us back again to Daniélou and the Traditionalists; just as we saw that music, math and metaphysics are linked, so is metaphysics and anti-globalism; as Alan Watts said, metaphysics is rockily practical.

In the Traditional metaphysics common to the East and West, the act of creation involves sound; entities are *called into* being (And God said . . . ; in the beginning was the Word). If we were as powerful as God, we too could create, using the correct Names of things. Such is the nature of Magic. Even so, our limited powers are able to approximate such Names, and using music—with proper intervals, of course—we can *evoke* (Sanskrit *vak*, Latin *vox*) beings—"speak of the Devil"—and psychological states.[30]

Certain intervals between tones *resonate within the body* more than others. According to this view, the most *physically compelling* intervals are those in the simplest proportions of one to another. (Harlan, p. 5)

---

[30] Consider, giving credit where credit is due, Wagner's famous evocation of the Rhine with only a series of figurations of the chord of E flat major

Thus the title of Daniélou's treatise in its revised English language edition: *Music and the Power of Sound.*[31]

Needless to say, even that reduced level of efficacy is impossible in the Western system, where intervals are inaccurate and their effects are judged to be purely customary or "merely psychological." Thus, while when a Hindu musician plays a certain raga, even the animals sense the approaching rainstorm, Richard Strauss, at the end of the West's "progress," gave up entirely and dragged a wind machine onstage.

Indeed, the effect of random intervals chosen for superficial effects can be positively harmful, both to one's own body and the body politic.

> The *Yue ji* declares: In periods of disorder, rites are altered and music is licentious. Then sad sounds are lacking in dignity, joyful sounds lack in calm. . . . When the spirit of opposition manifests itself, indecent music comes into being . . . when the spirit or conformity manifests itself, harmonious music appears. . . . So that, under the effect of music, the five social duties are without admixture, the eyes and the ears are clear, the blood and the vital spirits are balanced, habits are reformed, customs are improved, the Empire is in complete peace.[32]

By varying the intervals, inventing new combinations solely to create superficial effects, one endangers both the individual soul and the larger soul known as the State, and even the World Soul of the Universe.

George (posing as a Nazi organizer): "Well, it's just a game. Remember that, kids."

Tim (a fan of "his" book): "'Just a game.' He's so humble. Don't forget what you wrote in the epilogue, *the fate of the*

---

[31] See especially Chapter One, "Metaphysical Correspondences."

[32] Cited by M. Courant, "Essai sur la musique classique des Chinois," *Dictionnaire du Conservatoire,* pp. 206–7.

world depends on the outcome of this 'game'."

George: "Well, I was exaggerating a bit, just for effect."[33]

Away with this System, both played out but still dangerous in its very putrescence! Rather than seeking to preserve the Germanic classical heritage like some dead tooth, we must, in the spirit of archeofuturism, return to the roots in our ever present past and "make new" a White Tradition of our own, using our newest technology. In short, Aryan Futurist Music.[34]

PART TWO:
HARRY PARTCH — AMERICAN COMPOSER, HOBO, ARCHEOFUTURIST

Rejecting the equal temperament and concert traditions that have dominated western music, Harry Partch adopted the pure intervals of just intonation and devised a 43-tone-to-the-octave scale, which in turn forced him into inventing numerous musical instruments. His compositions realize his ideal of a corporeal music that unites music, dance, and theater.[35]

Having already questioned the value of Wagner for the alt-Right I might fairly be asked, "Well, what then? What have you to offer us instead?"

One proof of the irrational, quasi-cultic hold of Wagner on the Right is the way one must acknowledge him as possessing all positive predicates, however contradictory. Thus, he is not only the great innovator and pioneer and revolutionary, he is also the great exemplar of Western, or European, musical tradition, the very voice of musical tradition, which must not be questioned. Wagner, in short, was no Wagnerite.

---

[33] "The Limo," http://www.seinfeldscripts.com/TheLimo.html.

[34] As I've said in "I'll Have a White Rock Please," Varg Virkernes, than whom no one is whiter, more Activist, or more Metal, has shown us the way to what I call Blackened New Age. See the *Homo and the Negro.*

[35] Cover blurb for Thomas McGeary, ed., *Bitter Music: Collected Journals, Essays, Introductions, and Librettos* (Champaign, Il.: University of Illinois Press, 2000).

But even Wagner's "innovation" lies merely in pioneering some new, more dissonant harmonies, a couple of new instruments, and some stagecraft; he still operates within The System, the 12-tone, equally tempered system designed to fit his Erard piano, with its accompanying orchestra, opera houses, music schools and critics.[36] Some rebel.

If innovation within the form is laudable, surely questioning, and indeed replacing where necessary, the form itself is even more laudable. And this is precisely what Wagner did not do.

How about a real revolutionary? How about someone who, like Wagner, dreamed of great *Gesamtkunstwerke* based on ancient Aryan myths, performed by new instruments of his own design, in similarly innovative theaters? What if in addition he performed a fundamental critique of the Western musical system, but, never having the advantage of a princely patron, spent his life as a hobo and recluse?

---

[36] Ironically, as Daniélou points out, it is precisely the equally tempered orthodoxy of today, in which even musicians—especially musicians—have never heard a truly consonant chord, which prevents us from appreciating exactly how revolutionary Wagner's dissonances were. Or, indeed, any pre-20th Century music. Kyle Gann, after savaging ET, adds that: "Equal temperament—the bland, equal spacing of the 12 pitches of the octave—is pretty much a 20th-century phenomenon. It was known about in Europe as early as the early 17th century, and in China much earlier. But it wasn't used, because the consensus was that it sounded awful: out of tune and characterless. During the 19th century (for reasons we'll discuss later), keyboard tuning drifted closer and closer to equal temperament over the protest of many of the more sensitive musicians. Not until 1917 was a method devised for tuning exact equal temperament. [. . .] Nineteenth-century musicians used to argue about what colors the various keys represented; whether Eb major was gold, for example, and D major red. Twentieth-century musicians have dismissed such arguments as sentimental nonsense, but when you play 19th-century music in well temperament, you begin to hear the differences of color. Is it far-fetched to suggest that Mozart and Beethoven wrote keyboard music with certain key-colors in mind, and that we miss subtle but pervasive qualities in the music when we homogenize it into equal temperament? (http://www.kylegann.com/histune.html).

And what if he was an American, born in this century?[37] One of us![38] Just a slob, like one of us?[39]

Enter Harry Partch.

A: THE LIFE

"Depictions of Partch's tumultuous existence are a fascinating study of 20th-century American life even when told independently." (Harlan, p. 52)

For reasons that will become clear, the life and work of Harry Partch are best seen as of a piece, one—an integral whole, a unison, 1:1, if you will.[40] The study of both has been immensely benefited by the labors of Bob Gilmore, whose *Harry Partch: A Biography* (Yale, 1998) is a pretty definitive account of a man who, even when he wasn't a real live dagnabbit hobo still managed to leave almost as little trace of himself as Don Draper. For a "thumbnail history" you can take a look at Marc Wolf's "Harry Partch: America's first Microtonal Composer,"[41] which also supplies the photos, especially of the self-made instruments, that would have been one improvement for Gilmore's book. Rather than recapitulate these accounts, I want to skim through hitting some of the highlights that stand out when both his life and his art are looked at for Aryan motifs.

First, though, now that the word "integrity" has popped up, I must start by quoting this sad little summary provided by one of Partch's actual friends and followers, Ben Johnston.

---

[37] President John F. Kennedy, Inaugural Address.

[38] Tod Browning, *Freaks*.

[39] Joan Osborne, "One of Us."

[40] "Partch projected his self-image through his works." From the "Abstract" of the appropriately named dissertation, *One Voice: A Reconciliation of Harry Partch's Disparate Theories* by Brian Timothy Harlan, available on Google Books.

[41] http://marcjwolf.com/articles/harry-partch-america-s-first-microtonal-composer/

> He was so possessive of his artistic creations that notwith-
> standing the manifest impossibility that *any one person* could
> be artistically skilled, let alone talented, let alone genius-en-
> dowed in all areas of a complex multimedia art work, Partch
> was yet unwilling, even unable, to collaborate. He either
> dictated to his collaborators in their own area or he fought
> them all the way to an estrangement. . . . In his attitude to
> society he demanded support for his own work as far as
> possible without any strings attached while he was capable
> of even violating a contract with another artist. . . . This goes
> far *beyond artistic integrity*; indeed *the word integrity is an
> ironic one to use at all in this context*. He orchestrated and all
> but guaranteed the oblivion his work so obviously courts.[42]

Is there any other musician this combination of genius and amoral cussedness reminds one of? Of course: Wagner.[43]

Partch was born in 1901 and lived until 1974, thus neatly encompassing the period when White America reached its apogee.[44]

> His interest in non-Western musics was instilled upon him
> at a young age from his parents, who had been missionaries
> in China. Both his parents spoke Mandarin, and his mother
> would sing him Chinese lullabies while accompanying her-
> self on their reed organ. Later his parents purchased Edison
> cylinders of Hebrew chants, Congo dances, and Cantonese
> opera. All of these musics had a lasting effect on Partch.

---

[42] Gilmore, p. 252.

[43] For the lowdown on Wagner, see Deems Taylor, "The Monster," another part of the Counter-Currents Wagner Bicentennial Symposium, http://www.counter-currents.com/2013/05/the-monster/.

[44] We've frequently identified the period of circa 1972-76, admittedly our own Young Manhood, as the peak of White Western Civilization, it being, despite the myths of Liberal "progress," all downhill culturally, economically, social, since the Boomers took over. And yes, I know that 1901 is no longer "this century" but that's what Kennedy meant, and I'm sticking to it. As Gary Wills mordantly observed in *Nixon Agonistes*, Kennedy meant to rudely insult the departing Eisenhower, and wound up lauding the even more elderly Reagan.

(Harlan, p. 40)

His parents, of English, Scotch, and Irish ancestry, had fled the Boxer Rebellion[45] and settled in the Southwest for his mother's health. His father worked for the immigration services; apparently, the border was just as porous then as now, but at that time the flood was coming from Chinese trying to circumvent restrictions on the Pacific coast. Of course, none of these hordes spoke the Mandarin dialect, but then as now, the Immigration Service knew no better. Partch's father rejoiced in the title of "Chinese Inspector," and apparently his job was to roam around checking out saloons, restaurants, and laundries for suspiciously Oriental types, like Kwai Chang Caine.

More traumatic was Jennie's decision to circumcise Partch at the age of eight, for which he openly resented her. The incident was still troubling for him in his seventies. He later called circumcision a conspiracy between doctors and mothers who want to symbolically castrate their sons. "If they can castrate them," he said "they can keep them close" (Harlan, p. 54).

Well, there we are; I told you circumcision would crop up again.[46] Partch clearly saw this as an attempt to separate him from his father and brothers, and indeed most males at the time; a clear indication of his tacit sense that the male *Männerbund* was being attacked by Woman and Judeo-Christianity, as becomes clearer in Gilmore's unedited (ahem) quote:

But my mother decided I was going to be different. I was going to be a modern child who was going to be cleansed, as it were, by having a little piece of skin cut off [the Pythagorean Comma!]. — I didn't object to this humiliation so much as that I was then different from everybody else, *except for*

---

[45] At the end of his life, Partch had a sign on his door that threatened visitors with "Another Boxer Rebellion."

[46] And, as we anticipated, Partch will also wind up, like Bert Cooper, with "no balls at all," due to either having had mumps, untreated by his Christian Science mother, resulting in sterility, or a medical condition known as "undescended testicles," resulting in same.

the Jews. . . . this is a cabal,[47] a conspiracy between doctors and mothers—mothers who want their children symbolically castrated. (Gilmore, p. 23)

This was not the kind of "difference" and "innovation" that

---

[47] I've found at least one other bit of evidence of Partch's racial realism; in one of his most sustained pieces of satire—comparable to the "routines" developed by his fellow American Crank, William Burroughs, during his own time among the *Männerbund* of the down and out, or "beat"—Partch mocks the local booster notions that the "pioneer spirit" of San Francisco's "49er" descendants would produce a "real American music."

> To demonstrate this neo-pioneer spirit, they build a four million dollar opera house which allows descendants of 49ers to repose their fulsome fundaments in a diamond horseshoe, from which they support "American" music. . . . As a final demonstration of pioneering . . . *persons with shattered English and long noses are engaged to conduct* 90 piece orchestras. (*Bitter Music*, pp. 50–51)

While "looking down one's nose" is a common metaphor for snobbery, I can't help but find a trace of anti-Judaism here, not as a knee-jerk obsession but as something sensed, or "smelled out"—in the artificially implanted German-Jewish *Kultur* system I noted before. I feel confirmed in that suspicion by the way Partch immediately segues into a reminiscence of pounding the streets of New York, confronting "long dark faces" that surely are not those of Sutton Place. One thinks of Lovecraft's feverish vision of Levantine swarms during his New York stay. While as we've seen Partch is otherwise a very different American breed, open to the very "Levantine pipes" that so tormented Lovecraft in his sleep that he turned them into the blind idiot god Azathoth's piping at the heart of Chaos, both share a loyalty to the possibilities of a real American culture, and a sense of it being submerged by a tide of foreign dreck, whether elite *Kultur*, immigrant *Yiddishkeit*, or today's "vibrant diversity." As Christopher Pankhurst says in a slightly different context (reviewing Richard King's *How Soon is Now*?) "There is a stubborn urge to authenticity within indie music that is entirely in keeping with the mind-set that can lead one to forbidden political places" (http://www.counter-currents.com/ 2013/06/how-soon-is-nowthe-madmen-mavericks-who-made-independent-Gint-music-1975-2005/).

Partch would champion, but the opposite: it represented separation from the natural and submergence in the new, regimented, modern, pseudo-scientifically enlightened masses.[48]

Another "humiliation" occurred when the first-grade Partch drew a stallion, complete with "his symbol of fertility . . . long and portentous," only to be banged on the head by the girl sitting next to him, who then "vigorously rubbed the sex out of my horse" and redrew it as "presumably female or ambiguous." "Thus in early years did this Christian abstract female age cow me."

As Gilmore notes, this "Christian female abstract age" would continue to represent to Partch the threat to not just virility but the wholeness and integrity of the body itself, what would eventually identify in his music as *the corporeal.*[49]

> Another motivating factor Partch's critical perspective revolved around [was] music education, and particularly the teaching of music in academia. He felt strongly that creativity was stifled in education at every turn: for composers by the emphasis on the imitation of historic styles, and for performers by the emphasis on virtuosic proficiency. (Harlan, p. 38)

Partch, like millions of others, met the same quandary — personal integrity vs. "join the modern cabal" — in college, but unlike most others, he did something about it — he quit. After moving to Los Angeles and enrolling in UCLA, Partch realized that his "teachers" were idiots, men who knew nothing about the actual, physical nature of sound or music, but instead repeated rote nonsense about "harmonic laws"[50] and above all tried to implant an

---

[48] These comments were made in his seventies, during the making of a biographical film; in a different context, he complained about some aspects of the editing thus: "I am far more interesting with my integrity intact" (Gilmore, p. 380).

[49] Gilmore, pp. 30–31.

[50] Sort of the same way economics consists of fancy theories with little or no relevance to reality: "I've found that economic theory is a useful servant for understanding facts, but many bright people seem to view

artificial European culture that Partch had no use for.[51] After three months he left and completed his education in the public library, where he could take up—and discard—any book as needed. "I had virtually given up on both music schools and private teachers, and had begun to ransack public libraries, doing suggested exercises and writing music free from the infantilisms and inanities of professors as I had experienced them."[52]

Meanwhile, a job as an usher acquainted him with the European concert repertoire, as well as the social system involved —a "sea of blue-haired ladies"—that left him with a lasting distaste for all the social snobbery it involved. Although, as he gleefully pointed out, he never paid a nickel for a ticket.[53] "Before I was twenty, I had tentatively rejected both the intonational system of modern Europe and the concert system, although I did not realize either the ultimate scope or the consequences of that rejection."[54]

The rejection of the intonational system was made possible by his discovery, in the library, of Helmholtz's *On the Sensations of Tone as a Physiological Basis for the Theory of Music* (Longmans, Green, 1912; published 1885; downloadable from Google Books), whose explanation of the "natural affinities" of physical acoustics and musical aesthetics provided Partch with a rational and integral basis for musical creativity; he "began to take wing."[55]

Thus was born Partch's devotion to Just Intonation, an alternative to the modern European—though crypto-Talmudic—Equal Temperament system that was both scientifically based (uniting art and science, mind and body) as well as more truly, or more profoundly, Western. Musically, at least, Partch would be able to

---

theory as the master to which their awareness of reality must be enslaved." Steve Sailer, "How Immigration Can Hurt a Country" in theory, not just in reality," http://isteve.blogspot.com/2013/06/how-immigration-can-hurt-country-in.html

[51] Gilmore, pp. 35ff.

[52] Partch, *Genesis of a Music*, p. vii.

[53] About this time he began a romance with Latin heartthrob Ramon Novarro, which would end when the latter's film career took off; see Gilmore, p. 47.

[54] Partch, *Genesis*, p. vii.

[55] Gilmore, p. 49 and *Genesis*, p. vii.

reverse his circumcision.

> [A]ccording to Partch Western music had forgotten this an-
> cient practice. To reinstate this practice, however, he needed
> not only to *erase the arbitrary distinction* between music,
> dance, and drama, but also to *return to the use* of "infinitely
> varied melodic and harmonic subtlety." Just intonation was
> thus a key aspect of Partch's project *to transcend his own era*,
> an effort he believed was a primary obligation of the artist.
> What made just intonation so attractive was that it was both
> an expression of the harmonic series that *revealed a connec-
> tion to our physical being*, and *a system used by historically and
> culturally diverse groups.* (Harlan, p. 41)

Partch soon realized that a new intonation system required
new instruments — integrity again — and he began to construct his
famous Partch instruments; first a 43-tone keyboard, the Chromatic Organ, and then, inspired by reconstructions of the Greek
kithara, the ancestor of the lute and basically all string instruments, he built his own in 1938, followed by another 43-tone organ, the Chromolodeon, in 1942. He would later describe himself
as "a philosophic music man seduced into carpentry."[56]
But in the middle of all this the Depression took hold, and
Partch began a nine-year period, from 1935 to 1944, as a transient,
mostly as a hobo, a period documented by a journal, *Bitter Music*,
eventually published as part of a collection of writings under that
title in 2000. Nor would later foundation grants — always too little,
too late — and music school appointments — always limited, inadequate, and isolated from the academic "insiders" — make much
difference. In the mid-'60s he said, with some wonderment, "For
over 20 years I have been the strangest kind of hobo — a hobo with
over two tons of 'weird' instruments to take, wherever."[57]

B: THE MAN

I've suggested that integrity is the leitmotiv of Partch's life and

---

[56] Gilmore, p. 260.
[57] Gilmore, p. 330.

work (their unity being another kind of integrity), symbolized by the unison, 1:1.[58] We first encounter it in his rejection of an ossified "tradition" of musical education and concert-going, and in his subsequent search for a more meaningful, more truthful, system of musical intonation.[59] The discovery of Helmholtz's work suggested a way to unify the body and spirit, science and art, with a musical system soundly based in acoustical fact, not academic custom.[60]

The eventual 43-tone system required its own notation, and its own instruments, whose large size suggest that they could become a part of the stage setting itself, and the musicians become singers and dancers as well when not otherwise occupied.

---

[58] Which also reminds one of the ithyphallic Egyptian statutes, facing each other, arms to the sky, that Evola discusses in *The Hermetic Tradition*.

[59] I would suggest that Partch's search for a musical system that remains rooted in actual human acoustic experience, not abstract theory, parallels the idea that Evola discusses in "The Idea of Initiatic Knowledge," in which ordinary experience is transcended not by abstract cogitation — science — nor religious belief, but by a higher form of empirical experience itself. This essay can be found in his collective work *Introduction to Magic*.

[60] "O Freunde, *nicht diese Töne! / Sondern laßt uns angenehmere anstimmen*, und freudenvollere. . . . Deine Zauber *binden wieder / Was die Mode streng geteilt*. . . . Ja, wer auch *nur eine Seele/Sein nennt* auf dem Erdenrund!" Despite his antipathy to the concert tradition, Partch admitted a liking for the emotional intensity of Beethoven. Although Partch's most obvious classical *Doppelgänger* is Wagner, or perhaps Scriabin, for polemical purposes his Old Guy for the tradition is usually Beethoven, while when intonation in particular is on the table it's Bach. In both cases, he is at pains to note that he likes the music, sure. An "audibly drunk" Partch recorded in 1966 crows "I've never heard anyone play Chopin as well as I do" (Gann, p. 191). But he just doesn't think that justifies creating a whole totalitarian culture of imitation, privileging "virtuosity" and interpretation (and we know Who the virtuosi and interpreters are) over creativity. As for classical institutions, such as music schools, concert halls, and opera houses, they are anathema, dead and deadening, useful only as figures of mockery.

The composer could build, compose for, and train musicians to perform on a new set of instruments. This last seemingly insurmountable option was the path chosen by Harry Partch. Partch's use of just intonation must be understood in the larger context of what he was trying to achieve artistically. In the simplest of explanations, Partch used just intonation because it allowed him to compose for intoned voice, which helped to create the dramatic effect he was trying to achieve in his music. To accompany the voice in his music Partch needed instruments to play the 43-tone just scale he developed. Over the course of his career he designed and built some 40 unique instruments.

Beginning with *King Oedipus*, Partch's first theatrical production, his instruments began to appear onstage as part of the set design. Such staging was used in all of Partch's theatrical works, and as a result, the musicians were more easily integrated into the drama as actors, singers, and dancers. Thus, for Partch, the idea to use just intonation was embedded within a matrix of ideas that served a broader goal. All of these devices, his integration of drama with music and dance, his use of invented instruments tuned to just intonation, his 43-tone scale, his use of intoned voice, as well as his reliance on percussive techniques, and settings of plots inspired by ritualistic practices, were tools for Partch. (Harlan, pp. 36–37)

Gilmore too speaks of Partch's "misunderstood theories," "cryptic notation," and "strange instruments" as being, despite the unhelpful attention they drew and continue to draw, merely his "tools," his paints and brushes, what Heidegger might call his "ensemble."[61] But just as Harlan speaks of a "matrix" Gilmore also makes the important point that Partch frequently spoke of the tonal resources of Just Intonation not as a scale but as a *fabric*, with the metaphorical implications of an indefinite interweaving that lays down a total pitch space. Gilmore explicitly contrasts this with the *closed circle* of Pythagoras, as we have earlier, but we

---

[61] Gilmore, p. 201.

could also point out that Guénon also explicitly develops the transition from the spiral to "the symbolism of weaving" in outlining the nature of Universal Manifestation.[62]

It would be quite wrong, though tempting, to see all this as yet more "avant-garde" tinkering and *épater le bourgeois* tomfoolery. Partch always saw himself as part of the Western tradition—an individual, but a Western, indeed, West Coast, individual[63]—but that *it was the ET system that had strayed.* From his essay "Bach and Harmony":

> Music was *veering away* from the linear, becoming harmonic, and attaining a status *independent* of poetry and the dance. Consequently, instruments with harmonic versatility—keyboard instruments—became the intellect of the new music.
>
> [T]he whole trend of music since Gregorian chant has been *a tangent to the main historic stream.* The ancient Greek and Chinese conception—as old as history—that music is poetry has deteriorated . . . the voice is just another violin . . .
>
> [W]as the ancient conception lost? By no means. It was obscured, left to folk peoples. . . . But it flowed on in a broad stream [including] the Meistersingers of Nuremberg . . . Negro spirituals . . . and . . . Wagner. [64]

To understand that surprising reference to Wagner, first let's notice his recurrent notes of disdain for the false, abstract—of "the intellect"—notion of separating music from dance and theatre, while at the same time rejecting the idea of the voice being treated as just another violin. Unity does not mean uniformity. The latter is rather a result of the bloodless, bodiless abstraction of the ET system.[65]

---

[62] See Chapter 14 of *The Symbolism of the Cross.*

[63] "I've no business living anywhere east of the Rocky Mountains. . . . No sun in days" (Gilmore, p. 255).

[64] *Bitter Music,* pp. 162–63.

[65] In constructing his instruments, Partch always deferred to the integrity or "the daimon" of the instruments; see Gilmore p. 314.

The notion of Partch himself as a Romantic composer is compelling. . . . His emphasis on self-expression and composer as sole author of a work [*integrity!*] also support this view. In fact one of his earliest compositions after attending university, which he later burned, was a symphonic poem. Yet, according to his statements it was *the large forces often required to realize Romantic works* that discouraged him from pursuing that style. He also perceived a general *lack of intimacy between performer and audience* in performances, *and particularly between composer and audience.* (Harlan, p. 61)

Richard Wagner's music dramas ostensibly fit this model as well, yet in many ways Wagner's music dramas equally symbolized what 20th-century music theater composers were retaliating against. Partch, for one, applauded Wagner's condemnation of Italian and French opera, and his condemnation of "absolute" music for its lack of connection to speech and dance. He was particularly attracted to Wagner's endeavor to create works that fused poetry, music, and visual spectacle. *Yet he was not convinced by Wagner's operas. Wagner's use of a large orchestra and the great importance he placed on harmony gave his music obvious predominance over the dramatic action.* (Harlan, p. 134)

Partch:

In the wrestling match between Wagner's music drama and his symphony orchestra, Wagner's symphony orchestra (with yeoman help from his arias) gets both shoulders of Wagner's music dramas on the floor within five minutes after the curtain rises and for the following two or three hours jumps up and down on the unconscious form.[66]

---

[66] Harry Partch "Oedipus" (1954), reprinted in *Bitter Music*, 219. Cf. Kyle Gann: "He may have written opera, but he was closer to . . . Balinese Monkey Chant, ancient Greek drama, early Florentine opera, the blues — any genre that which *uses music to enhance, not dominate, a story* (*Music Downtown: Writings from The Village Voice*, p. 191).

Like Wagner, Partch was unsatisfied with the contemporary state of the musical tradition; unlike Wagner, he located the problem not in a relatively superficial Frenchification of the operatic genre, but more fundamentally: in the inexpressiveness of the equal temperament system itself. While Wagner had gamed the system with a will, glorying in the creation of ever more abstruse and surprising modulations, such as the famous "Tristan Chord," by Partch's day the system had been clearly played out.

Such effects, of which Wagner was perhaps indeed The Master, depended on surprise; while any chimp could pound on a keyboard, the rules of the game required one not just to invent new sounds but show how they ultimately fit back into the system — "resolve" them. Composers could only go so far, and then the lines would snap.

Moreover, Partch realized that the obsession with harmonic effects had resulted in an everlasting divorce — lack of integrity! — between the voice and the mass orchestra (remember "the voice as just another violin"?). For Partch, integrity meant both the unity of voice and music, as well as respect for the nature — or what he called, in discussing his instruments, the "daimon" — of each. If, as Nietzsche thought, Wagner's music/dramas were a rebirth of Greek tragedy, it was fatally botched by the mind-forged manacles of the post-Bach (anti-)tradition:

> It is likely that his experiences attending Chinese operas as a young man in San Francisco helped him to realize his recreation of the ancient Greek dramas. His early attempt to do this with *King Oedipus* infused epic poetry and music according to the ancient aesthetic that *did not strictly differentiate between these two elements*. In his later works he also included dance. (Harlan, p. 40)

Partch, in short, recognizes his search for musical integrity as analogous to Wagner's *Gesamtkunstwerk*, but finds the latter to ultimately fail due its adherence to the wayward system of ET harmony and the bourgeois concert-system. "The music of the symphony . . . is an art of . . . massed tones . . . and hearers are transported by sheer mass and volume. . . . The music of the historic concept involves the greatest economy of materials, and hearers are transported not by mass but subtlety."[67]

Partch would try a different, more radical path. Rather than suggesting a few changes in stagecraft or adding another equally tempered instrument or two, rather than superficially appropriating the legendary *Meistersingers* and shoehorning them into just another opera, he would return to the roots of the Western music that such guilds had tried to preserve, to find out what went wrong long ago, and rebuild a new music for our times. "It was not that Partch rejected the Western tradition, but rather that he felt it should be revered 'dynamically.' He vehemently upheld that tradition should be under constant review in order to verify its continued relevance" (Harlan p. 37).

In short, archeofuturism, or radical traditionalism.[68] "The Classics" were fine, but devotion to them, limited to reproducing them

---

[67] "Bach and Temperament" in *Bitter Music*, p. 163. These are the "mass" effects that Daniélou identified as typical of the attempts of Western composers to supplement the loss of expression in ET. "Eastern listeners often make such remarks as 'The Beethoven symphonies are very interesting, but why have all those chords been introduced, spoiling the charm of the melodies'"? Needless to say, this was before Nehru, Mao, and others put their people into re-education camps to "modernize" them so as to become Chopin virtuosi, like Red Indians exulting in their glass beads. One thinks of one of Harry Haller's hallucinations in the Magic Theatre of *Steppenwolf*: Brahms and Wagner in Hades, condemned to leading hordes of black clad masses over hill and dale—the notes they wasted. These "mass" effects correspond to mass production, mass media, and other characteristics of the increasingly "quantified" modern world, and make the idea of Wagner's Ring Cycle as a "critique" of capitalism rather ironic. In the unpublished satire "On G-String Formality" Partch ironically confides "Confidentially, there will never be One World until *everyone* loves Bach as much as we do" (Gilmore, p. 171).

[68] Cf. Alex Kurtagić: "Conservatism is the negation of the new; tradition is the ongoing affirmation of the old, of the archaic. And therefore it's endlessly regenerating, constantly renewing" ("Masters of the Universe" Revisited—An Interview with Alex Kurtagic, http://alternativeright.com/blog/2013/6/19/masters-of-the-universe-revisited-an-interview-with-alex-kurtagic, June 19, 2013 by George Whale).

with some kind of merely external "virtuosity" added, must not be confused with real creativity with the tradition.

Lacking the notion of radical traditionalism, Partch's audiences tended to misunderstand him, by assimilating him to either of two reassuringly familiar anti-Western roles: as either an "Orientalist" or some kind of "avant-garde" radical.

These were two things that infuriated Partch as failures to understand what he was doing. The first, beloved of lazy though positive reviewers and polite guests, was to say something like "It's very Oriental, isn't it?"[69] In a very superficial sense, it is—it seems mostly gongs and mallets, with nary a string instrument to be found—no room of the blood-warm romance of the *shtetl* and swooning ladies in the private boxes.

More profoundly, the "Oriental" tag is a reflection of an ingenuous perception of what René Guénon has discussed in the context of metaphysics and the "crisis of the modern [Western] world"; that the "modern" West has amounted to a cultural wrong turn which had the effect of isolating itself from not only the East but its own past, and thus become a monstrous historical anomaly. By refusing to continue on that road, and instead returning to its roots to find a new direction, Partch winds up sounding "oriental" when he is actually *au profond*—or rockily, as Alan Watts might say—Western.

As Guénon, Evola, and other Traditionalists insisted, in such situations as today's "Crisis of the Modern World" one must turn to other traditions, not to join them, or to combine them into some "New Age" syncretism, but to discover there elements missing or distorted in one's own Western tradition, *and thus the means to renew it, not abandon it.* Writing to encourage a discouraged friend, who sounds like a typical reader of Evola or Counter-Currents, Partch says:

I must part with you, when you say—". . . there's virtually

---

[69] Partch wryly noted that "The bewilderment of many Orientals is easily equal to the bewilderment of many Caucasians." Quoted in Mina Yang, *California Polyphony: Ethnic Voices, Musical Crossroads* (Champaign, Il.: University of Illinois Press, 2008), p. 57.

nothing left, nothing retrievable from the European past, no signs along the way, and nothing to lean on." I've said it many times, and I'll say it again. In three thousand years the West has abandoned values, beautiful and significant things, that *in toto* are at least as important as what we have preserved. But it is tough—no instruments, the culture, the milieu are absent. But they can be re-created or imagined. With Oriental music, you don't have to re-create or imagine. In either case, what you come up with is something new. (Gilmore, p. 384)

As we have seen, Partch's background—Chinese missionary parents, childhood and young adulthood in the Southwest and West Coast—gave him much exposure to "alien" music, from Chinese theatre to Zuni rituals. Partch always saw himself not as an antiquarian or a folklorist, but as his own man, and fundamentally a Western man, of the American Southwest.

The more I see of fashions, the more I discern, with infinite clarity, another path—that of Man, the bright adventurer, the magic maker.[70] When I feel optimistic, it holds brilliant promise, like an Arizona morning before dawn, with its cardboard stage set and dark eastern silhouette in honor of the sun's holy rising. . . . The truly path-breaking step can never be predicted, and certainly not by the person who makes it at the time he makes it. He clears as he goes, evolves his own techniques, devises his own tools, ignores where he must. And his path cannot be retraced, because each of us is an original being.[71]

---

[70] The note of "Faustian Man" here derives perhaps from Partch's reading of Spengler, although he otherwise had little use for Spengler's views on music or Eastern culture.

[71] Gilmore, p. 356, from Partch's *Genesis of a Music*, pp. xii, xi; compare Crowley's "Every man or woman is a star." Lest all this talk of "integrity" sound too sanctimonious, it must be noted that Partch had an odd method of coming to decisions by arguing the two positions with himself, often aloud. He was quite open about the method, and recommended it to others. A kind of integrity, I guess. Gilmore (p. 379) quotes

He also despised the "avant-garde," especially "Cagean gim-mickry" that he saw as at best a surrender of the responsibility of the composer, as worse, mere showmanship. "Drinking orange juice down an amplified gullet" he snorted, reporting on an actual Cage stunt—I mean, "concert." He "distrusted all types of avant-gardism on the grounds they were contrivances of over-civilized cliques."[72] "Composers with 'advanced techniques' . . . enshrine the bodiless brain. The bodiless brain really needs no sounds at all, only theories."[73]

Nor, despite living for long periods (for him) in such haunts as San Francisco, Big Sur, and Sausalito, did he have any interest in "The Beats." "Harry had no use for the Beat Generation" one West Coast friend remembers. While becoming a more and more fero-cious drinker as he aged, Partch had no interest in marijuana or other "recreational" drugs, nor joining a little clique of "hipsters," which he compared to "Going around in a circle and meeting the same people every five degrees"—and we know how much he hated circles![74]

But above all, he regarded the Beat "jazz poetry" as just another kind of "avant-garde" gimmickry. His critique illustrates his de-mand for both technical knowledge and integrity, as well as a sense of "different" that did not reduce to mere contrariness:

Poetry-*cum*-jazz: I've heard a few very simple things I like,

---

a houseguest who overstayed his welcome being awoken one night to sounds of argument in the next room, and realizing first it was about what to do with him, and second, that both voices were Partch's. I can't help but be reminded of the composer Adrian Leverkuhn coolly tran-scribing his hallucinated conversation with the Devil in Mann's *Doktor Faustus.*

[72] Yang, *California Polyphony*, p. 56. On the other hand, Partch had cordial and encouraging relations throughout his career with Howard Hanson, a very comfortably Romantic composer who never the less rec-ognized Partch as a fellow independent-minded Aryan-American.

[73] From a letter quoted by Gilmore, p. 259.

[74] Nor did Partch have any use for Alan Watts, despite being a fellow goateed Northern California Japanophile, with a similar shyness-in-duced tendency to drink too much. See Gilmore, p. 218 and elsewhere.

but mostly, it seems to me, both poetry and jazz need more *cum*. They should be more *with it*. When poets are jazzmen, and jazzmen poets we'll be closer to an art. I see little evidence that poets have studied the sounds of their own voices, and rhythms, to say nothing of the frequency sounds of their voices, and no evidence whatever that the jazzmen are doing anything different than they've always done. (Gilmore, p. 234)

Ultimately, Partch's immersion in the European tradition took him all the way back to the earliest cave paintings, and the tradition, commonplace in the West through the Middle Ages, of atavistic anonymity.[75] Ironically, while being filmed for a portrait of the artist called *The Dreamer that Remains*, Partch exclaims

I would choose to be anonymous. Of course! I'm thinking of those fantastic cave drawings in southern France and in northern Spain, at Altamira I think it is. And there's no author there! And what a treasure they are! And who cares who did them, how many thousands of years ago. Of course, I'm not saying that anything I do is going to last that long. But who cares what the name was! (Gilmore, p. 283)

Part of that "anonymity" would be his disdain for the "gay liberation" bandwagon when it reached him in the—and his—seventies. For Partch, his homosexuality was a purely personal concern, not political. "Coming out" seemed to him less an avowal of personal liberty than a political alignment, as well as falsely assuming a "fixed sexual identity that could be confidently declared in public." Contra the "gay liberation" fanatics, this "identity politics" as we call it today was again only a counterfeit of integrity: "true love is ambidextrous."[76]

---

[75] See Guénon's *Reign of Quantity*, chapter 9: "The Two-Fold Significance of Anonymity."

[76] Gilmore, pp. 378–80. Gilmore himself thinks Partch was just "old-fashioned." Partch was about as "old fashioned" as William Burroughs, another "cultural outlaw" (p. 156) who viewed marriage as "a biological trap" (p. 193). Both were old-fashioned only in their commitment to the

In the words of Lou Harrison, the Californian composer who has to a degree assumed Partch's mantle: "Harry told the truth about tune, as Kinsey did about sex."[77]

C: THE MUSIC

As someone once said, writing about music is like dancing about architecture, so perhaps it would be best to take advantage of our modern intertubes and refer the reader to the audio and video resources listed below. I would, however, like to do two things before ending; first, reassure the reader who may have suffered from one too many college music performances, and then give some indication of how his works fit into his archeofuturist development sketched above.

One is first and most impressed with how normal — how, dare I say it, natural — it all sounds.[78] Of course, I have been exposed, willingly or not, to a fair about of "modern" or "avant-garde" music. But even the most innocent ears should not expect to hear the tormented shrieks of dodecaphony nor the easily parodied boredom of Judaic "minimalism" nor *épater le bourgeois* assaults from police sirens or shotguns, nor long stretches of silence impudently put forward as "music."

> Microtonal music can be tonal music; and . . . Partch's tuning system, which was grounded on the idea that all

---

values of the *Männerbund*, although Partch, with his Southwestern background and years of wandering as a hobo, really lived the life that Burroughs only read about — in such books as Jack Black's turn of the century crime memoir *You Can't Win* — or wrote about — such as his Dead Roads Trilogy.

[77] Quoted in Wilfred Mellers' review of *Bitter Music* in the *Times Literary Supplement*, with Mellers adding that Partch's collected writings "Leaves us in no doubt that for Partch *life and music were one*; personal reflection intermingles with snatches of hobo speech and song, presented in rudimentary notations that demonstrate how 'words are music,' in rock-bottom America no less than in ancient Greece, in Gregorian chant, or Provencal troubadour song."

[78] Harlan thinks otherwise: "Indeed, the effect of microtonal melodies and harmonies performed with acoustic instruments and voice is nearly as 'eerie' sounding today as it was when Partch received his first concert reviews in 1931" (p. 51) but I think he's wrong here.

tones manifest proportionately from 1:1, was an extreme example of a tonal system. For Partch, the use of just intonation to develop Western music was an alternative to other contemporaneous attempts to resolve the modern crisis of tonality. [. . .]

While other composers were attempting to expand the acceptance of dissonance, Partch placed his efforts in expanding the realm of consonance. "It is not necessary", he said, "to assume antimusic or nonmusic attitudes. It is not necessary to resort to noise or nonrhythmic music, or even excessive dissonance to achieve dynamism in creative art."(Harlan, p. 23; quoting Partch's "Monoliths in Music," [1966] in *Bitter Music*, p. 195)

Partch's instruments, no matter how outré in form or sound, and however "one with" the sets, are always perceived as musical instruments, created and played by humans, and in this respect he certainly compares favorably with the increasingly synthesized — and synthetic — music created in the pop world since the '80s.

It is a vindication of Partch's philosophy, and his methods. When ET has been first theoretically stripped of its pretensions to being natural, or inevitable, or optimal, and revealed instead as an unnatural, abstract, and entirely played-out imposition by *Kulturphilistinen*; and when a truly natural scale was created, along with the instruments needed to play it, the results were, as Hindu or Chinese theorists would have predicted, naturally harmonious and pleasing to the ear. As the Situationist slogan from Paris '68 had it, "Beneath the pavement — the beach." It is, if you will, archeofuturism.

As for the musical works themselves, they followed an evolution similar to Partch's own — archeofuturist with unity or integrity as its leading motive. "He came to believe that the future of music — and indeed, of civilization — lay in a rebirth of the instinctual springs of life that had animated ancient cultures, and this rebirth called, inevitably, for the recreation of the media through which the spirit was to be made manifest."[79]

---

[79] Wilfred Mellers, *Music in a New Found Land* (New York: Knopf,

Partch's work — at least after his potbellied *auto de fé* — like the Greeks, was originally monophonic, not in the sense of recorded in one channel, but a single instrument, perhaps even a single string, accompanying one voice. "His music *has* to be monophonic and in Just Intonation, *because* it is a corporeal theatre ritual [like Classical drama or Noh]. . . . His works, like Aristophanes and Japanese Kabuki, use monophonic chant, slapstick, and juggling for socio-religious purposes."[80]

This was because his original idea was that music had evolved from speech, and so was essentially intoned speech. Music should realize the expressive forces latent in speech (hence, already we see whence his dissatisfaction with the overwhelming Wagnerian orchestra). This already sounded "oriental" enough, especially when setting, say, the poems of Li Po.

With the production of *King Oedipus*, however, Partch reacted to the experience of collaboration on sets and dance with a seismic shift in his conception of music, towards a basically percussive sound, thus becoming even more "oriental" (the *New York Times* sneered that he had "reinvented the gamelan for his own purposes"[81]). But even more importantly, it was, as we have seen, a new vision of a total theatre work, integrating music, voice, dance, set design, into one whole.

> The transition from the intoned speech manner to a percussive dance idiom follows his realization that the theatre could be a suitable medium for both. . . . Moreover, [the director's] acceptance of his instruments as dramatically compelling presences on stage both vindicated and transformed Partch's attitude to his instrument-building activity, and confirmed his belief in the sculptural and kinesthetic appeal of instruments as visual forms. (Gilmore, p. 216)

Once again, the idea was to learn from the East, and one's own experience, to overcome modern abstraction and return, archeo-futuristically, to a more corporeal Western past: "[I]n the orient

---

1964), p. 170.

[80] Mellers, p. 171

[81] Gilmore, p. 276.

there has never been any great separation of the theater arts, and therefore no need to conceive of *integration*. . . . [I think] in terms of revitalization of the over-specialized Western theater, through transfusion of old and profound concepts" (Gilmore, p. 298).

Partch's large, beautifully constructed instruments would now be integral parts of the stage setting, not hidden away underneath the stage,[82] and the musicians, instead of sitting around waiting for their cues, would be expected to be part of the action as singers, dancers, or mimes.

The result was *The Bewitched*, which took its theme — the "un-witching" of human beings from our comfortable existences[83] — from Partch's perception of his players as "lost musicians" who had "achieved a kind of magic perception through their music."[84]

Originally a dance work, central to the concept is that the Lost Musicians are co-conspirators with the Witch, and form a kind of Greek chorus, singing, dancing, stamping feet, "their presence on the stage forming an indispensable part of the dramatic action."[85]

Bewitched remains a pivotal work for Partch. It marked a drastic shift from his monadic songs for voice and a small number of instruments, to large-scale productions that *integrated* a sizable ensemble of musicians, dramatic narrative, and dance. The combination of these elements is one of the

---

[82] "Partch says that watching his instruments being played is part of the experience" (Mellers, p. 173).

[83] Gilmore, p. 227.

[84] Gilmore, p. 219; Mellers, p. 173, calls them "primitives in their acceptance of magic as real." During late-night sessions, Partch began to take on a guru-like status, taking on a "willing acceptance of artistic responsibility" and "an involvement with the concerns and aspirations of a younger generation." In short, creating a musical *Männerbund*, although Partch's peripatetic life would prevent any long-term group from being established. One might also find in the magical "Lost Musicians" an echo of the role played by the Master Musicians of Joujouka in the life and work of William Burroughs; the Witch, an "ancient, pre-Christian symbol" (Gilmore, p. 228) corresponds to their Pan festival's ritual of a young boy dressed as "Bou Jeloud, the Goat God."

[85] Gilmore, p. 227.

best known characterizations of Partch's work, and is an important aspect of his concept of Corporealism.

On a superficial level the integration of dance, drama, and music in the production of *Bewitched* was a success. The reason Partch considered it a failure was because the integration was designed to be realized by a blending of the traditional roles of the dancer, actor, and musician. The dancer/actor/musical performer, like the "idea and the music" *was intended to be one, and therefore Partch wanted the same performer to alternate between dancing, acting, and playing an instrument.* (Harlan, p. 110)[86]

Partch's next major work would return to the classical world, but while *Oedipus* had been safely classical, now he would "*bodily* transfer Euripides' *The Bacchae* to an American setting." Based on the "assumption that 'the mobbing of young male singers by semihysterical women is recognizable as a sex ritual for a godhead'," the resulting work, *Revelation in the Courthouse Park*, would be

A dramatic hybrid of an unusual kind, setting a "straight" version of an ancient Greek play alongside a contemporary drama that is closer to the territory of musical than opera. The score that Partch produced is likewise of a hybrid nature, amounting almost to a resume of his compositional techniques to that time.[87]

---

[86] Ironically, *The Bewitched*, though the first of his series of increasingly massive productions, born of inspiration at the collaborative work on *King Oedipus*, would be a complete, almost hysterical disaster, as far as Partch was concerned, though everyone else thought it a triumph. This was the production that inspired Johnston's portrait, cited above, of Partch as self-destructive.

[87] Gilmore, p. 280. Mellers also draws the comparison to American musical theatre. Weirdly, *Revelation* was written in 1959, one year previous to *Bye Bye Birdie*. Reviewing the Broadway revival—which, in its 1960 version, also featured in a pivotal episode of *Mad Men* that season, in which Sal inadvertently outs himself to his wife—the *Village Voice* slyly commented "Something weird is happening in Middle America:

By alternating the action between a modern American courthouse park and the palace of ancient Thebes, the intention was to point up the "psychological parallel" between the erotio-religious frenzy of the Bacchae, the female followers of the god Dionysus, and the hedonism and submissiveness of American teenagers and those "not so young" (as the text puts it) to rock 'n' roll idols, represented in *Revelation* by the sensuous Dion.[88]

Revelation would also give Partch a chance to deal with his, shall we say, mother "issues." It's a somewhat unsatisfying work, though, as the contemporary music seems not particularly parodistic, nor particularly authentic—actual rock 'n' roll makes no appearance, for example. As Gilmore notes, the full force of Partch's music only makes itself felt "at the last minute appearance of Apollonian clarity," a symbolic point that renders the rest of the music somewhat pointless.

In any event, Partch certainly evades a problem that has beset Wagner: by slapping a "modern" version of the same mythical action right next to it, he neatly forestalls all those attempts to "modernize" Wagner by "updating" his settings with modern décor, dress, and concerns.[89]

By most accounts, *Delusion of the Fury* is Partch's masterpiece. Here he abandons classical pretense altogether in favor of borrowing from similar but living traditions, with Act One based on a

---

You can see it in Conrad Birdie's revelation in the courthouse park, howling a hymn to the American Virtue before a stiffly assertive obelisk bollocked by screaming stone eagles"(http://www.villagevoice.com/2004-07-20/film/resurrecting-trad-the-twist-and-a-rude-birdie/full/).

Myself, I can see even clearer parallels to the bifurcated shows of Hedwig and Tommy Gnosis in *Hedwig and the Angry Inch*, especially the themes of castration—Burt, Harry, and Hedwig—life on the road, and of the desire and pursuit of the whole, or one.

[88] Gilmore, p. 279.

[89] I am reminded of Mark Twain's praise of Mary Baker Eddy for similarly forestalling any attempts to "reinterpret" her scriptures by requiring all Christian Science services to include nothing but reading from her own works, without any additional commentary.

Japanese Noh play, and Act Two based on an African folktale. Unlike *Revelation*, the tales are alternating versions of the same action; the work is unified by the use of the same actors in both parts, and by a deeper underlying theme. By combining both these living traditions Partch gives rebirth to the Greek festival, with a tragedy followed by a satyr play on the same topic.[90]

This is real "cultural diversity," not the inane liberal version. Partch reduces these vastly different plots to their common theme: the futility of anger. In the one, a noble warrior realizes that anger is dishonorable, in the other, common people become involved in a ridiculous quarrel that brings even justice into disrepute. [91] The foolish Judge has the last word, for this is Partch's "reconciliation with the world" — his *Parsifal*. And why not — he was now living in his most palatial accommodations ever, not a Wagnerian Venetian palace, but a former laundromat in Venice, CA.

D: FINALE

Gilmore's epilogue tells the dispiriting, but perhaps inevitable, tale of the "schisms" that have developed among those attempting to safeguard and extend Partch's legacy. Ironically, most of them seem to revolve around interpretations of *integrity*: Ben Johnston having completed after Partch's death the project for an integrated system of just and tempered notation that Partch had abandoned in 1933, should his music be published in that more user-friendly way, or in its "original" form? Should Partch's filing cabinet of a lifetime's writing and ephemera be edited or even censored, or published "as is"?

Ultimately, it doesn't matter, much, if Partch's particular instruments are preserved, or his music ever played again. Nor does it matter whether you, after following the links below, listen to Partch's music and decide you "like" it, or not; or that it's "better" than Wagner, or not, whatever those words could mean.

What I've been suggesting in all this hoo-haw about tonality, has been that we need to stop idolizing Wagner, certainly stop

---

[90] Gilmore fails to note that the satyr play analogue in the African folk tale involves a goat, thus linking it by etymology to the first, tragic part.

[91] Gilmore, pp. 326–27.

imitating him, or anyone else, including Partch, but take Partch as a model and inspiration, far more relevant to our times than Wagner, and make our own Aryan music.

Contra my critics, I have no need to lure our youth away from Wagner, or the classical tradition. The music is just fine, and the kids can make up their own minds. But using classical samples to 4/4 rock songs is not the way forward for our culture. The system of ET is our prison, both musically and culturally.

Why not, then, admit the problem and look for a solution? Of course, slogans and programs are no good by themselves; they need, as Partch would say, corporeality; they need to be embodied in imitable figures. That is the function of mythology, or of the classical education given to the British Empire's future servants. That, I suppose, is the function of Wagner, and why his figure is treated as taboo.

As we've noted, Partch himself recognized Wagner as a forerunner, but he also recognized that Wagner failed; partly for his own idiosyncratic reasons, but also because of the system, ET, as well as the tradition of abstract music itself, both of which he expanded, to his credit, but failed to overcome.

Let us choose for ourselves, and let us chose a different figure.[92] A man of our time, and our nation. A man who, unlike Wagner, spurned the yoke of patronage, and like Siegfried, wandered in the wilderness until, like Siegfried, he returned to smash the system of ET as Siegfried broke Wotan's spear.

Writing about Robert Howard and his barbaric creation Conan, W. J. Guillaume has emphasized the strategic importance of that integrity of mind and body, art and science, that Partch called "corporeality":

> Through his genius Howard has provided us with a medium for re-awakening and generously nourishing our inner-Aryan essence and re-infusing ourselves with the instincts and intuitions—the crucial personal qualities—

---

[92] "Partch projected his self-image through his works. In doing so, *he created a model* that aimed to inspire others toward individual expression and artistic investigation" (Harlan).

which put us back in contact with ourselves individually and collectively. . . .

Conan teaches the critical lesson that intelligence coupled with will is what brings victory and survival: only when mind operates with muscle, brain with bulk, will their possessors triumph. In today's struggle the technician must be imbued with the ancient Aryan warrior spirit if he is to defeat the Jew and the colored swarms. He must become, in short, one of Nietzsche's "new barbarians," that superior stock of highly evolved White men who have *blended their pure, natural instincts with the scientific outlook.* Howard's Conan is a valuable catalyst in this blending of essences.[93]

Harry Partch: He's like our Wagner, only better.

RECOMMENDED FURTHER READING

Bob Gilmore, *Harry Partch: A Biography* (New Haven: Yale University Press, 1998).

Thomas McGeary, ed., *Bitter Music: Collected Journals, Essays, Introductions, and Librettos* (Champaign, Il.: University of Illinois Press, 2000).

Harry Partch, *Genesis of a Music,* second edition, enlarged (New York: Da Capo Press, 1974).

Corporeal Meadows, http://www.corporeal.com/, is an extensive site devoted to Partch by Jonathan Szanto.

RECOMMENDED LISTENING

Enclosure Six: Delusion of the Fury (Innova, 1999).

---

[93] W. J. Guillaume, "The Importance of Conan," http://www.counter-currents.com/2013/06/the-importance-of-conan/

For sheer sonic magic, and incorporating all of Partch's synthesis of music, drama, movement, and visual wonder, there couldn't be a more potent introduction to the sound of Harry Partch. Written late in his life, with the largest ensemble of instruments available (and performed by arguable his best ensemble), it is hard to overstate the importance of this recording being available again. Especially if your ears lean towards instrumental music, this is the one to place in the player and turn it up to 11![94]

The Bewitched — A Dance Satire (Composers Recordings, 1997).

Set in the mystical realm of the University of Illinois . . . Partch's 10 vignettes satirize aspects of collegiate life but in the style of ancient ritual theater . . . (representative titles: "Visions Fill the Eyes of a Defeated Basketball Team in the Shower Room," "The Cognoscenti Are Plunged into a Deep Descent While at Cocktails").

Musically, *The Bewitched* is a good introduction to Partch's longer pieces. It is written for a combination of his originally created instruments and some traditional wind and stringed instruments. While this music is definitely experimental, what hits me most as I grow older, is how familiar and assessable it really is. . . . Partch is a great composer to listen to, especially if you are new to the avant-garde and want to listen to something that is both challenging but not too discordant. And *The Bewitched* is a great place to start listening to this wonderful American eccentric. (Amazon reviews)

Harry Partch explains just intonation:
http://www.publicradio.org/tools/media/player/musicmavericks/talk_partch_explains_just_intonation

Partch explains his version of just intonation, "monophonic":

---

[94] http://www.corporeal.com/freshpix.html

http://www.publicradio.org/tools/media/player/mu-sicmavericks/talk_partch_monophonic_not_equal

Partch compares tempered triads with true triads:
http://www.publicradio.org/tools/media/player/mu-sicmavericks/talk_partch_true_vs_tempered

Bitter Music in Natural Acoustics with Harry Partch (A Collection of YouTube videos, including *Daphne of the Dunes*):
http://www.wilderutopia.com/performance/bitter-music-natural-acoustics-harry-partch/

Ralph Adams Cram:
Wild Boy of American Architecture

"We all understand that intriguing tribal rites are acted out beyond the groomed exteriors and purple-tinged bow windows of Louisburg Square, but except for what some literary, chosen-few Bostonians have divulged, we don't know what these coded rituals are, and never will."

—Truman Capote, "Hidden Gardens"[1]

"Great cathedrals, such as colonial Spain built between Mexico City and Buenos Aires, have had little appeal to a people disparaging greatness and grandeur."

—Michael O'Meara, *New Culture, New Right*[2]

Robert Crunden's *The Superfluous Men: Conservative Critics of American Culture, 1900–1945*[3] is a valuable collection of representative works—essays, chapters, letters, reviews—by the usual suspects of the "Old Right"—Mencken, Nock, Santayana, Davidson, Tate. It's a great second-hand bargain at Amazon, which makes up for the annoying little "introductions" Crunden contributes, which dismiss his, and his reader's, supposed objects of interest in such terms as "emotional extremism masquerading as cultural analysis" or "hardly rates as good political science," whatever that means; for someone with such PC contempt for those who dare to wade outside the "mainstream," it's puzzling

---

[1] Reprinted in Truman Capote, *A Capote Reader* (New York: Random House, 1987), p. 673.

[2] Michael O'Meara, *New Culture, New Right: Anti-Liberalism in Postmodern Europe* (Bloomington, Ind.: 1stBooks, 2004). Kindle location: 5727.

[3] Robert M. Crunden, ed., *The Superfluous Men: Critics of American Culture, 1900–1945* (Wilmington, Del.: ISI Books, 1999).

why he felt the need to spend the time on this anthology — which was supposedly originally twice as large.

One name was unfamiliar to me, at least, and even Crunden calls him "the most neglected" of his subjects: Ralph Adams Cram. And imagine my excitement when reading on and finding Cram described as: "[A]n Anglo-Saxon racist, an connoisseur of Oriental art forms, a decadent homosexual, an apostle of 'anti-modernism,' a hopeless political reactionary [hopeless? What other kind is there?] and the most gifted Gothic architect in [early XXth century America]." Sounds like Cram was one of the originals of what I've called, on my blog and in my book *The Homo and the Negro*, Wild Boys!

Apparently, there's only one "serious study" of Cram, a two volume work by Douglass Shand-Tucci[4] who, as you can guess from his fancy name, has "a very trendy obsession with issue of sexuality," although that's just Crude Crunden sticking his nose up again.

Since our first essay for Counter-Currents featured Noël Coward[5] as an exemplar of the "Bohemian Tory" ideal promoted by Russell Kirk, it's only appropriate that a far more positive review of the recently published second volume of Shand-Tucci's biography can be found in Kirk's journal *The University Bookman*.[6]

According to the Amazon listing, Cram basically built America's church and college landscape:

> Supervising architect at Princeton, consulting architect at Wellesley, and head of the MIT School of Architecture, he would also design most of New York's Cathedral of St. John the Divine and the campus of Rice University, as well as important church and collegiate structures throughout

---

[4] Douglass Shand-Tucci, *Ralph Adams Cram: Life and Architecture*. 2 volumes. *Boston Bohemia* (Amherst: University of Massachusetts Press, 1994); *Ralph Adams Cram: An Architect's Four Quests* (Amherst: University of Massachusetts Press, 2005).

[5] "Sir Noël Coward, 1899–1973," in *The Homo and the Negro*.

[6] Daniel McCarthy, "An Architect for all Purposes," *The University Bookman*, vol. 46, no. 1 (Spring 2008).

the country. By the 1920s Cram had become a household name, even appearing on the cover of *Time* magazine.

According to McCarthy's review, his achievements extended far beyond architecture, however:

He was a fine, and controversial, essayist; a novelist (Gothic, of course); a co-founder of *Commonweal* magazine, though Cram, a High Church Anglican, never became a Roman Catholic; also a co-founder in 1925 of the Medieval Academy of America and its journal, *Speculum*; and he was responsible for the first wide publication of Henry Adams's *Mont St. Michel and Chartres*, which Adams had been reluctant to put into print.

And all this, mind you, in addition to running what Shand-Tucci calls "a full-fledged homosexual monastery" at Caldey Abbey off the coast of Wales, while at the same time happily married to Elizabeth Read back in the USA. An architect's *Männerbund!*

And here's a link to yet another alt-Right favorite: among Cram's Gothic tales is "The Dead Valley," of which no less than H. P. Lovecraft himself wrote, "the eminent architect and mediævalist Ralph Adams Cram achieves a memorably potent degree of vague regional horror through subtleties of atmosphere and description."[7]

It turns up most recently in the new Library of America volume *American Fantastic Tales: Terror and the Uncanny from Poe to the Pulps*.[8] I can attest to the effect of the story, but I was unaware of the Lovecraftian way the threads of Mr. Cram's interests were circling around me.

And speaking of popular writers with distinctive but critically abused prose styles, Cram apparently even influenced Ayn Rand!

---

[7] H. P. Lovecraft, "Supernatural Horror in Literature," VIII, The Weird Tradition in America.

[8] Published in 2009, with a rather indifferent introduction by Peter Straub, who also did the Lovecraft volume in the same series.

While her Howard Roark is usually taken to be based on Frank Lloyd Wright, Tucci points out that Roark's contempt for modern pseudo-Gothic monstrosities ("buttresses supporting nothing" is Roark's dismissive conclusion) is fully in line with Cram's nuanced Medievalism, a kind of proto-archeofuturism, as expressed here: "Shall we restore a style? . . . Shall we recreate an amorphous medievalism and live listlessly in that fool's paradise? On the contrary . . . *We are retracing our steps to the great Christian Middle Ages, not that we may remain, but that we may achieve an adequate point of departure*: what follows must take care of itself."[9]

Rather than futilely boasting "I inherit nothing. I stand at the end of no tradition," as Roark does, Cram, as McCarthy says, wanted his architecture, "to be traditionalist without being antiquarian, to be modern without being rootless."[10]

Even the neo-con fuddy-duddies over at the *First Things* blog recently found some good in Cram:

> It's not, of course, that we shouldn't sometimes be frightened by full-throated architectural rhetoric. Far from it. It's just that I can think of those more deserving of our fears than Cram. In *The Fountainhead*, Ayn Rand created the architect Howard Roark (modeled after Wright), whose Wynand Building was to be "a gesture against the whole world . . . the last achievement of man on earth before

---

[9] See Tucci, *Ralph Adams Cram: An Architect's Four Quests*, p. 171. I would point out that this is also the real motivation behind the recent growth of "historically accurate" musical performance: not to futilely seek to recreate some imaginary "Medievalism" but to strip away layers of "Romantic" and "Modernist" traditions—and we know Who dominates those, don't we?—so that we can forge our own original relation to the past. Music: another field conquered by Cram!

[10] Contemporaneous with Cram, *The Decoration of Houses* (1897), co-written by Edith Wharton and her architect friend Ogden Codman, Jr., delivered a magisterial rebuke to the future Roarks: "Once this is clearly understood, the supposed conflict between originality and tradition is no conflict at all." Rev. and expanded ed. (New York: Norton: 1998), p. 11.

mankind destroys itself." In comparison to that, Cram was a kitten.[11]

Kitten, eh?[12] Let's see how "cute" our Wild Boy becomes when the subject of politics come up.

Like Lovecraft, Cram also came to approve of FDR's New Deal; like most "Old Rightists," he recognized the resemblance to Mussolini—but unlike these "old liberals," he approved! "Anglo-Democracy . . . [would] be a democracy of status and of diversified function, under an hierarchical, not an egalitarian system of organization. In a word, it will be *conditioned not by the quantitative standard but by the qualitative standard.*"[13]

"Anglo-Democracy" sounds a lot like Spengler's "Prussian Socialism" or Yockey's "Ethical Socialism," and as advocated from time to time on this blog.[14] It's interesting, terminologically, that Cram's "Anglo" qualifier picks out exactly what Spengler and Yockey would dissociate their ideas from; for them, England and the Anglo-Saxons were the veritable "nation of shopkeepers" promoting the money-centric idea of equality.

We can get a better idea of Cram's ideas on equality and elitism in one of the essays that Crunden reprints, which had decisively formed Albert J. Nock's "misanthropic" social philosophy. As McCarthy reports, Nock's "view of mass man's lowly level was crystallized by Cram's 1932 *American Mercury* essay, "Why We Do Not Behave Like Human Beings."

"We do not behave like human beings because most of us do not fall within that classification," Cram concluded, noting that only a handful of historically exceptional indi-

---

[11] Matthew Milliner, "Architecture and Absolutes," online at http://www.firstthings.com/blogs/firstthoughts/2010/08/27/archite cture-and-absolutes/

[12] "He's as gentle as a kitten"—Bela Lugosi referencing his hulking henchman, Tor Johnson, in Ed Wood's *Bride of the Monster.*

[13] From 1934, quoted by McCarthy, op. cit.

[14] See Greg Johnson's "Notes on Populism, Elitism, and Democracy," http://www.counter-currents.com/2012/09/notes-on-populism-elitism-and-democracy/

viduals haven risen above the mass of mediocrity and savagery. "What kinship is there between St. Francis and John Calvin; the Earl of Strafford and Thomas Cromwell; Robert E. Lee and Trotsky; Edison and Capone? None except their human form. They of the great list behave like our idea of the human being; they of the ignominious sub-stratum do not—because they are not." Cram's doctrine was not as misanthropic as it might seem: *He valued the herd of humanity as both precious in the eyes of God and as the seedbed from which the truly human few could arise. But he rejected egalitarianism*, presentism, and the thesis of evolutionary progress; civilization's "standard of today is no whit higher than that which obtained in the Middle Kingdom of Egypt, Periclean Athens, the Byzantium of Justinian or the Europe of St. Louis," he averred.

Again, the credo of the Bohemian Tory, who loves the masses—at least, his own people, such as Cram's Anglo-Saxon race—as a necessary seedbed for creating the great men that other races will never be able to equal or surpass; rather than as raw material for some impossible utopia of equality after suitable . . . re-educating.

Is it any surprise that such a towering figure of the American spirit is unknown today?

Admit it, you've never heard of him before. And why should you have, since our "disseminators of culture" are doing all they can to hide him in plain sight—so much more effective than a ban, which might make him *interesting*.

The recently published (2010) Penguin Classic edition of *Book of Tea* for example, provides a bare handful of notes, unlike the usual massive armature, one of which refers the reader to a contemporaneous but reversed appreciation, West to East, in a work by another Boston aesthete, identified as "Ralph N. Cram"—admittedly, the author's original error, but apparently not worthy of correction by the famous Penguin editors.

Meanwhile, 2010 also brought us the Tuttle reissue of the work referred to, *Impressions of Japanese Architecture and the Allied Arts*, which, while at least getting the author's name right, is shorn of its subtitle, as well as its first chapter. No explanation of the first change is given, but the editor, one Mira Locher, informs us that

> Although in many ways Ralph Adams Cram was a radical thinker for his time, he was still a product of an era in which the "Oriental" race was understood as essentially different from and incomprehensible to Westerners. . . . Hence the publisher has chosen omit [sic] the chapter and . . . [his] musings on race.[15]

Radical good, but not *too* radical. Yes, the little academic harridan, herself or her publisher unable to compose a grammatical sentence in English, dares to fiddle with the prose of a master certified by Lovecraft himself! One wonders why if, as implied, Cram thought the Japanese to be "incomprehensible," he would bother to write about them at all. Why not discuss the language of whales instead?

Here, then, is the conclusion of the chapter from whose Lovecraftian horror Ms. Locher has shielded your innocent eyes (thanks to the folks at archive.org):

> I do not mean to imply by what I have said above that it is impossible to judge it by western standards: *in so far as these are universal and neither local nor special, Japanese art stands the test as well as that of our own race.* Indeed, I am not sure that it may not possess a distinct value in enabling us to discriminate between those standards universally accepted, which are fixed and for all time, and those others, equally accepted, but arbitrary, ephemeral, unsound. *All art meets and is judged on one common and indestructible basis: but each manifestation possesses numberless other qualities, many of them of almost equal value, but peculiar, intimate, and personal.* These must be judged by other standards, and it is here that I think we shall fail in our estimate of Japanese

---

[15] Ralph Adams Cram, *Impressions of Japanese Architecture.* With a new foreword by Mira Locher (Rutland, Vt.: Tuttle, 2010), pp. 20–21.

art, since the two races are at present absolutely unable to think in the same terms. If, failing to apprehend *these minor qualities*, we can separate them, and lay them, for the time, to one side, so *revealing the kernel which contains the very essence of all*, we shall be able, if not to judge Japanese art justly, at least *to realize the position it takes in the body of art that belongs to mankind as Man*. (pp. 23–24)

Brrr, the blood positively runs cold! "The body of art that belongs to mankind as Man"? Hitler reborn!

Cram, a Traditionalist in architecture, was as capable as, say, René Guénon, a Traditionalist in metaphysics, of appreciating the principles of another tradition, and perhaps being influenced by them, even admitting their superiority to one's own, without failing to realize that their particular historical form was an local adaptation by a distinct culture—or dare we say it, *race*—and hence not directly usable by ourselves short of a crude imitation, arbitrary syncretism, or parody. Some of us can tell the difference between Debussy and "Chopsticks."

But this editor is unable to make such relatively subtle distinctions, and must have thought the slightest hint of "they're not like us" especially at the start would lead "modern" readers to throw the book aside in disgust. Perhaps she is correct, but whose fault is it, other than that of academic Grundies and Pecksniffs like herself?

And his Cathedral, the largest Gothic church in the world and the second largest church of all—eclipsed only by St Peter's Basilica in Rome? We can read this on a tourist blog:

> The cornerstone was laid in 1892 but the grand plan envisioned by the noted ecclesiastical architect Ralph Adams Cram and the firm of Heins & LaFarge (designers of the legendary City Hall subway station and the Bronx Zoo) has proceeded fitfully, and now, 113 years later, the still unfinished building has fallen on hard times. Most of the grounds are fenced off with nasty looking chain link. The scaffolding still in place for the southwest tower looks like it is rusting on the stonework, and the northwest tower

remains un-begun. The north transept was ravaged by fire in 2001, and the cathedral has struggled to recover from that tragic event.

It is hard to escape the feeling that St John the Divine as a cathedral building is a hopeless cause. It had been about 18 years since my last visit, and in spite of the progress on the south tower (all made at least a decade ago) the cathedral still looks obviously unfinished and is even beginning to show signs of neglect. It stands as a sad, poor relation to other edifices of similar scale, such as the Washington National Cathedral.

There's that word again, "hopeless." As René Guénon relentless documented in *The Reign of Quantity*, there is no room today for those who would be *conditioned not by the quantitative standard but by the qualitative standard.*

Still, like Tradition, the cathedral remains. Someone once said of Evola that "he was our Marcuse, only better." As for Ralph Adams Cram, the Wild Boy of American architecture: "He was America's John Ruskin. But our Ruskin could *build.*"[16]

Counter-Currents/North American New Right
January 23, 2011

---

[16] Matthew Milliner, "Just Another Routine Lecture at the Yale School of Art," http://www.firstthings.com/blogs/firstthoughts/2010/08/26/just-another-routine-lecture-at-the-yale-school-of-art-2/

THE ETERNAL OUTSIDER:
VEBLEN ON THE GENTLEMAN & THE JEW

Jack Donovan has done us a great service—or at least, done one for me—in his recent Counter-Currents essay "The Manly Barbarian: Masculinity and Exploit in Veblen's *Theory of the Leisure Class*."[1] Veblen being one of those "names" one always hears and sees referred to, I have several time tried to read him, to no avail. As Jack says, it all seems "a lot of rambling, convoluted writing and thinking," typical of a kind of dated, Edwardian "fine writing" in the social sciences that predates the current mathematical obsession, which replaced purple prose and "elegant variation" with supposedly more scientific "hard" numbers and graphs. As readers of this site know, I'm not afraid of the dense and repetitive writing of James, Lovecraft, or indeed Evola—I even have a theory about it[2]—but Veblen just seems like a bore in a seersucker suit and straw boater.

However, Jack's suggestion that all the good stuff is in the first chapter of *Theory* appeals to my delight in finding distilled essences in lieu of wading through tedious volumes of old forgotten lore—part lazybones, part decadent aesthete[3]—and even better, the free sample chapter of one of the Kindle editions at Amazon contains the whole first chapter, as well as some swell pictures of horsies and such like illustrations of "conspicuous consumption."

I was particularly struck by his observation that the rest of the book also "suffers from a middle class bookworm's *ressentiment*

---

[1] http://www.counter-currents.com/2012/10/the-manly-barbarian/

[2] See "The Eldritch Evola" chapter 1, above.

[3] Joris-Karl Huysmans' *À Rebours* is in some ways an account of dozens of ways of attempting to trap the "essence" of one experience, sensual delight or art after another; at least that is how Wilde's Dorian Gray read it, while "Lord Henry's corrupting 'influence' is described as a series of distilled 'poisons', 'poisons' that a receptive Dorian imbibes until he begins to receive their 'great reward'." See M. M. Kaylor's *Secreted Desires: The Major Uranians: Hopkins, Pater and Wilde* at p. 317; first published in 2006 by Masaryk University and now available free online at http://mmkaylor.com/.

toward both "delinquent" bullies and predatory elitists (who he thinks have a lot in common)."

Academics like Martha Banta, in her recent Oxford World Classics edition, think otherwise, on both style and value: "Twelve more tightly packed chapters lay ahead, each with insights . . . into . . . our times." Such insights, according to Banta, include:

Veblen only overtly reveals his distaste when describing the dogs and horses put on display by members of the leisure class.

Display of good manners and good forms is a waste of time.

Modern day gentlemen are merely most discreet than feudal lords who gnawed on beef-bones.

The craving for gold and diamonds is lacking all social use.[4]

Church worship is another form of "honorific waste."

Team sports and gambling follow the same impulse that leads to belief in God, since all are based on "animistic beliefs and anthropomorphic creeds."

Philanthropy is further proof of social inadequacy.

Academic honors have little use in the modern world.[5]

Reading this, and Jack's account of Veblen's sneering views of

---

[4] A meme recently re-activated by no less than Warren Buffett's buddy Charles Munger; see "Charlie Munger, "Gold Is For Holocaust-Era Jewish Families To Sew Into Their Garments; Civilized People Don't Buy Gold," http://www.zerohedge.com/news/charlie-munger-civilzied-people-dont-buy-gold-only-pre-holocaust-jews-sew-it-their-garments

[5] Thorstein Veblen, *The Theory of the Leisure Class*, ed. with an introduction and notes by Martha Banta (New York: Oxford University Press, 2007).

such "barbaric" pursuits as hunting, etc., made me smell something more specific than a "middle class bookworm's *ressentiment*" towards jocks. It occurred to me that I had read something like this before, from a similar period, but in much more vigorous prose (I mean Veblen's, not Jack's).

Then it hit me: Maurice Samuel, author of *You Gentiles* and *The Gentleman and the Jew*! Two works that would be classics in the literature of anti-Semitism, but for the fact that Samuel was a Jew, and thought he was defending, nay, writing an encomium to, the bitter, timeless hatred of the Judaic for the *goyim*.[6]

As a reviewer at Amazon says, to Samuel

> Gentiles are not even remotely close to being God-people, but are more like children; they are not as serious and their worldview is shaped by sport. This sporting mentality manifests itself in war, competition, business, religion, scholarship and a host of other worldly activities. Samuel believes that Jews can partake in these affairs as well, but they aren't as good at it as the Gentiles. This is because Jews see these sporting activities as ridiculous. All activity for a Jew should be directed to religious study and reflection on God. Jews will fight in a war, but only if they have to, and then they want to finish the business as quickly as possible. A Jew, according to Samuel, will never revel in the sporting "rush" from an event as much as a Gentile will. Samuel does make an interesting observation when he examines Plato's idea of utopia that is found in The Republic. Samuel is amazed that in this ideal society, war still exists. This is because of the sporting mentality. Even in our ideals, we have to have competition through sport.

Well, there you have it: Western Civilization, from Homer to

---

[6] Maurice Samuel, *The Gentleman and the Jew: Twenty-Five Centuries of Conflict in Manners and Morals* (New York: Knopf, 1950); republished by Behrman House as "A Jewish Legacy" book in 1978; *You Gentiles*, from 1924, is available free at archive.org; or you can get his *Selected Writings* for $0.01 at Amazon.

Hemingway, from Alcibiades to Lee to Patton, just a bunch of dumb as rocks jocks. Think Winkelvoss twins, rowing away like it was *Brideshead Revisited,* thinking Larry Summers will make Zuckerberg "play fair."

It's not surprising that Veblen and Samuel, each undoubtedly unaware of the other, started to sound the same as they gazed at and puzzled over the Establishment that had rejected them both. They've both unconsciously stumbled on the same truth, which we've been trying to hammer into the hard heads of the Hard Right for years: Western or Aryan Civilization has its origins not in hard work, strict morality, and family values, but in the primitive *Männerbund;* art, religion, the military, all arise out of the barbaric play of the Wild Boys. If the Right wants to "conserve" the institutions of the Gentleman, he needs to cultivate Jack's Barbarian, not, as the neo-cons would advise them, the Mormon Family Man. And of course, if you wanted to destroy our culture, you couldn't do better than to take Veblen or Samuel to heart and subject it to a "scientific" or "rational" or "moral" regime—and who could object to that?—reducing culture to "sensible" things like reproducing or money-making.

Although after the upheavals of the '60s we've come to think of the Protestant Establishment as, well, The Establishment (The Man, if you will), it must be remembered that they are, after all, Protest-ants. From Luther himself through the Puritans to the New England busy-bodies to the Progressives, there has been a outsider strain in Nordic Protestants, derived from the Judaic elements in Christianity, representing what MacDonald has called an ethical in-group mentality. This is the "I'm an outsider because I'm morally superior" attitude taken up by Veblen which takes him almost entirely onto the side of the Judaic. The Northern WASPs only became "the" Establishment after righteously exterminating the Southern Cavalier class.

Thus Banta is correct in distinguishing Veblen's Nordicism from that of the National Socialists, who themselves comprised a fairly broad spectrum from almost New Age pagans like Hess, through Aryan mystics like Himmler, to accomodationists like Hitler. Rosenberg most closely resembles Veblen; one of the most prominent exponents of the so-called German Church (i.e., Chris-

tianity without Judaism), he none the less was sufficiently Luther-
an to indulge in what Evola found to be the most primitive kind
of anti-Catholic, Germans versus Romans rhetoric. As Evola insisted, and we agree, the German nation, like all nations, was a
mixture of various racial strains; the task of the racial hygienist is
to select the one that is to become dominant; ideally, the least Judaic.

THE VEBLEN QUESTION

If Veblen's complaints about "barbarians" sound like Samuel's
jaundiced Judaic eye on Gentiles, the question arises, was Veblen
a Jew?

Although easily proven not to be, he is, as one of Hermann
Hesse's characters calls Harry "The Steppenwolf" Haller, a "rotten patriot" for a supposed Aryan. Even Banta notices something
a little off:

> But although Veblen's family was of Nordic descent, the
> emphasis he places upon the ruthless nature of the "doli-
> cho-blond" shares none of the pride later expressed by
> members of the Nazi Party. Instead, Veblen's negative re-
> marks anticipate the attacks launched in 1918 by Cyril
> Briggs, editor of the radical black journal *The Crusades*,
> against "the blond beast" — the bloodthirsty, ape-like preda-
> tor of the "mongrel" European race. (Kindle Loc 222)

Yes, these ape-like mongrels are truly not "God-people."
Even the Jews have asked the question, and quite recently. According to no less a source than "Tzvee's Talmudic Blog" (aka
יבצ לש ידומלתה גולבה) the question remains:

> Was Thorstein Veblen Jewish?
> No the famous social critic and economist, Thorstein
> Veblen was not a Jew. He was a Lutheran from Minnesota.[7]

Why even raise the issue?

---

[7] http://tzvee.blogspot.com/2010/01/was-thorstein-veblen-
jewish.html

The reason that we ask is that *Wired* magazine in an article this month "Accept Defeat: The Neuroscience of Screwing Up," by Jonah Lehrer, discusses Veblen's analysis of Zionism and Jewish intellectualism.

The results of his thinking 92 years ago, summarized by the magazine, are provocative.

Indeed. As *Wired* tells the tale:

In 1918, sociologist Thorstein Veblen was commissioned by a popular magazine devoted to American Jewry to write an essay on how Jewish "intellectual productivity" would be changed if Jews were given a homeland. At the time, Zionism was becoming a potent political movement, and the magazine editor assumed that Veblen would make the obvious argument: A Jewish state would lead to an intellectual boom, as Jews would no longer be held back by institutional anti-Semitism. But Veblen, always the provocateur, turned the premise on its head. He argued instead that the scientific achievements of Jews—at the time, Albert Einstein was about to win the Nobel Prize and Sigmund Freud was a best-selling author—were due largely to their marginal status. In other words, persecution wasn't holding the Jewish community back—it was pushing it forward.

The reason, according to Veblen, was that Jews were perpetual outsiders, which filled them with a "skeptical animus." Because they had no vested interest in "the alien lines of gentile inquiry," they were able to question everything, even the most cherished of assumptions. Just look at Einstein, who did much of his most radical work as a lowly patent clerk in Bern, Switzerland. According to Veblen's logic, if Einstein had gotten tenure at an elite German university, he would have become just another physics professor with a vested interest in the space-time status quo. He would never have noticed the anomalies that led him to develop the theory of relativity.[8]

---

[8] http://www.wired.com/magazine/2009/12/fail_accept_defeat

Indeed, a provocative thesis.[9] It explains why Veblen is suspected of being a Jew: Veblen too was an alienated outsider cynically critiquing White civilization. Furthermore, although Veblen's thesis is enough to earn the "suspicion" of anti-Semitism through its anti-Zionism, it's really just another version of the same old vaudeville routine: "without us Jews you *goyim* are nothing!"

One wonders how Babylon, Athens, Rome, the Christian Middle Ages, the Holy Roman Empire, the Elizabethans, managed to do anything at all. Not a good deli in sight. You might as well kill yourself!

Moreover, a glance at the great cultural centers of today's Jewry, New York and Tel Aviv, would easily belie any such notion. Tel Aviv, well, *meh*. As for New York, its reputation as a world capital of culture and everything else is a function of well-known Jewish logrolling or ethnic networking: J-artists "discovered" by J-gallery owners, pumped by J-critics in J-periodicals, sold for big bucks to J-"patrons" (the ones still whining, after nearly a century, for the "return" of "their" artworks that were liberated by the forces of the European Revolution) and ultimately for bigger bucks to bemused *goyishe* patrons (blue bloods or Junkers as the

/all/1

[9] And bearing as well some resemblance to Daniel Harris' *The Rise and Fall of Gay Culture* (New York: Hyperion, 1997), which provoked many reviewers, such as Alisa Solomon in the *Village Voice*, to tantrums of outrage over its apparent thesis that gays were much more highbrow and, well, interesting, before they were co-opted by the mainstream, and, well, should just get back in the closet and write more wonderful musicals! Or in this case, back to the Patent Office, or the unheated tenement, or even the *shtetl*, and scribble some more! There's more to Harris' thesis than Thorstein's, as I shall argue, and it also is kind of a twisted version of my own thesis, derived from Alisdair Clarke and spelled out most clearly in the first chapter of *The Homo and the Negro*, that pre-Stonewall gays were hardly cowering in closets (as illustrated by my essays on Noël Coward in *The Homo and the Negro* and Ralph Adams Cram, above) and that when given the opportunity to leave the supposed closet should have re-assumed their role as creators of Western Culture rather than joining the Left's "rainbow coalition" of culture-destroyers.

case may be); substitute any other area of society *ad lib*.

The truth, as always, is exactly the opposite: rather than bringing the light to the benighted Aryan, it is the Aryan who has, always and everywhere, created culture, and the Judaic who, unable to do so, exists only as a parasitical hanger-on, at best; a destroyer, at worst. Any "contributions" have indeed been just that, something added onto a pre-existing Aryan structure, which had been totally absent from native Hebrew society from Genesis to the granting of civil liberties by Napoleon.

The Judaic is not an "outsider" just coming in to lend a hand or a new pair of eyes; he is an underminer, and so is Veblen, for that matter.[10]

Of course at this point someone will bring up "the Moslem contribution to Western Civilization," which is fine with me, since Moslems are effectively a Semitic people who, like the Romans and Germans, recognized the value of what Athens had created and chose to emulate it, thus earning the eternal enmity of their "brothers" the Judeans. But then, the Judeans hate everybody, always and everywhere; the Romans coined the word "misanthrope" to describe this turbulent race; and the Judean, as always, projects this onto US, making him the innocent victim of an unmotivated, irrational hatred—what Kevin MacDonald has called the "lachrymose" version of Judaic history.[11]

At this point someone will also mention Israel. Always the go-to counter-example for stereotypes of Jewish helplessness or ineffectuality—first, after the 1948 land grab (the very first episode of *Mad Men* shows the Men, all WASPS— "Have we ever hired a Jew? Not on my watch"—shouting and jumping around like school kids over the battle scenes in the movie *Exodus*—"First they're in camps, then they're on the beach with machine guns!"); then, after the "Six Day War" becoming incongruous models of dark, hairy manhood—Woody Allen on the *Times* Op-Ed page no

---

[10] "The rats are underneath the piles. The jew is underneath the lot." —"Burbank with a Baedeker: Bleistein with a Cigar," T. S. Eliot, 1920.

[11] http://www.alternativeright.com/main/the-magazine/remaking-the-right/

less, exclaimed, "Jews with machine guns? Come on!"[12]

Anyway, the much vaunted, much promoted—by the Judaic-minded media, of course—"Jewish State" is largely a vanity project (more Judaic preening), a paper tiger or Potemkin village:

> No matter what the "Clean Break" document aspires to, Israel's whole survival strategy has always been to rely on aid from the outside: without the billions that flow from the US Treasury into Israeli coffers, the entire Zionist project would have failed long ago. It has been kept on life support all these years by money from abroad, and by the hopes of the Israeli leadership that more Jews will emigrate to the Promised Land. The main problem, however, is that American Jews are so thoroughly assimilated that the idea of taking up residence in Israel never occurs to them: for American Jews, *America* is the Promised Land. Aside from that, the appeal of moving to a country that sees itself as besieged—and whose leaders every day assert that they are sitting on the edge of a second Holocaust—is necessarily quite limited.[13]

Alas for the Zionists, things have turned out pretty much as Veblen suggested they would.

The Outsider as Insider

But the important work MacDonald and others have done to document the extent of ethnic networking leads to another problem with the Outside Contributor thesis. Even if we granted Veblen the "contributions" of the Jews, due to their outsider status, that would hardly be relevant today, when Judaics dominate all the relevant fields (especially if we consider, and I do, those *goyim* in name only that Evola would say

---

[12] I'll soon have a piece on another Preminger film, *Advise and Consent,* and its influence or not on *Mad Men.*

[13] "The Israel Lobby and the Road to War; Part III of 'Roots of the Iranian 'Crisis'," by Justin Raimondo, October 12, 2012, online at http://original.antiwar.com/justin/2012/10/11/the-israel-lobby-and-the-road-to-war/

had a "Jewish soul").

How much "outsider" perspective can the Judaic provide, once they dominate a given field?

Thus we see the "outsider" meme as an excuse, a ruse, in fact, to provide cover for the reality of domination through ethnic networking.

Anyway, anyone who's had to work around God's Chosen knows this much vaunted "objective" or "critical" perspective is really just a matter of taking a snide and supercilious attitude of sneers and jeers to everything anyone else believes, and the holier the better.

> M: No it can't. An argument is a connected series of statements intended to establish a proposition.
> A: No it isn't.
> M: Yes it is! It's not just contradiction.
> A: Look, if I argue with you, I must take up a contrary position.
> M: Yes, but that's not just saying "No it isn't."
> A: Yes it is!
> M: No it isn't![14]

To see the sneering smugness that constitutes the "outsider perspective" in reality, consider the case of Paul Krugman, Princeton professor (hired by Ben Bernanke), *New York Times* columnist, and, oh yes, "Nobel" Laureate.[15] How's that for being connected? But look what happens when someone dares to question this inside-outsider:

> But if you just can't get enough of the pugilistic Krugman fighting, you may want to check out the video of him at an economic debate in Spain over the weekend, at which he

---

[14] Monty Python, "The Argument Skit," The Money Programme (episode 29; aired 2 November 1972; recorded 4 December 1971).

[15] The fake "Nobel" Prize in Economics is itself a wonderful example of their impudent fakery, solemnly announced every year and never exposed by the compliant media.

accused Pedro Schwartz, a Spanish [*sic*] economics professor, of "pulling credentials" in their debate about Keynesian economics, then fully gave him the "talk to the hand" gesture when Schwartz denied it. That happens around 49 minutes into the video.[16]

So much for "openness to dissent" etc. As always, it's free trade (the libertarian-capitalist) and free speech (the ACLU Liberal) for us, until we take over, then not so much (bank bailouts and speech codes). As we would expect, the demands for "free speech" last only long enough to oust the WASPs and establish a Jewish elite, then a Talmudic orthodoxy reigns.

The aforementioned Huysmans, though, or because, of his "decadent" mindset, had their number already in the 1880s:

> At the same time, he noticed that the free thinkers, the doctrinaires of the bourgeoisie, people who claimed every liberty that they might stifle the opinions of others, were greedy and shameless puritans whom, in education, he esteemed inferior to the corner shoemaker.[17]

The Ferment of Nuclear Fission

Since *Wired* thinks that Jewish "outsiders" are so valuable to scientific progress, let's take a look at a well-known case with important, nay tragic, consequences: the Bomb.

There's a persistent myth among "educated" Westerners, like the notion of human-skin lampshades, that German science suffered from a lack of Judaics, which supposed lack then supposedly led to their defeat. Oh, the irony! Or as Bela Lugosi would say, "How iron-ick!"

As Savitri Devi pointed out, this idea completely misunderstands how science works. It matters not whether Einstein publishes in Berlin, New York, or Buenos Aires; published work is, well, public, and available to all.[18]

---

[16] *À Rebours*, translated by John Howard as *Against the Grain*, chapter 1.

[17] *À Rebours*, chapter 1.

[18] Unless the Judaic lawyers start whining about licenses and

And since, as Eliot observed, "reasons of race and religion combine to make any large number of free-thinking Jews undesirable,"[19] why should a society not remove the plague from its bosom, while still reaping the rewards, if any, of their tiny little researches? A point to which we shall return at the end.

But in any event, the real story is that German scientists actually foot-dragged on the project, to prevent the development of such a terrible weapon. Aryan scientists, left to their own devices, reached an ethical conclusion: Aryan morality would not allow the use of such a weapon.

> Heisenberg himself . . . had realized by now, just like a handful of scientists the world over, how unbelievably hideous and horrible the new invention might turn out on the practical level. . . .
> When Professor Hahn, who looked and behaved like a quintessential patrician out of a Thomas Mann novel, met Heisenberg shortly after the latter's installment, he declared unequivocally: *"I'd rather die than build the bomb!"*
> And that was that.

> And would have been, if not for those much-lauded "outsiders" and "victims"

> . . . Heisenberg and the small inner circle of his staff, all men with a strong Christian foundation, knew what would happen eventually. Namely that other countries might feel less encumbered by moral restraints and indeed build the terrible weapon. Particularly the USA, where so many Jewish

---

trademarks; oh, the irony. Again, the "free speech" that America uses to climb to the top becomes "intellectual property" and "trade secrets" when the Chinese want to avail themselves of it.

[19] The Page-Barbour Lectures delivered at the University of Virginia in April-May 1933 and published in 1934 under the title *After Strange Gods;* too dangerous to be allowed in print today, of course—free speech, indeed!—but available online at archive.org. Also see Kerry Bolton, "T. S. Eliot," Part One, online at http://www.counter-currents.com/2012/09/t-s-eliot-part-1/

scientists had found refuge after their enforced German exodus. And who all nourished a massive grudge against their former country of birth.[20]

Yes indeed, the so-called "eternal victims of history" once more prove to be its consummate predators. Judaic scientists in the US, led of course by the little prince, Albert, were nagging and cajoling Roosevelt to "hurry up" and develop a bomb for America to use in exterminating the Nordic Amalekites. Well, they didn't quite get their wish, but needless to say, they couldn't wait to steal the atomic secrets and hand them over to Stalin.

The next step was to hand it all over to their proposed new Golem, the UN, but there Stalin threw in a monkey wrench, refusing to surrender Russian sovereignty. The resulting shift of alliances resulted in the US retaining its role as Golem, protector of Israel, while the Soviets took up the White Man's Burden (hence the Israeli and neo-con obsession with "freeing" Judaics from Russia and overthrowing the Soviets), a change that seems to have escaped the occluded minds of the American Right, other than, of course, Francis Parker Yockey.[21] And we know what happened to him . . .

Eventually, of course, the Israelis, who never signed onto the Non-Proliferation Treaty (unlike Iran), developed their own nukes (again, unlike Iran) which everyone knows but no one mentions, even to rib Bibi a bit about the hypocrisy of waving around cartoon bombs at the UN (whose job, of course, as just pointed out above, is to ensure that other nations don't get The Bomb, but not Israel).

Once again and as always: the news of the day is the opposite of what you've been told — oh, what to do about the Iranian threat to poor Israel; and our "principles" apply only to thee, never to me.

---

[20] See Michael Colhaze, "Werner Karl Heisenberg: Absolution vs. Damnation, Part 2, " http://www.theoccidentalobserver.net/2012/05/werner-karl-heisenberg-absolution-vs-damnation-part-2/

[21] See Francis Parker Yockey, "The Prague Treason Trial: What is Behind the Hanging of the Eleven Jews in Prague?" from December 1952, http://www.counter-currents.com/2011/06/the-prague-treason-trial/

The Judaic obsession with nukes, then and now, is really quite striking and creepy, and suggests a close, perhaps essential connection of the two, in line with Guénon's comments about the "sinister" nature of so-called "sub-atomic" physics, the ultimate expression of the Reign of Quantity, and thus the prelude to the true and final dissolution: "*Solvet sæclum in favilla.*"

Indeed, one has to wonder, how much of Israel's public nagging about Iran and nukes is something of a double fake-out, designed to push and prod until Iran (which as an Aryan nation would naturally eschew, as did the National Socialist, the barbarity of nukes—the Chief Ayatollah has, in fact, already ruled out developing or using such weapons as explicitly "un-Islamic"—one can only imagine the Chief Rabbi—who has declared that providing medical assistance to victims of the IDF is an abomination—issuing a similar pronouncement only if adding the proviso "unless used to defend the Jews")—is forced into getting some, if only to "grab these insolent Jews by their throats and shut their lying mouths!" as an exasperated Dr. Goebbels said of the Weimar media.

Paradigm Enforcers vs. Free Inquirers

Finally, and once again taking the big picture view, *Wired*'s invoking Thomas Kuhn to laud Judaics as "paradigm breakers" is ludicrous. As Paul Feyerabend has lamented, the lessons drawn from Kuhn have been the exact opposite: that the way to transform a chaotic pseudo-science like sociology or economics into a "real" science is to just decide on a "paradigm," condemn everything else as "junk science," and go on your merry tenured, grant-grubbing way. Ever and always, free speech until our ethnic networking is complete, then just shut up.

This applies *a fortiori* to "scientific" issues that also have political or religious penumbrae. There's no judicially enforced "law" of gravity, and flat-earthers are harmless eccentrics, but just try questioning "The Six Million" (unless, of course, you're a *Landsman*, like Raul Hilberg, and perhaps not even then—ask Norman Finkelstein) or the teaching of "natural selection" in your children's school.

In fact, one might think that there is a direct, inverse relation here: the more actual evidence you have, the less you need to shame, fire, or imprison the doubters. And one can't help but notice again, which ethnic group receives the benefit.[22]

Feyerabend, a true Aryan philosopher — and an ex-Luftwaffe pilot! — called for a separation of Science and State for these very reasons, and noted that his anti-method of "Anything Goes" would hardly spell the end of science.[23] While Greece rose to greatness on the backs of unwilling slaves, we can rise to greater heights on the back of willing slaves, foolish blinkered nerds and geeks who, like Huxley's gammas, or the denizens of TV's *The Big Bang Theory* (produced by Charlie Sheen's Judaic nemesis, Chuck Lorre) delight in having a chance to wear mental chains while we, mentally free, are also free to make use of the mechanical toys they produce.[24]

---

[22] Ordinarily I'd chalk up the Creationists to the Judaic side, if it were a war between knowledge and faith, but in this context the evolvers are the equally Judaic atheists; remember, the Judaic controls both sides, and can take whatever position needed. As Evola noted, the same principle applied in different contexts may produce quite different effects, and so each case must be judged on its own merits; very similar and valuable advice advise was given by A. E. Housman to aspiring textual critics; see for example "The Application of Thought to Textual Criticism" in *Proceedings of the Classical Association*, August 1921.

[23] See his *Against Method: Outline of an Anarchist Theory of Knowledge* (London: Verso, 1975; 4th ed., 2010) and *Science in a Free Society* (London: Verso, 1978).

[24] Or not, if we choose. Ultimately, the whole science and tech thing may need some re-thinking. As Guénon observed, traditional societies "failed" to develop science and technology in our sense, due to their having little or no interest in studying the ever-fading away material universe, or improving their creature comforts, preferring to focus their attention, and their society, on "the one thing needful." There is indeed something Judaic about science itself, deriving perhaps from the arrogant notion the world as an artifact, and a faulty one at that, needing *tikkun olam*. This is perhaps the point at which White culture reveals its fatal susceptibility to the Judaic infection, its Death Star thermal exhaust portal: our Faustian need to "control and manipulate [the] environment" (See Collin Cleary, "Asatru and the Politi-

Instead our world is increasingly under the control of these very Judaics and Judaic-souled ones, who have moved far beyond — if ever they were at all — the role of "critical outsiders" and now constitute instead the New Inquisition of Zionce.

I wonder what Veben would say today? Feyerabend, it seems, would side with Jack Donovan against Veblen's Judaic smarties: ". . . when sophistication loses content then the only way of keeping in touch with reality is to be crude and superficial. This is what I intend to be."[25]

A barbarian, if you will.

Counter-Currents/North American New Right
January 23, 2011

---

cal," http://www.counter-currents.com/2012/10/asatru-and-the-political/).

[25] Paul Feyerabend, "How to defend society against science" (1975), http://www.galilean-library.org/manuscript.php?postid=43842

THE WINKLE TWINS WIN ONE!
OWEN WISTER'S *PHILOSOPHY 4: A TALE OF HARVARD UNIVERSITY*

Owen Wister
Philosophy 4: A Story of Harvard University
New York: Macmillan, 1903
Kindle annotated edition by Daniel P. B. Smith, with original illustrations, 2012.

> "When you call me that, *smile*." —Owen Wister, *The Virginian*

> "I can scare the stupid out of you but the lazy runs deep." —The Wisdom of Paris Geller

If you had asked me, before I read James Neill's *The Origins and Role of Same-Sex Relations in Human Societies*,[1] what "The Virginian" was, I would have identified a somewhat faded old TV western series.

Filmed in color, *The Virginian* became television's first 90-minute western series. Immensely successful, it ran for nine seasons—television's third longest running western.

Looks like there was a TV movie later on.

What I didn't know is that it was not only based on a novel, but a pretty significant one too: *The Virginian, a Horseman of the Plains*, by Owen Wister (1860–1938), which apparently was filmed several times but more importantly, it was, again according to Wikipedia, "[T]he first true western written, aside from short stories and pulp dime novels. It paved the way for many more westerns by famous authors such as Zane Grey, Louis L'Amour, and several others."

---

[1] James Neill, *The Origins and Role of Same-Sex Relations in Human Societies* (Jefferson, N.C.: McFarland, 2009). See my Kindle Single, *A Review of James Neill's "The Origins and Role of Same-Sex Relations in Human Societies"* (Amazon.com, 2013).

According to Neill, *The Virginian* documents the sexually free lifestyle of the American cowboy, which Wister discovered when visiting the West for his health. Already in 1885 he was writing (to his mother!) that "this life has a psychological effect on you" and that cowboys were "[A] queer episode in the history of the country" and "without any moral sense whatsoever."[2]

Neill calls it "an all-male world, away from women, where male bonds frame the emotional lives of the heroes" -- in short, our beloved Wild Boys. Most (all?) readers miss this, Neill observes, because, in line with the custom of the times, and most healthy societies, Wister is quite—entirely—reticent about actual physical relations.[3]

Wister himself was eminently an Easterner, and *Philosophy 4*, written a year after the success of *The Virginian* as part of a publisher's idea for a series of "little novels by favorite authors," gives him a chance to go back to an Eastern equivalent to the cowboy world; it represents his retelling an anecdote supposedly first retailed to him in his undergraduate days at, yes, Harvard.

The tale basically involves two undergraduates, Billy and Bertie, and their attempts to cram for a final exam in, of course, Philosophy 4 (i.e., second semester sophomore year).[4] Being rich and indolent, they have hired a poorer but brighter sophomore, one Oscar Maironi, whose parents had not "owned town and country houses in New York" but "came over in the steerage." Unable to face another all-day session with Oscar they decide to give him the slip and head out to the countryside, planning to settle a bet by finding a legendary tavern. Hilarity ensues, and the boys learn enough about philosophy in practice to ace the

---

[2] David McCullough, *Mornings On Horseback* (New York: Simon & Schuster, 1981), p. 320; quoted from John M. Kearns, *The Cowboy Composite: Theodore Roosevelt and the Birth of American Cowboy Romanticism*, http://scholarworks.csun.edu/xmlui/bitstream/handle/10211.2/1856 /JkearnsThesisDraftFinal.pdf?sequence=1

[3] See "The Sex Life of Cowboys" in Neill, esp. pp. 419-21 on Wister.

[4] Academics might amuse themselves by glancing over the questions, which Wister provides, and asking themselves if a sophomore today, or even a graduate student, could answer more than a few of them.

exam, beating even Oscar's score.

It's a slight tale, but a pleasant way to soak for a bit in real Old America and although you can find it free online I recommend the kindle, which for only a buck more adds original illustrations as well as Mr. Smith's somewhat obsessive annotations, speculative reconstructions and photos. Smith is smart as a whip, and on his webpage asks two questions that locate the additional interest this tale should have for Counter-Currents readers:

❖ Are we intended to understand that Oscar Maironi is Jewish? Is Wister expressing a mild anti-Semitism? Does he take it for granted that the reader shares it?

❖ Is there a trace of homophilia [i.e., male-bonding viewed through the lenses of post-Stonewall gay liberation] in the narrator's own attitude toward his subjects? (I sometimes think I notice this in *The Virginian* as well).

Kudos for that *Virginian* insight, ten years before Neill! The Old America (Dylan and Harry Smith's "old weird America"') was indeed a land of cowboys without "moral sense," naked wrasslin', and a powerful suspicion of people whose folks came over in steerage, whether or not they had a townhouse.

Smith notes that we see Harvard at the end of its transformation from a state university (yes!) to a massively endowed finishing school for the elite—that is, the WASP elite. At this point foreigners are beginning to muscle their way in—poorer Whites on scholarships, and outright infidels. Is Maironi not merely Italian but a Jew? Seems clear: "Oscar could lay his hand upon his studious heart and await the Day of Judgment like—I had nearly said a Christian!"

Then there's this bit that Smith and I both throw our hands up at: WTF? Asked to leave his notes for the boys to look over in the morning

Oscar's hand almost moved to cover and hold his precious property, for this instinct was the deepest in him. But it did not so move, because his intelligence controlled his instinct nearly, though not quite, always. His shiny little eyes, however, became furtive and antagonistic—something the boys did not at first make out.

OK, acquisitive instinct, cleverly dissembled, shiny little eyes, check. "My precious" indeed. But then this follows:

> "I do not ever leave my notes with anybody. Mr.Woodridge asked for my History 3 notes, and Mr. Bailey wanted my notes for Fine Arts 1, and I could not let them have them. If Mr. Woodridge was to hear—"
>
> "But what in the dickens are you afraid of?"
>
> "Well, gentlemen, I would rather not. You would take good care, I know, but there are sometimes things which happen that we cannot help. One time a fire—"
>
> At this racial suggestion both boys made the room joyous with mirth.

Not wanting to share his notes might be construed as Judaic (he's being paid $5 an hour to tutor them, so why let them have a freebie?) but why is the fire excuse—pretty sound, I'd say, in those rickety old Harvard buildings—somehow "racial'? Does it make him sound like he's lived in tenement firetraps? Again, look who's talking. But the finale brings us back on point: "Oscar stood uneasily contemplating them. He would never be able to understand them, not as long as he lived, nor they him."

There's the note, the Judaic as psychological outsider, able—perhaps uniquely qualified—to memorize and compile 300 page sets of notes on Western Philosophy, but able to really understand it—or any other part of our culture.

This is the message of the tale as a whole; the rowdy boys, precisely by giving Oscar the slip—he passive-aggressively comes back each hour on the hour, leaving a note each time - and carousing all night, acquire an insight into philosophical problems such as "the duality of the self" (remember, this is the high tide of academic Hegelianism) that outshines the little fact-grubber.

And Billy's suggestions concerning the inherency of time and space in the mind the Professor had also found very striking and independent, particularly his reasoning based upon the well-known distortions of time and space which hashish and other drugs produce in us. This was the sort of thing which the Professor had wanted from his students: free comment and discussions, the spirit of the course, rather than any strict adherence to the letter. He had constructed his questions to elicit as much individual discussion as possible and had been somewhat disappointed in his hopes.

One has to wonder if the Professor is William James, with that bit about wanting his students to make free comments about hashish. Oscar the tutor is not happy, and the Judaic whine about "fairness" begins:

> "There is some mistake," said Oscar to them when they told him; and he hastened to the Professor with his tale. "There is no mistake," said the Professor. Oscar smiled with increased deference. "But," he urged, "I assure you, sir, those young men knew absolutely nothing. I was their tutor, and they knew nothing at all. I taught them all their information myself." "In that case," replied the Professor, not pleased with Oscar's tale-bearing, "you must have given them more than you could spare. Good morning."
>
> Oscar never understood.

The dénouement shows us how things have changed:

> But he graduated considerably higher than Bertie and Billy, who were not able to discover many other courses so favorable to "orriginal rresearch" as was Philosophy 4. That is twenty years ago. To-day Bertie is treasurer of the New Amsterdam Trust Company, in Wall Street; Billy is superintendent of passenger traffic of the New York and Chicago Air Line. Oscar is successful too. He has acquired a lot of information. His smile is unchanged. He has published a careful work entitled *The Minor Poets of Cinquecento,* and he writes book reviews for the *Evening Post.*

What little we learn of Oscar's life off campus shows us that he is using his fact grubbing to insinuate himself into the salons of various blue-haired society types; he we see the Judaic plan of attack, gradually taking over our cultural institutions. Why, there was a time when Columbia University didn't think Lionel Trilling was fit to teach the humanities without the danger of corrupting the youth!

Today, of course, Oscar's scions would be running the business enterprises, as well as what remains of scholarship and magazines. Billy and Bertie? Likely performing exquisite cultural duties on the board of some nonprofit organization or some other socially irrelevant enterprise.

There must be a whole genre of such college idylls, which I confess is unfamiliar to me as such, but definitely something I'd like to explore. For now, several works from my own random lifetime reading suggest themselves.

Right in the first sentence, the pink shirts worn by the two boys brings to mind Phineas's pink shirt in *A Separate Peace*; arousing comment in the '40s, today it would no doubt lead to either a beat-down or an unwanted invitation to the LGBT formal.[5]

The pink shirts are worn with tennis flannels, and that certainly helps conjure up the similar ramble taken by Charles and Sebastian in Chapter One of *Brideshead Revisted*.

Thus, our boys the next day: "One hour later they met. Shaving and a cold bath and summer flannels, not only clean but beautiful, invested them with the radiant innocence of flowers."

And in Waugh, "Sebastian entered—dove-grey flannel, white

---

[5] Those with *proper* upbringing would *know*, of course, that pink is one of the go-to-hell colors favored by those with too much money to care about fashion; see *The Official Preppy Handbook* by Lisa Birnbach (New York: Workman, 1980)—note the author's name—and note that its sad little follow-up, *True Prep: It's a Whole New Old World* by Birnbach and one "Chip" Kidd (New York: Knopf, 2010) demonstrates the social decline we are discussing by, among other things, nominating Barack Obama to its updated Prep Pantheon, having converted Prep, like the United States, from a cultural heritage to a proposition anyone can buy into—literally.

crepe-de-chine, a Charvet tie, my tie as it happened, a pattern of postage stamps."

And they're off on their little adventure: "In their field among the soft new grass sat Bertie and Billy some ten yards apart, each with his back against an apple tree."

A similar pose is taken in by Charles and Sebastian, although they bring the strawberries with, rather than consume them the night before (*after* Oscar leaves).

> [Billy and Bertie] reached Harvard Square. Not your Harvard Square, gentle reader, that place populous with careless youths and careful maidens and reticent persons with books, but one of sleeping windows and clear, cool air and few sounds; a Harvard Square of emptiness and conspicuous sparrows and milk wagons and early street-car conductors in long coats going to their breakfast; and over all this the sweetness of the arching elms."

Recalls a later excursion by Charles of a Sunday in Oxford:

> I walked down the empty Broad to breakfast as I often did on Sundays at a tea-shop opposite Balliol. The air was full of bells from the surrounding spires and the sun, casting long shadows across the open spaces, dispelled the fears of night. The tea-shop was hushed as a library, a few solitary men in bedroom slippers from Balliol and Trinity looked up as I entered, then turned back to their Sunday newspapers. I ate my scrambled eggs and bitter marmalade with the zest which in youth follows a restless night. I lit a cigarette and sat on, while one by one the Balliol and Trinity men paid their bills and shuffled away, slip-slop, across the street to their colleges. It was nearly eleven when I left, and during my walk I heard the change-ringing cease and, all over the town, give place to the single chime which warned the city that service was about to start. None but churchgoers seemed abroad that morning; undergraduates and graduates and wives and tradespeople, walking with that unmistakable English church-going pace which es-

chewed equally both haste and idle sauntering; holding, bound in black lamb-skin and white celluloid, the liturgics of half a dozen conflicting sects; on their way to St Barnabas, St Columba, St Aloysius, St Mary's, Pusey House, Blackfriars, and heaven knows where besides; to restored Norman and revived Gothic, to travesties of, Venice and Athens; all in the summer sunshine going to the temples of their race. Four proud infidels alone proclaimed their dissent, four Indians from the gates of Balliol, in freshly-laundered white flannels and neatly pressed blazers with snow-white turbans on their, heads, and in their plump, brown hands bright cushions, a picnic basket and the Plays Unpleasant of Bernard Shaw, making for the river.

Even in the '20s, but four infidels! But I guess all the Judaics are "Anglicans."

It's interesting that Waugh, writing in WWII England, doesn't try to really hide what the boys are up to, although he does sugar-coat it with lots of high-falutin' verbiage and quasi-theology.

Now, that summer term with Sebastian, it seemed as though I was being given a brief spell of what I had never known, a happy childhood, and though its toys were silk shirts and liqueurs and cigars and its naughtiness high in the catalogue of grave sins, there was something of nursery freshness about us that fell little short of the joy of innocence.

Waugh, in short, cloaks Charles and Sebastian in some kind of Edenic childhood[6] while offloading all the "degeneracy" and "corruption" onto the serpentine Anthony Blanche.

------

[6] The late Victorians were suckers for the nursery; those who bemoan adults today reading *Harry Potter* and *Twilight* should reflect on this: Kenneth Grahames' *The Golden Age*, "a collection of sketches of the lives of five orphaned late-Victorian children, was said to be the favorite bedtime reading of Kaiser Wilhelm II on his royal yacht. President Roosevelt tried to persuade the author to visit the White House." That's Teddy Roosevelt, Wister's Western buddy-boy.

Wister, on the other hand, simply gives us an equally "innocent" scene—the "boys bathing" loved by the *fin de siècle* types, along with some Laurentian wrestling—without the elbow in the ribs[7]—"it's really innocent, you know"—in his blunt, Old West way:

> "I'm going in," said Bertie, suddenly, as Billy was crediting himself with a fifty-cent gain. "What's your score?"
>
> "Two seventy-five, counting your break on Parmenides. It'll be cold."
>
> "No, it won't. Well, I'm only a quarter behind you." And Bertie puffed off his shoes. Soon he splashed into the stream where the bend made a hole of some depth.
>
> "Cold?" inquired Billy on the bank. Bertie closed his eyes dreamily. "Delicious," said he, and sank luxuriously beneath the surface with slow strokes.
>
> Billy had his clothes off in a moment, and, taking the plunge, screamed loudly "You liar!" he yelled, as he came up. And he made for Bertie.
>
> Delight rendered Bertie weak and helpless; he was caught and ducked; and after some vigorous wrestling both came out of the icy water.
>
> "Now we've got no towels, you fool," said Billy.
>
> "Use your notes," said Bertie, and he rolled in the grass. Then they chased each other round the apple trees, and the black gelding watched them by the wall, its ears well forward.

Editor Smith wonders about why they took horses, and spends not a little time on "equestrian newsgroups" online (sounds pretty dirty to me!) to find out speed and mileage figures. I'd say the reason is obvious: to have a horse along to set the Old West atmos' in Old Jamaica Plain.[8]

---

[7] Richie: "Please, I've only got so many ribs, Noël Coward." Rik Mayall, *Bottom*, Episode 1 "Smells."

[8] The Granada TV version gives us a view of their backsides in a later scene, although since the frontsides are presumably facing Sebas-

On our other topic, "anti-Semitism," Waugh is much friendlier with the Jewish boy, again Anthony Blanche, although he still may be repulsive to any normal person. The academic grind here is Mr. Samgrass, whose toadying with Lady Marchmain's set recalls Maironi's cultivation of literary ladies; he's not particularly Jewish but his trip with Sebastian to the Levant is at least equivocal. The real outsider is Rex Mottram—a Canadian!—whose social climbing—we last see him in Parliament, on his way to the Cabinet, and an appeaser! —and dull fact-grubbing without understanding context and tradition (his Catholic conversion classes are a comic highlight) make him and the Flyte family mutually incomprehensible, like Oscar and the WASP elite. Charles, after a gruesome "gourmet" dinner with the nouveau riche Rex:

> "[Rex] lit his cigar and sat back at peace with the world; I, too, was at peace in another world than his. We both were happy. He talked of Julia and I heard his voice, unintelligible at a great distance, like a dog's barking miles away on a still night."

Julia later describes Rex to Charles as

> "[Not] a complete human being at all. He was a tiny bit of one, unnaturally developed; something in a bottle, an organ kept alive in a laboratory. I thought he was a sort of primitive savage, but he was something absolutely modern and up-to-date that only this ghastly age could produce. A tiny bit of a man pretending to be whole."

The British decline was accelerated by the war:
> "If you ask me, sir, it's all on account of the war. It couldn't have happened but for that." For this was 1923 and for Lunt, as for thousands of others, things could never be the same as they had been in 1914. . . . "It all came in with the

---

tian's little sister Cordelia, I'm not sure why this was thought to be an improvement.

men back from the war. They were too old and they didn't know and they wouldn't learn. That's the truth."

The Second World War brought in another load of louts, later known as the Angry Young Men, who demanded culture and all the goodies but with none of that toffee-nosed class business that seemed designed to keep them out. Kingsley Amis's *Lucky Jim* is the Ur-Text here,[9] although Amis concern with culture was authentic enough to eventually distance him from the tearers- and dumbers-down in the schools.[10]

In America, by the '90s, things were pretty well shot. Whit Stillman's *Metropolitan* shows us the class-anxious interaction of scholarship boy Tom with the prep-school elite of the Sally Fowler Rat Pack, including a lugubrious type that meditates on the decline of the UHB or "urban haute bourgeoise." Tom gives a wonderful epitome of the triumph of the implicitly Judaic Scholarship Boy over mere WASP culture:

Audrey Rouget: What Jane Austen novels have you read?

Tom Townsend: None. I don't read novels. I prefer good literary criticism. That way you get both the novelists' ideas as well as the critics' thinking. With fiction I can never forget that none of it really happened, that it's all just made up by the author.

Metropolitan also starred a Stillman regular, Chris Eigeman,

---

[9] Although often classed with them, Colin Wilson was a self-educated working class bloke who had no chip on his shoulder about it. Amis once threatened to throw him off a rooftop. See *The Angry Years: A Literary Chronicle* by Colin Wilson (London: Robson, 2007).

[10] See his "Why Lucky Jim Turned Right" in *What Became of Jane Austen? And Other Questions* by Kingsley Amis (New York: Harcourt Brace Jovanovich 1971). Amis eventually became such a pillar of the Establishment that he was able to diagnose both factors of the social decline we're observing, here: "I've finally worked out why I don't like Americans. . . . Because everyone there is either a Jew or a hick" (http://en.wikipedia.org/wiki/Kingsley_Amis#cite_note-29).

who turned up in the 2000s on *The Gilmore Girls*, whose self-parodying exploration of the over-privileged Connecticut elite has been my subject on several occasions.[11]

On *GG* the Billy and Bertie role seems obviously to be Madeline and Louise, but in fact they are airheads focused on fashion and dating. No doubt this is exactly how the Judaic nerd views his Aryan rivals. Indeed, many a fan has wondered how, no matter how rich their parents are, these two arrived at and graduated from a supposedly exclusive prep school. We might imagine that, as in Wister's tale, there are tutored with a great deal of sighing and eye-rolling by their best friend, who just happens to be the smartest, most driven, most repellent girl in the school (until of course our supposed heroine, Rory Gilmore, arrives), the blonde Judaic Paris Geller.

The rivalry of Paris and Rory—which falls under the category of "vitriolic best buds"—shows how uncomfortable Hollywood is with our current elite's need to have stereotypically smart but abrasive Judaics cast as attractive characters. Rory should, like Billy or Bert, be easy-going and casually smart in a non-Asperger's way, showing up Paris at every turn, but the producers have, in their Judaic way, imagined her as impossibly, ridiculously bookish (how else be schmart?), and given her a mother who is so relentlessly "nontraditional"—though, with typical SPWL hypocrisy, insistent that she attend both a private school (the expense of which drives her to an uneasy agreement with her estranged parents, which sets the series plot in motion)—as to make the family, like Demian's, essentially the token Judaics of their small town. Although five generations of Gellers have attended Harvard, plot contrivances result in both winding up at Yale.

So the confused result is that instead of Wister's pairing, Paris and Rory are essentially not really so much friends but *Doppelgängers*, so much so that Liza Weil was originally cast as Rory, and when the role was given to Alexis Bledel, the producers cre-

---

[11] See my "The Gilmore Girls Occupy Wall Street" in *The Homo and the Negro* and "From Groundhog Day to Gilmore Girls" online at http://www.counter-currents.com/2013/05/from-groundhog-day-to-gilmore-girls/

ated the Paris role for her, which required her to *dye her hair blonde* to distinguish her from the blue-eyed brunette Rory. Along with the hair, she shares with Tory (Rory?) Spelling a strong jawline and a proneness to a pop-eyed stare, but seems to be able to bring it off better.[12]

And such is the magic of TV, or the charm of Ms. Weil, that Paris quickly became my favorite character, rather than the loathsome mother and daughter Gilmore, though perhaps tied with Edward Herrmann's definitive WASP *pater familias*.[13]

Finally, lest the reader complain that all I talk about are old books and movies and TV shows, and to get around to that title you may have wondered about, let's get right up to date: is this not the saga of the Winklevoss Twins? As Matt Parrott describes it:

> The basic idea of Facebook, creating a simple and exclusive alternative to MySpace, isn't Jewish. But the project was hijacked when the gullible Winklevoss twins entrusted Mark Zuckerberg and his accomplice, Eduardo Saverin, to help execute the project. (See also Kevin MacDonald's review.) The movie adaptation of this true story is a fevered Jewish revenge fantasy against their hapless arch-enemies, the reviled WASP "insiders." Both the book, by Ben Mezrich, and the screenplay, by Aaron Sorkin, wallow in defeating the earnest brothers, heaping these two iconic American Christians with humiliation after humiliation.[14]

------

[12] The show is so ethnically confused that Rory eventually winds up dating a scion of the supposedly upper class—get this—*Huntzbergers*, who all have obvious arriviste names like Logan and Mitchum, and even deign to look down upon the Gilmores, who arrived on the Mayflower!

[13] I was very happy to take the Which Gilmore Girls Character Are You Test and get Paris, although I confess I did cheat; I mean, come on, "Are you fluent in Mandarin and Portuguese?"

[14] Matt Parrott, "How Jewish is *The Social Network*?" online at http://www.theoccidentalobserver.net/2011/01/how-jewish-is-the-social-network/

Mezrich expounds:

> Like Zuckerberg and Saverin, he attended Harvard, where he was a self-confessed "geeky kid," and acknowledges that as a Jewish boy from Brooklyn who had not come from "a long line of people who had gone to Harvard," there were opportunities that were not open to him. "There are these groups where there is this old world aristocracy going on," he says. "People like me—and Mark—couldn't really be a part of that."

The Social Network is essentially *Philosophy 4*, re-written by the victors, and greatly expanded to include all the sadistic fantasies of "retribution" Oscar and his kind have nursed over the centuries. Even that old fool of a Professor is re-vamped; as Kevin MacDonald notes in his review, "Did anyone else note the scene in which the Winkelvii appeal to Larry Summers, then president of Harvard to intervene in the matter, and Summers refuses?"

Only the WinkleTwins could be so dense as to imagine a tribesman like Summers would "play fair."

So, in answer to Smith's pertinent questions, Wister is "a bit" of an "anti-Semite" as the term is understood today, and yes, he did expect his readers to share his views.[15]

After all, this was America—before the flood! And as Thomas Gossett blandly asserts, "No American writers have done more to publicize race theories and to glorify the Anglo-Saxons than

---

[15] He's also the author of *Lady Baltimore*, which in addition to being reprinted in the Southern Classics Series, provoked this know-nothing review on Amazon:

> Wister shows much sympathy for the plight of the upper echelon white Southerners who felt they lost a complete way of life after the Civil War. This is where Wister's lousy viewpoint comes in: it's really hard to stomach all the ballyhooing over Southern honor and Romanticism. Only Wister's talent as a writer allows him to get away with it.

So you know this will be next on my reading list!

have Frank Norris, Jack London, and Owen Wister."[16]

To which he smugly adds "None of these authors is a major figure in American literature . . ." for which opinion I don't give a hoot, but I'm more interested in his concession that ". . . all of them . . . wrote books which sold a great many copies."

So do your part, and buy an Owen Wister book today!

Counter-Currents/*North American New Right*
January 23, 2011

---

[16] Thomas F. Gossett, *Race: The History of an Idea in America* (Dallas: Southern Methodist University Press, 1963), pp. 198–99.

Light Entertainment:
The (Implicitly) White Music of Scott Walker

No Regrets: Writings on Scott Walker
Edited by Rob Young
London: Orion, 2012.

> "I've come far from chains/From metal and stone/From makeshift designs/And seeking a star"
>
> —Scott Walker, "Rhymes of Goodbye"

> "Searching for a more authentic life than just as another puppet on a string he withdrew into the world of his own music"
>
> —Derek Walmsley[1]

> "For in this medley the worlds of high art and 'pop' art . . . all meet."
>
> —Harold Beaver[2]

The ongoing "career"—to use the inevitable but rather misleading term—of Scott Walker, from '60s teen idol to '70s Jack Jones-style crooner to '80s recluse to 21st-century *avant garde* icon, is perhaps the most problematic in pop history, even surpassing, perhaps, "Elvis—What Happened?"

No Regrets is a collection of around a dozen new essays, along with a couple of interviews, arranged chronologically by album release, that attempt to explain—at least in the sense of "make the details known," if not exactly "make plain or comprehensible," or "provide a motive for"—that unique trajectory of life

---

[1] Derek Walmsley, "Didn't Time Sound Sweet," *No Regrets*, pp. 59–60.

[2] Harold Beaver, "Introduction" to Herman Melville, *Moby-Dick*, ed. Harold Beaver (New York: Penguin, 1972), p. 25.

and work.

No one's life or work, or life's work, is likely "explainable" so there's cause for complaint—no regrets!—if the unprecedented phenomenon of Scott Walker remains a mystery. Rather, the reader should appreciate the offer of enormous amounts of detail about not only Scott's life—most of which, if known, is rather banal: parents' divorce, life on both coasts of the US, petty juvenile delinquency, but still managing to make his Broadway debut and his first 45 while still in high school; screaming, bloodthirsty female fans; endless lucrative touring, both as a group and later solo; shopping sprees and self-medication with vodka and valium to cope therewith; then seclusion, save for an occasional orange juice commercial to make ends meet, releasing increasingly hermetic records every decade or so to acclaim from smaller, less violent mobs of fans—but also about the social and cultural atmosphere—such as the union rules that broke up sessions for mandatory tea breaks "just when you got something going" and forced Scott to break into the studio after hours to do overdubs without the contractually required presence of live musicians—in which he created his own contribution to that '60s sound phenomenon Phil Spector once called "little symphonies for the kids" but, in Scott's case, more influenced by Sibelius, Bartok, or even Ligeti than Beethoven or Brahms.

The reader shouldn't expect "the answer(s)" about such a cultural phenomenon, and certainly not some "Very Short Introduction" or even "Complete Idiot's Guide" to Scott, but rather enjoy the opportunity to take a private, after-hours tour, curated by expert docents, around various facets and angles of a rare work of art—rather like the book of essays on Joyce's equally hermetic late work by Beckett and others published in 1929 as *Our Exagmination Round His Factification for Incamination of Work in Progress*—and so come "to experience the awe and mystery"—to use the catchphrase from *The Outer Limits*, the *Twilight Zone* knock-off that was just finishing its run the year Scott's plane set down in London—of Scott Walker.

Naturally, though each is devoted to one or more of Scott's albums, the essays vary widely in tone, length, and value. Oddly, the ones devoted to some of Scott's most important albums—

Nina Power on the first solo albums, *Scott* and *Scott* 2 and Brian Morton's on the 1986 *avant garde* return *Tilt*—are the least valuable. Power's is too short to say anything, while Morton throws around some opaque grad school terms like "significs" that shed no light; and while several essays take T. S. Eliot as a reference point for Scott's physical and mental exile from America, with more or less insight, Morton says Walker's "European sensibility" has "a distinctively American phenomenology" (see what I mean) that can only be compared to . . . Susan Sontag—the notion of Sontag being typically "American" about anything leading the reader to gag and even Sontag to spit at the author.

Smack in the middle, and taking up about a third of the whole book, is the longest and most daring essay here, Ian Penman's, which caught my attention right from the title, "A Dandy in Aspic," taken from a favorite '60s British spy novel and film, which I plan to review at some length in the coming year. In fact, the whole essay, in its barely controlled run-on of McLuhanesque "probes" tossed out and left behind, paradoxically combined with a sharp focus on the tiniest of details, reminds me, and perhaps the reader, of my own work[3]—so good for him! But especially since it's the longest essay here and centrally placed, I'd like to zero in on it a bit to give you some idea of its intriguingly allusive qualities.

A Dandy in Aspic, the film,[4] opens with a Saul Bass-style sequence in which the credits appear over a dancing puppet that eventually become entangled in its strings and collapses. Penman starts "Dandy" right off by telling us that the contemporary

---

[3] Collected in *The Homo and the Negro*.

[4] There's no record of Scott's interest in or even awareness of the film, but the theme, existential doubt in a Euro-Brit, Cold War setting, is similar to what he was gropingly exploring in the albums he was making at the same time, both originals and compilations of movie songs. He'd eventually contribute a song of his own to a James Bond film—such a downer it was dropped from the film and relegated to the soundtrack album, in a kind of karmic payback for those late '60s potboilers of his. His early career was short-circuited when his patron, Eddie Fisher, was dumped by Liz for Richard Burton, who played the definitive '60s existentialist agent in *The Spy Who Came in from the Cold*.

icon of British MOR, and Scott's presumed role model, Matt Monro (who sang the title song in *From Russia with Love*) was no "swarthy puppet on razzle-dazzle strings" but a working man like Ian's dad and his chums, whose ascent to lounge stardom appealed because it exposed "the business of class" as "a world of illusion, strings pulled"(pp. 76–77). Through Monro, we are subliminally—Penman never makes the point explicitly, like some of Scott's opaque lyrics—led to the film's dandy, a double agent sent against his will from England to Europe, as Scott fled first America then England for Amsterdam and Sweden, both under assumed names: the spy's is "Dancer," while Scott's is "Walker" (The Walker Brothers was a Righteous Brothers knock-off comprising neither brothers nor Walkers).

Penman goes on to mount a spirited defense of the idea that "critical consensus" be damned, Middle Scott is the best Scott, really the Heart of Scott. For dedicated fans who fell in love with, or to, "the early stuff," but, while glad he's found some revered place in the history of pop, find the "later stuff" a little off-putting, it's mighty welcome to have Penman on our side.

Penman reminds us that in the actual world of the '60s things were not so clear cut as they may seem "after the (youth) revolution" which was itself just a marketing scheme that meant little more than selling hippie wigs at Woolworths, while Jimmy Page did session work not just with The Who but Tom Jones and Harry Seacombe, "the Bow Tie Brigade" he calls them. In that context, Scott's "lost years" period of post-Brothers, post-solo albums, the period of movie soundtrack songs, ersatz "Country Western" made by middle-aged Brits in London, a TV variety show, and pub tours seems less incongruous, less of a challenge to the understanding.

Some might even find it ideal: "the sudden illumination of serious art, mixed in with the cheap and heady cocktail rush of popular idiom" (p. 81). Eliot, another American exile, did something like that in the confines of "The Wasteland," and Rob Young, the editor of this collection, reminds us that Scott arrived in London the month after Eliot's death. Like the code phrase for the spy's death in *Dandy*, it is "the passing of the buck" from Old Tom to Young Scott. Much of the pop cultural coverage on

Counter-Currents fits that description, since only the despised pop or lowbrow cultural artifacts fly low enough under the elite radar to smuggle in some Traditionalist meaning.

And despite touring with Hendrix, Scott was already "far nearer the MOR realm of Matt Monro," even on those solo albums his fans consider to be the "real" Scott.

> The music *pulls* off the trick of looking in two directions at once, without feeling like it's *pulling in two directions* at all. The surface may feel initially slight and bland, all *quivering strings — but then you're hooked, can't turn away, keep returning*. Songs with subtly shape everyday language into something oddly memorable. Some detail or undertow. You listen and things go dark. (pp. 82–83, my emphasis)

Again, strings are pulled, but they're yours, not his.

And speaking of those "details" that hook you, Penman steps back from his defense of Scott's unfashionable period to deliver a self-conscious defense of his own procedures, which could just as easily be used to defend my own, reviewing movies and TV shows from a high-minded Traditionalist perspective:

> Am I projecting too much on to mere makeweight songs? Or isn't that the whole point and glory of such songs? That being slight or fluffy is no barrier to smuggling themselves illegally into places within our listening hearts . . . [unlike] the rock cult of 'hidden meaning' [there's] the thrill of exposing something for yourself, finding something surprising in the sonic shadows you had no reason to suspect would be there. . . . The simplest word or phrase can end up freighted with impossible richness and ambiguity. (pp. 117–18)

As Penman sums up Scott's output during these MOR years:

> Of course Middle Scott is all surface; but as we well know, surface can become quite fugue-like with the right degree of concentration. This is the entire basis of the secrets of

spell-casting and invocation. (p. 124)

And as the British archetypal poet Jeremy Reed insists, the fan's obsession with pop ephemera is a relation of the poet's eye on the mundane, so it's no surprise that Reed has produced several poems and even a rather stalkerish biography devoted to Scott.

Unfortunately, Penman's essay drawls down and peters out without really making much of a point—the titular *Dandy in Aspic* reference that got me all hopped up never becomes as explicit as I've made it here and ultimately goes nowhere—and one feels the editor should really have put his foot down and demanded one more rewrite. Still, Penman leaves us with this lovely image, a YouTube video of Scott, vintage 1972, singing some desolate Euro-MOR to some dissolute Euro-crowd, nicely dressed like the Rat Pack but mod; or mod enough but without a cravat or lace cuff to suggest Austin Powers, and even so intimating his secret nature, pop industry puppet no longer, now the Chakravartin, the Taoist Realized Man of no-action, the unmoved mover at the center of the cosmic wheel, the still point of the chaotic post-War era: "He is *compellingly un-animated. A still point.* He could be the unhappiest, drunkest man in Europe—but he looks like a perfectly Scandinavian picture of health" (p. 135, my emphasis).

From blond American teen idol in England to Scandinavian lounge singer? On that note, let's turn back to the collection as a whole. Each reader, of course, will have his own area of interest—which others might call his 'bias'—and those who recall my previous discussion[5] of Scott in *The Homo and the Negro* will know that my own is using Scott Walker as a model for a future Aryan Musician, a proud maker of White Music. And so I was most interested in the evidence provided throughout the essays here of Scott's exemplary Whiteness; indeed, many of his "mysteries" evaporate when one realizes, as most of the authors do not and likely would be horrified to consider, that one is dealing

---

[5] "I'll Have a White Rock, Please—Implicit Whiteness, Aryan Futurism and the Godlike Genius of Scott Walker," in *The Homo and the Negro.*

with not some Judaic crooner — even if Eddie Fisher gave him his first job, and there's been a few Israeli managers and "collaborators" here and there since — but with a true Aryan.[6]

---

[6] Rather than vaguely insinuating what "White" is, I base myself here on Baron Evola's discussion of the ideal type of the "Roman Spirit" found in *Men Among the Ruins*:

This original Roman spirit was based on a human type characterized by a group of typical dispositions. Among them we should include self-control, an enlightened boldness, a concise speech and determined and coherent conduct, and a cold dominating attitude, exempt from personalism and vanity. . . . The same style is characterized by deliberate actions, without grand gestures; a realism that is not materialism but rather love for the essential; the ideal of clarity, which eventually turned into rationalism in only some Latin peoples; an inner equilibrium and a healthy suspicion for every confused form of mysticism — a love for boundaries; the readiness to unite, as free human beings and without losing one's identity, in view of a higher goal or for an idea. We may also add *religio* and *pietas*, which do not mean "religiosity" in the Christian sense of the word, but instead signify for a Roman an attitude of respectful and dignified veneration for the gods and, at the same time, of trust and reconnection with the supernatural, which was experienced as omnipresent and effective in terms of individual, collective, and historical forces. Obviously, I am far from suggesting that every Roman man and woman embodied these traits; however, they represented the "dominant factor" and were embodied in the ideal that everybody perceived to be specifically Roman. [. . .]

The Roman chastity or sobriety of speech, expression, and gesture is contrasted by the gesticulating, noisy, and disordered exuberance of the Mediterranean type, by his mania for communication and effusiveness, and by his feeble sense of boundaries, hierarchy, and silent subordination. The counterpart of these traits is often a lack of character, the tendency to get excited and become drunk with words: verbosity, a flaunted and conventional sense of honor, susceptibility, concern for appearances but with little or no substance. The expression "Pobre in palabras pew in obras largo" [Poor of words but rich in deeds], which characterized the ancient Spanish aristocratic type, should be

Since I think most of my readers share this interest, at least to some extent, and so I'll give some indication of what these essays provide us, likely unknowingly, to flesh our idea of Scott Walker, White Musician in the modern age—or indeed, as the film biography calls him, the "30 Century Man."[7] So here are some of the Aryan themes that are implicitly referenced throughout the book:

First off, the name. As I've already noted, it's not "really" Scott Walker, but Noel Scott Engle. A couple of writers here note how "Engle" relates to "Angle," that is, the Anglo people who settled England, making England his natural home and Scott a synecdoche for the nation, or, as we would say, the White race. And a few others make the same connection as Pope Gregory—*non Angli, sed angeli*—while Penman, of course, goes recklessly further, linking his hermaphroditic beauty and melancholy Eurocentrism to *Der Blaue Engel* and "Walker" to Baudelaire's *flâneur*, the angel as wandering ghost.

The Walker Brothers act extended both the name play and the beauty. His agent's secretary recalls "They were these American male gods who looked perfect" (p. 31); the front men were, as Greg Johnson recently said in another context, "both tall and blonde, which at one time was considered quintessentially "California.""[8]

It wasn't really about the music alone, though. As I've suggested, based on the work of Michael Hoffman, classic rock, especially heavy metal and psychedelic, are the contemporary versions of pagan Mystery rites (and hence, of course, their implicit

---

compared with Moltke's characterization: "Talk little, do much, and be more than you appear to be"; all this points to the "Roman" style. (p. 259)

[7] *Scott Walker: 30 Century Man*, directed by Stephen Kijak, 2007 The title comes from one of Scott's compositions on his *Scott 3* album—the cover of which reduces him to a single, cover-filling eye, at once anonymous and icon of Aryan genetics. The song is perhaps most generally familiar from its use in *The Life Aquatic*.

[8] Greg Johnson, "Plastic Christmas," online at: http://www.counter-currents.com/2012/12/plastic-christmas/

Whiteness). In the case of the Walkers, the "concerts were less about the music and more about playing out a ritualistic ceremony where the blond American gods appeared in the flesh before their braying worshippers" (p. 39).

The flesh of the gods, of course, is provided by the entheogenic drugs accompanying such performances. While Bowie could only suggest that "we could be heroes just for one day" Scott, on the album that seemed to have provided Bowie and Eno with the template for their Berlin adventures, assured us on *Nite Flights* that "We will be gods."

Unfortunately for his career, and his record company, Scott was actually too Aryan to tolerate for long the messy unpleasantness of '60s stage performance (screaming teenyboppers and endless touring on British Rail), and "the emerging counterculture and hippie underground made him shudder" (p. 150). The aforementioned secretary recalls that "Scott was very aloof. There was a certain amount of arrogance." Indeed, Scott sounds a bit like Archie Bunker or even one of the Mobile Infantry of *Starship Troopers* as he recalls that "The place was crawling with hippies and there was no way around that, if you weren't in their uniform. It was tough" (p. 152). Interestingly, Scott, like Alan Watts at the same moment, picks up on the real phoniness of the hippies' supposedly "liberated" rags.

So Scott retreated to—that is to say, took his stand in—the studio. Not that it was a big change, really. The Walkers "did not adhere to any accepted notion of authenticity as a group, either on stage or in the studio." With a non-playing drummer and two guitarists who let session men handle the chores, they were "a mythical beast, spawned and constructed under laboratory conditions in the Phillips studios" (pp. 32–33).

Again, it's the whole notion of "authenticity" that puts Scott at odds with the modern "counter-culture," where "the paradigm of authentic expression was interminable electric blues rock" (p. 89). Rock (which, Penman reminds us, was best described by the *National Lampoon* as "black roots music played by longhaired English homosexuals") hates MOR because it's "too smart . . . too implacably adult, it luxuriates in its stylized lack of passion . . . thoroughly 'square'. No edge, no soul" (p. 90). I'll say it, as Penman won't: *too White*.

Instead of grubby, yet ultimately fake "authenticity," the White musician seeks technological perfection, producing a smooth, flawless result that is, *ipso facto*, truly authentic, because it is his own. "Pulse-free Muzak" (p. 88); "American music created in stilted laboratory conditions in Britain" (p. 13). By contrast, "Things were so primitive when I was performing . . . I simply could not achieve the results I was after. It was all quite so traumatic for me as a young man" (p. 40). "*Scott 3* emerged at the height of psychedelics, and while it eschewed its methods, ideals, and its morality, it nevertheless makes ruptures in time and space that match any record of that era" (p. 67).

How on Earth did he accomplish that? Two factors were key: the White pursuit of technological superiority in the studio is at the service of a Faustian quest for The New in sound; and respect for the Logos or Word: "All that guitar based stuff—I just feel that I've heard it before so many times. It goes on and on and never seems to end. It's just the same narrow ground being worked over. I would drive me mad to have to work within those parameters" (p. 7). "Some guy strumming away, telling you the story of his life . . ." (p. 248).

Or as Eno says in his interview in *30 Century Man*: "I have to say it's humiliating to hear this . . . you just think 'Christ we haven't got any further!' I just keep hearing all these bands that sound like bloody Roxy Music and Talking Heads. We haven't got any further than this. It's a disgrace really!"

"[I]t's never about the meltdown of logic" but rather the opposite: "being allowed to record exactly how he visualizes everything" (p. 89), Scott was able to use the studio system with artistic precision due to another Aryan trait, his very un-hippie professionalism.[9] Middle Scott "was a pro. He huddles with the ses-

---

[9] As Penman notes, the old time soul revues were, for all their "funk" rather like MOR than rock: professionalism, crowd-pleasing, matching outfits, and elaborate choreography. James Brown was proud to be "the hardest working man in show business." *Les extrêmes se touchent*: I suggest, as I did in my earlier essay, that the White man impresses the Negro not by imitating him—dancing around like a monkey—but precisely by taking his Whiteness "up to 11" and being him-

sion guys and arrangers and gets the albums done. He doesn't sink or slip away into drunk afternoon decrepitude" (p. 84).[10]

Unlike tedious generations of White trash "rock stars" and "rap artists" that the Judaic music industry has chewed up and spit out bankrupt or dead, Scott had found a way to "ride the tiger."

"This is how you disappear" as the Scott lyric so frequently repeated in this collection goes. Cranking out "product" without the vulgarity of suicide or living out forgotten years in a Sunset Boulevard mansion. Hiding in plain sight, like the Russian double agent Eberlin/Krasnevin in *Aspic*, home "an improbable image," "internal exile" in a "Siberia of the soul" even "inside your own [fake] name." You're "between checkpoints, a sonic no-man's land . . . right inside the song itself" (pp. 86–87).

By *Scott 3* there were already "few of the trappings of rock" that would "*time-stamp* the album;" the songs were "untethered by percussion and *stretch* out endlessly . . . as if moving in zero gravity" (pp. 64–65, my emphasis).[11] As I suggested in the same essay, White music is proudly un-rhythmic, reaching for the Infinite by means of new technologies and instruments free of the "slavery of time."

Secondly, the lyrics: the key was to "focus on the word," the

---

self to the nth degree—true authenticity. Grandmaster Flash was knocked out by the motionless Kraftwerk: "They were so stiff, *they swung!*"

[10] Bogart was a similar professional, who keep the drinking, though heavy, after work hours, and also like Scott, that "easy to work with" image helped keep him in demand with producers where more "temperamental" *artistes* might have been exiled. See my essay on Bogart reprinted in *The Homo and the Negro*. Oddly enough, Brian Dillon, in his review of this book, refers to Scott as "Bacall-beautiful": "Brian Dillon on Scott Walker's manic pop stardom and long vanishing act." *The Guardian*, Friday, July 27, 2012.

[11] "Stretch" was Scott's nickname, for his height, and the title of one of his MOR albums; "endlessly" recalls Kraftwerk's "Europe Endless" and again, the puppet strings of *Dandy in Aspic*. David Toop's essay describes Scott's music as "flexing, sagging, cracking, breathing, *stretched* over bloody fluidity."

Aryan Logos, "with the song at its service" (p. 71). Hence the interest or obsession, with the French chanson, *à la* Jacques Brel. At the same time, he wanted to "progress without becoming unmusical" (p. 57). Already in 1969's *Scott 3* the "lyrics" are as impenetrable as they'll be on such later work as 1995's *Tilt* — "Every single sound on the track is related to the lyric in some way" as he says in a 1995 interview (p. 199) — or 2006's *The Drift*, where, in an interview that year Scott insists that even where there are "no beautiful string arrangements" but just "big blocks of sound and noises" you "always have to keep matching it to the lyrics" (p. 248).

"Literary allusions and livid visions are crow-barred into dense, awkwardly scanning lines that need to be unpacked by the listener" while delivered by a voice "not always so far from Vegas" and "none of the wild style studio tricks that rock was exploring at the same time" (p. 73).

Those lyrics, however abstruse, reflect a realistic Aryan individualism: "Scott's prostitutes, hustlers, transvestites are not lumped together" — "the Masses" fit for self-congratulatory bleeding hearts to weep for at a distance — "but dealt with . . . individually . . ." (p. 108); as well as the high status of women in Aryan societies: "Not only does he not share the casual sexism of his rock/pop contemporaries, but some of Scott's best songs are sung from a woman's point of view" (p. 108).

"Everything right out in the open but hardly anyone seems to have noticed. Why? Because it was set not to a twelve-bar blues but to a gorgeous caroming Broadway melody?" (p. 111) Indeed, more than that: "it has the sheer ease and economy and space of jazz. It has the balls of classic show tunes. It has the anger of protest. It has the unassuming cleverness of a Sondheim. Maybe that's the problem — how much it jumps around" (p. 115). But it has to, since each song is about an individual, "a different person, a different nationality, a different era," each one a "link in a chain of wasted lives" — "heartbreakers without kitsch" (p. 52).

Just as the operatic and implicitly White rock of Jim Steinman (Meat Loaf) has been described (with a sneer) as "camp for straight people," Stephen Kijak, director of the Scott bio film, *30 Century Man*, recalls someone calling Scott's music "Judy Garland for gays who grew up writing poetry and wearing black turtlenecks." But "queer culture" is bigger than that, a "gap in our culture" (Kijak again) where Scott has placed himself, "insider looking out," renouncing everything "we are supposed to want — money, sex fame" to "become a nobody, a place to work or not to work."[12]

Like Bartelby, he would prefer not to. So the realized man, as Coomaraswamy reiterated, has abandoned the ego and become nobody, his epitaph *hic jacet nemo* ("Nobody special" as Suzuki described himself), and as the Chakravartin, no longer the puppet controlled by others but the Universal Man in the Center, pulls all the strings himself, and works by not-working.

That brings us back to the spiritual elements in Scott's work, a spirituality of endlessly renewed struggle (again, "Europe Endless") quite opposed to that of the passive Christian mentality (what Evola would call a "confused form of mysticism"): "Most of my stuff is about frustration, of being unable to hold on to a spiritual moment, always losing it" (p. 250). "I'm a man who struggles with spirituality whereas he [David Sylvain]'s given in to it. [My albums] are about struggle in a Dostoyevskian sense. It's a real fight for me in every line. Whereas he's given in to a state of grace" (p. 201).

However difficult the struggle, the White Man finds it worth it; the reward is adulthood, and above all, Light, even if it is in the form of Ice or Glass. Even, or as Penman would have it, especially, in his MOR work: *'Til the Band Comes In* is just as obscurely *avant garde* as *Climate of Hunter*, but it is "his lightest work: light because adult, and adult because confident enough to be light" (p. 109). "Easy on the ear melodies that feel distinctly *icy*, with a weight of compacted absence, sadness, wasted time. *Flawless like cheap glassware* – pretty songs with no real prettiness. Light entertainment that *lets no light escape*" (p. 121, my emphasis).

---

[12] From the essay "Black Sheep Boy," pp. 56–57 — the title comes from a song on one of Scott's solo albums, but it's also the title of Joel Grey's solo album, who is best known for his performance in *Cabaret* with Garland's daughter, Liza.

In Cesare della Riviera's "The Magical World of the Heroes" (*Il mondo magico de gli heroi*), written in 1605 and edited by Evola in the early 20th century, there is an Italian pun that alchemists would return to over the centuries:

ANGELO = ANtico GELO, i.e. the "Angel = Ancient Ice"

Even if I haven't convinced you that Scott Walker is the ultimate White musician and worthy of your attention for that reason alone, this book will appeal to anyone with an interest in the mechanics of the post-war pop music industry or just some damned fine cultural writing. It's really quite exciting to see such implicitly White music, both *avant garde* and MOR, receiving serious critical attention. White Nationalists should be heartened by it, and should encourage this unexpected entry point into the mainstream by purchasing multiple copies for family and friends!

Counter-Currents/*North American New Right*
January 23, 2011

ANDY NOWICKI'S
THE COLUMBINE PILGRIM

Andy Nowicki
The Columbine Pilgrim
San Francisco: Counter-Currents, 2011

> "Anyway, the day I was there I saw this huge cockroach crawling across the floor. I don't think I've ever seen a bigger, more repulsive-looking bug in my life. Without even thinking, I just smooshed it with my foot, and then all of a sudden Tony got really mad at me.
>
> "I'll always remember this moment. He gasped, like he'd just witnessed an awful atrocity. Then he looked at me with an expression of . . . just stinging reproach. 'Isn't nature cruel enough already?' he practically shouted, 'without us adding to the cruelty that's already there?? What'd that roach ever do to you, anyway???'
>
> "Then he tenderly picked up the dead roach body with his bare hand. He gazed at it with forlorn pity, and I thought he was about to break down crying. It was weird as hell."
>
> —From Andy Nowicki's *The Columbine Pilgrim*

It's not surprising that Tony Meander, the insect patriot of the passage just quoted, a man for whom the word "introverted" is as sadly inadequate as the man himself, should suddenly express tender concern for a cockroach.

He is the hero, or at least the protagonist, of *The Columbine Pilgrim*, a novel by Andy Nowicki, self-described "reactionary Catholic" and author of *The Psychology of Liberalism* as well as proprietor of the Dyspeptic Myopic blog; it's also the first work of fiction published by Greg Johnson's estimable Counter-Currents Publishing house.

Tony might be said to have peaked in high school, but not in any football hero sense. He is the ultimate Loser. His torments at the hands of his teenage cohorts, excessive but emblematic for all that, have stayed with him, endlessly revisited, becoming the hard core of what passes for his identity. Eventually he finds some ways to deal with them, including Nietzschean megalomania, until he finds the inspiration he needs in the Columbine shootings. He visits the scene, like Hitler laying a wreath at Bayreuth, then returns to what passes for "home" to wreak his vengeance.

In purely literary terms, I would describe the writing as straightforward rather than flashy, in keeping with the models it appropriates — the lone gunman's journal and nonfiction crime — although the hallucination scenes, featuring taunting figures floating in the middle distance, perhaps show the influence of Philip K. Dick (*Ubik, Three Stigmata of Palmer Eldritch*). But leaving aside literary thrills, this is a book whose themes and ideas will need to be grappled with and overcome by those who think of themselves as being against society and on the Right.

Superficially, but as we shall see, only superficially, Nowicki's *Pilgrim* seems another example of the 20th century's unique contribution to art, which I have called Cockroach Literature. In this genre our "antihero," smugly superior or sympathetically put-upon, does battle with the uncomprehending and unappreciative Yahoos of his particular society.

But unlike the hero of a Grail romance, or a Raymond Chandler detective story, or even a conventional "middlebrow" novel, our boy (it's almost always a boy) has no sense of defending the Truth and the Right; in fact, he is precisely "smart enough" to know that there is no Truth, no Justice; Truth and Right are the tools of oppression, and really, "everything's phony."

Nor, like the protagonist of a German *Bildungsroman* or Scandinavian "family business saga," does he eventually learn that society, or some particular institution that holds him in its grip, has, after all, some reason, some right, of its own, and so find his place in it.

While Jim Dixon, Kingsley Amis' angry young yobbo battling *Lucky Jim*'s academic stuffed shirts, might finally earn his ironic nickname with an implausible job offer to London (a sign of Amis's latent conservatism; the true Cockroach disdains anything like a job), usually The Man triumphs through prison (Judaic Paul Newman's blond haired, blue eyed *Cool Hand Luke*) or the mental institution (*One Flew Over the Cuckoo's Nest*) or the draft board (Richard Farina's masterpiece of hipster Castroite misogyny *Been Down So Low It Looks Like Up to Me*); or else he accidentally blows himself up in a gas-filled attic, like Beckett's solipsistic proto-slacker *Murphy,* or jumps on a bus to anywhere as we fade out (*The Graduate*). Think of the contrasting worlds where first James Gould Cozzens' sympathetic study of wartime airmen dealing with boredom and duty in *Guard of Honor,* then Joseph Heller's malicious hatchet job on the same theme, *Catch-22,* could be both best-selling and showered with honors. Never heard of Cozzens? — that's my point.

The archetypal Cockroach is, of course, Gregor Samsa in Kafka's *The Metamorphosis,* and this is quite appropriate, since the Cockroach and his literature is both the product, and the instrument, of the Judaic strategy of demoralizing *goyische* society by "uncovering" the "truth" behind its ideals.

But as I said, the resemblance is only superficial; neither Nowicki nor his protagonist is a Cockroach. However, before Gregor Samsa awoke from his uneasy dreams, there was Dostoyevsky's Underground Man.

Again superficially, our Pilgrim's tale does resemble *Notes from the Underground* at least in structure. Part One of the latter gives us the voice of the Underground Man, narrating his current feelings and the events of the recent past. Part Two, though still his narration, allows us to see the Underground Man in action, his "rescue" of a prostitute, with whom he can think of nothing to do but ruin her life anyway.

Likewise, Nowicki's Prologue gives us the voice of the Pilgrim himself, traveling, making his titular Pilgrimage to the very site of the Columbine shootings, compulsively thinking and reminiscing, ultimately unto the point of hallucinatory madness in a Hunter Thompson-style hotel freak-out. This is followed by Chapter One (the only chapter, oddly, although I think we will eventually see the reason here) which abandons first person narration and gives us a presumably objective account of his re-engagement with "objective" reality, if revisiting your Columbine-worthy high school tormentors via a convenient reunion can be called "reality"; desperate, murderous actions, narrated as if in a "true crime" account.

While Dostoyevsky may have created the template for the Cockroaches to come, his work, like Nowicki's, is decidedly different. They are not examples of Cockroach Literature but desperate attempts to understand and overcome it. Dostoyevsky, and his U-Man, know that he is a cockroach, suffer from such knowledge, and most importantly, will know the reason why.

Notes is conceived at a frontal attack on rationalism, secularism, progressivism, and their smug public face, Optimism.

Nowicki is not as straightforward in laying out the grounds of Meander's grudge against the world. His high school humiliations, though rendered in toe-curlingly abject detail, seem almost programmatically complete, running the whole gamut from pants-pissing to "faggot" cat-calling to cheerleader emasculation, and involve most races and both sexes.

Yet even so, they are more common than not, and hardly any real world victims return 15 years later to execute their tormentors (who, also programmatically, are all present and literally accounted for in the handy sign-in book).

This should tell us that Nowicki has more on his mind than critiquing high school fascism and contemporary educational theory, and the clue is Meander's turn to philosophy in college, and to Nietzsche in particular. Tony Meander, like Hesse's Harry Haller (*The Steppenwolf* being another work, in the shadow of Dostoyevsky, but saved from Cockroachhood not by Russian Orthodoxy but by the informing presence of Nietzsche), is one of those who are not just born out of time, but fated to suffer their time more than the others around them, right to the dregs.

What makes them suffer is what Nietzsche called nihilism, the loss of man's center consequent on the loss of God and the "higher world" in exchange for, as the New Testament would say, "the whole [finite] world." Titus Burckhardt has succinctly described the origin and stages of the crisis:

> The image of man . . . is succeeded by the image of autonomous man, of man glorifying himself. . . . This illusory autonomy implied from the first the 'loss of the center,' for man is no longer truly man when he no longer has his center in God; thereafter *the image of man decomposes*; first it is

replaced, as regards dignity, by other aspects of nature, and then it is *progressively destroyed; its systematic negation and disfigurement is the goal of modern art. . . .*

As soon as man's center, the contemplative intellect or the heart, is abandoned or obscured, his other faculties are divided among themselves . . . thus, Renaissance art is *rationalistic . . .* and *also passional, its passion having a global character:* the affirmation of the ego in general, a *thirst for what is big and without limit.*

Thrown back on himself, the artist sought new sources of inspiration . . . he released a new force, independent of the world of experience, *uncontrollable by ordinary reason, and contagiously suggestive.*[1]

Nietzsche taught the self-overcoming Overman as the alternative to his version of the Cockroach, the Last Man. Nowicki's Pilgrim passes through the stages Burckhardt descried, first the rationalism of philosophy, then the affirmation of the Ego without limit ("Du bist Gott," his God-hallucination helpfully informs him) and then violence, uncontrollable and contagious.

"He was conscious of himself changing, of becoming a self-made creation, his own God," claims one student. . . . "Tony would say he was God some days, then would laugh it off, like he wasn't sure how seriously to take himself. But I could tell that these were ideas that he was scrutinizing very closely. I had a feeling that he was at the point of making a major decision."

Still looking through Dostoyevsky's prism, we can usefully contrast his Underground Man with Nowicki's Pilgrim. The Underground Man's revolt is brief, futile, and rather than rescuing a fellow human being he even makes the prostitute's life worse; ultimately it's all tears and delusions. Our Pilgrim is better organized, perhaps due to the guidance provided by the Colum-

---

[1] *The Essential Titus Burckhardt: Reflections on Sacred Art, Faiths, and Civilizations* (Bloomington, Indiana: World Wisdom Books, 2003), pp. 141, 197.

bine *Alte Kämpfer*. He gets to line up his old enemies, humiliate, and destroy them, while also getting, though grotesquely, the cheerleader. Even that remaining high school fear, teenage pregnancy, metamorphoses into a posthumous triumph:

> All of them have confirmed that Patricia is far from traumatized, but instead is "nearly euphoric" over the news.
>
> "She can't wait to be a mom," said one friend.
>
> "Patty never wanted a kid before," commented another. "She thought it would be a drag, and that it would make her look fat. But now she's incredibly excited. It's the weirdest thing I've seen in my life!"

What explains such relative success? Perhaps, our Pilgrim has chosen better myths.

One clue may lie here:

> Certain witnesses report that he appeared to be laughing to himself at some unknown joke, and one even claimed to hear the exact words he muttered to himself: "Huh! Eleven. One for each disciple. Every apostle a martyr. But not anymore. No bullet for Judas. Huh!"

Indeed, there's a lot of laughter for a book of this sort, about 30 occurrences in a little over 100 pages. "Indeed, he now laughed, easily, as a man sitting on the couch watching his favorite sitcom drinking a beer after a hard day might laugh. He was having a grand old time."

Who is it that laughs easily, having a grand old time, at a massacre, especially a massacre of saints and apostles, even if he's doing the shooting? One answer comes to mind: The Joker. Indeed, the idea of crashing a party, lining everyone up, humiliating, killing and (at least by implication) raping the cute ones, while cracking oneself up with bad puns and insults, is a pretty clear Joker trope.

As Trevor Lynch has insightfully noted in his review of *The Dark Knight*, the Joker weaponizes the ideas of Tradition, using "irrational contingency" to shatter the chains and illusions of planning and Progress.[2] By contrast, Dostoyevsky's Christianity, the ultimate root of the idea of Progress and God's Plan, renders the Underground Man's revolt futile.

And like the Joker, the Pilgrim is not afraid of death.[3]

Still, the Joker analogy fails, or rather, Tony is not able to live up to it. He is too much the man of *ressentiment*, in Nietzsche's terms, too fixated on his past humiliations, too self-pitying. It's the Cockroach again. The film Joker mocks this tired old trope with his ever-ready, ever-changing accounts of his "origins." The Joker has transcended any concern for his "past" while Tony is still living in his high school locker.

Tony's *ressentiment* makes him a sucker for Christianity and its myths of transcendence, the "long suffering" Jehovah, or his vengeful Son. Always the fixation on origins and debts to be repaid (while the Joker just burns his stack of money).

Unable to transcend himself, Tony must die, but his death does not result in the Christian fulfillment he may have expected.

Just as we can re-purpose his life of *ressentiment* for ourselves, making it a test case of how not to overcome, we can also form our own understanding of his death. Like many modern men, he has been mistaken about his myth. He is not fated to be some sacrificial Jesus, as he thought, but rather to be Sigmund, and his own son ("'It's *definitely* a boy' . . .") conceived in violence and betrayal, will avenge his dead father and bring down the (false) gods.[4]

---

[2] Trevor Lynch, *Trevor Lynch's White Nationalist Guide to the Movies*, ed. Greg Johnson, Foreword by Kevin MacDonald (San Francisco: Counter-Currents, 2012).

[3] There may also be an echo here of what Baron Evola writes in his book, *Saggi sull'Idealismo Magico* ("Essays on Magical Idealism"), published in 1925. As paraphrased at the Gornahoor.net site: In this trial, he must destroy every such mental and emotional support. He must "deny every faith, violate every moral land social law, scorn every sentiment of humanity, every love and generosity, every passion, affirm an implacable and all-pervasive skepticism, reaching finally a conscious and critical madness."

[4] One might also find a hint of make your own Hitler plan in *The Boys from Brazil* as well. As an intermediate form, we might consid-

And now we know why there is only one chapter here . . . the rest is to come. As Burckhardt says, the violence unleashed is *contagiously suggestive*.

But we will not have long to wait. Having moved from the inadequate Christian mythology of the One Lord, our Siegfried, like the original mythological hero, is born and reborn every day, everywhere. We will hear from more "Me-anders," everywhere, and soon . . .

Earlier, I called the writing merely straightforward. But then we don't go to writers like Dostoyevsky for modernist verbal fireworks. To an aesthete like Nabokov, "Dostoevsky's . . . monotonous dealings with persons suffering with pre-Freudian complexes, the way he has of wallowing in the tragic misadventures of human dignity — all this is difficult to admire."[5]

But real people like us turn to literature for some insight into our lives, and maybe some guidance. Can we admire such a madman as Tony Meander? Surely not; yet as Lynch has also observed, such criminals, lunatics, and monsters are the only channels that Tradition has to express its ideas within what Dick called the Black Iron Prison of liberal cultural hegemony.

There are many like the Pilgrim in or attracted to the "Rightist" milieu, and Nowicki gives us some insight into where they come from, what makes them failures to be avoided at all costs, and how we can learn not to become them ourselves. It makes a fine addition to that small, wholly admirable genre: the literature of the Outsiders.

Counter-Currents/*North American New Right*
March 23, 2011

---

er *Taxi Driver*, the creation of Paul Schrader and Martin Scorsese, whose backgrounds — strong, religious communities — have provided relative immunity to the Cockroach. De Niro's Travis Bickel refuses to join the cockroaches in the streets, and successfully, though murderously, rescues the child prostitute; he even, ironically, fails at suicide and becomes an urban hero.

[5] Vladimir Nabokov, *Lectures on Russian Literature*, ed. Fredson Bowers (Orlando, Fl.: Harcourt, 1981), p. 104.

The Huxley of the Alternative Right

Andy Nowicki
The Doctor and the Heretic and Other Stories
Rockford, Ill.: Black Oak Media, 2011.

"'If this is grace,' he muttered through clenched teeth, 'then why does it feel like Hell?'"

> —"Tears of the Damned: A Counterfactual Tale"

"Turning a page in Huxley you say, 'There but for the grace of God …' — and suddenly you wonder whether Divine Grace has intervened in time."

> —Charles J. Rolo, *The World of Aldous Huxley*, "Introduction"

No sooner has the world had the chance to digest *The Columbine Pilgrim* (fat chance, that) than Andy Nowicki, like a demented TV cooking contestant, pops up with this poisonous little *amuse-bouche*.

The reader coming from the *Pilgrim* and wanting more of the same might be well advised to turn to the middle of the book and the second tale, "Tears of the Damned: A Counterfactual Tale." With a protagonist who boldly announces himself as "Dylan Klebold," we are now in sci-fi-fantasy territory, where Nowicki addresses his Columbine demons with an intriguing premise: an alternative timeline in which the two teens become not mass murderers but solid, even heroic, citizens, their crimes appearing only in obsessive dreams. Or are these dreams? They seem much more real than their "real" lives. In a twist worthy of the old *Twilight Zone*, it seems that crime can be sidestepped, but not guilt and punishment—an interesting explanation for our general despair.

Speaking of crime and punishment, the next tale returns to what I identified in my review of *Columbine* as cockroach territory. "Autobiography of a Violent Soul" gives us a vivid specimen, motionless on his filthy mattress; one who has reacted to the vicissitudes of life by seemingly taking Noël Coward's advice to "rise above it" but actually storing up a detailed inventory of grudges so extensive that only God could take the blame.

He's the sort of life of the party who, when the first girl he has the courage to call hangs up on him, launches into a meditation on "the Fall":

> Summer was over. Summer is always over before you know it, slain by the ubiquitous, unstoppable tyrant known as autumn, that ruthless season of death, always on the march, which captures and devours its prey in one murderous lunge. The air turns chill, the leaves shrivel and die, and their corpses fall from their branches and litter the ground Summer is the illusion—fall the reality. Life is the ephemera, death the essence.

The Fall, get it, *hypocrite lecteur*?

Indeed, when it comes to erudite whining he gives Beckett's equally mattress-bound schizophrenic Malone a run for his money:

> Through existing, I've gotten attached to existence. Bit by bit, I've been initiated into one after another successive degradations of being, and following each degradation, my soul has been further debased, reduced, polluted, and corrupted. After first suffering the misfortune of conception, I was born and proceeded through a mostly happy childhood. . . . I have complaints about my parents, of course. Who doesn't? I'm sure they had complaints about me too. But they loved me, fed me, sheltered me, clothed me, and kept me safe from harm, and I was happy.
>
> I don't blame them for what has become of me, far from

perfection as they might have been. I don't blame my mother and father, who in a sense were my "makers," but only biologically speaking. Rather, I blame my Maker; I blame the One who created me from scratch, *ex nihilo*, the one who gave me flesh and bone, and put me here to suffer, bleed, and die. It's He I indict. I am alone to blame for my mistakes, but He alone is to blame for the mistake of forcing my life upon me, of making me who I am and causing me to be who I have become.

Yes, I blame God!

And Malone:

I shall be neutral and inert. No difficulty there. Throes are the only trouble, I must be on my guard against throes. But I am less given to them now, since coming here. Of course I still have my little fits of impatience, from time to time, I must be on my guard against them, for the next fortnight or three weeks. Without exaggeration to be sure, quietly crying and laughing, without working myself up into a state. Yes, I shall be natural at last, I shall suffer more, then less, without drawing any conclusions, I shall pay less heed to myself, I shall be neither hot nor cold any more, I shall be tepid, I shall die tepid, without enthusiasm. I shall not watch myself die, that would spoil everything. Have I watched myself live?

Let me say before I go any further that I forgive nobody. I wish them all an atrocious life and then the fires and ice of hell and in the execrable generations to come an honored name. (p. 165)

Perhaps Beckett's decrepit protagonist has lived long enough with his ramblings to become more succinct, but the same spirit, composed of squalor and Gnosticism, is there, as well as in his final act of supposedly "poetic" violence—or would be, if only he could find a reason to get up off the mattress.

And speaking of getting off—sorry, too long an acquaintance with the cockroach does tend to coarsen one's sensibilities—the title story of this collection represents a change in polarity, taking us into the inner life of Dr. Carol Golden, an attractive, professionally successful but sexually unfulfilled widow, right down to her various fantasies, fleshly folds, and fluids.

The fluids are inspired by a *Penthouse*-style letter from an anonymous patient, demanding that she

> Wear a skirt, my love. Wear it, if you wish, during our session, but more importantly, wear it in your life! Let the spirit of life rush between your legs and buoy you up in grand ecstasy — be free from grief and pain.

She quickly identifies this as the work of Fenton Balonsky who, in the midst of 21st century America, is still Slavic enough to have seen, and even dwelt briefly, in Hell, and can smell "degeneracy and despair" even in his colleagues at the seminary he thought would provide refuge. He uses the Church to "ride the tiger" (Evola's phrase is quoted) until blossoming (like a man-eating plant) into another Ramen-eating, manifesto-writing Gnostic with an urge to tell all to a psychiatrist before killing himself.

This being Nowicki-land, one dreads their inevitable encounter, expecting either a humiliating mistake to be brooded on for years or an axe-murder, but doctor and heretic find they have more in common than they, or the reader, may have suspected, and Nowicki manages to contrive an ending that, for him, is almost worthy of a Hollywood rom-com, but without entirely betraying his dour *Weltanschauung*. Bravo!

Nowicki is seems to be shaping up as the Alternative Right's Aldous Huxley, who also blended an obsessive focus on the physical grotesquerie of ordinary existence (although even Nowicki has yet to top Huxley's lovers inundated with the exploded guts of a dog dropped from an airplane) with deep — or lofty, if you prefer — spiritual intimations, in the hope that by intensifying the one the other may be conjured into appearance.

Counter-Currents/*North American New Right*
January 23, 2011

Bright Lights, Big Nothing

Andy Nowicki
Under the Nihil
San Francisco: Counter-Currents, 2011

Like a hellhound on the heels of his last book, *The Doctor and the Heretic*, comes snarling in Andy Nowicki's *Under the Nihil* (pronounced, as the characters do, as "Nile," as in Land of the Dead).

Here we have another one of Nowicki's "cockroach" heroes—perhaps he really should get out more—but with a bit more gumption than usual, having early found the Church (or "run to it" as his brutish father sneers) and persevered through schoolmate taunts ("Bead boy! Peed Boy!"). You might think he's related to the titular heretic of his previous collection until he is undone by the Mother Church itself; its once hippy-dippy post-Vatican II superiors no longer interested in Kumbaya but desperate now to keep out the weirdos like . . . him.

Frederick Rolfe, another "spoiled priest" convinced of his vocation, took a thirty year vow of celibacy, sponged off a series of friends in lieu of secular employment, wrote a sequence of exquisitely unpublishable novels ("Caviar, but from a real fish," D. H. Lawrence called them) and then, his vow expired, perished in Venice during spell of "furious pederasty" (according to my old Penguin edition). Our unnamed narrator moves into a crack neighborhood rather than a working class rooming house, writes a blog rather than novels ("which shows you just how far away I truly was from salvation"), but the main difference is that he finds what Rolfe always wanted: a benefactor with a big checkbook. This "Mister X," who represents "a privately-run organization which sometimes consulted for the interests of American security," provides a weekly stipend in return for participation in the trial of a secret, experimental drug: Nihil.

But at this point I'd like to step back and take a look at the book's unusual narrative form.

The first thing you notice is that it's written in the second person. There must be something hard or unsatisfactory about such convention, since the number of second person narratives you can think of, to say nothing of whether you've read them, or if they're any good, can be counted on the fingers of, well, slightly less than one hand.

There's Faulkner's 1934 *Absalom! Absalom!* which, as you can tell from the title, no one reads. Then there's Edna O'Brien's 1970 novel *A Pagan Place,* but more recently, and more relevantly, Jay McInerney's *Bright Lights, Big City* (1984) – and that's the one you've probably read.

Asked by the *Paris Review* about her unusual choice, O'Brien said:

> The reason was psychological. As a child you are both your secret self and the "you" that your parents think you are. So the use of the second person was a way of combining the two identities. But I tend not to examine these things too closely – they just happen. (Edna O'Brien, interviewed by Shusha Guppy)

McInerney's use has a different psychological effect. Consider his novel's opening: "You are not the kind of guy who would be at a place like this at this time of the morning. But here you are, and you cannot say that the terrain is entirely unfamiliar, although the details are fuzzy."

The effect here is to implicate the reader – or rather listeners, given the conversational style – in the narrator's point of view. "You" means "If you were me right now at this here bar."

Nowicki's "you" however is not the reader but our "Mister X," who lassos the protagonist into a deranged "fight terrorism through drugs" scheme that seems all too plausible given the history of the half-assed "bright ideas" produced by the decayed Ivy Leaguers that make up our "intelligence community." (See Tim Weiner's excoriating history *Legacy of Ashes.*)

And like so many of our "best and brightest," his "Big Man on Campus bearing, incongruously clashing with the foot-shuffling false modesty" reaches the peak of annoyance with a Boston accent.

It's a small detail, that Nowicki goes on to milk for a few

laughs, but it does set up a series of reverberations in this reader's pop sensibilities, sort of like a round of "Kevin Bacon" (who appeared in *JFK*, which connects him to . . . you'll see).

Once the detail emerged, I began to hear Mr. X's interview, and his subsequent ones, in the tones of Martin Sheen's character in *The Departed*. Like the young men Sheen interviews there, Nowick's hero is playing a double game, going along with Mr. X in order to "punk the punkers." He thinks he's smarter than this James Bond wannabe played by Thurston Howell III, and, like most of the CIA's foreign "assets," he probably is.

The younger Sheen starred in *Apocalypse Now*, a fitting title for most of Nowiki's work, where he is pulled from a drunken, self-destructive delirium in a disheveled Saigon hotel room – comparable to Nowicki's "dump of an apartment, in the middle of a massive colony of roaches, rats, meth-labs, and gang-bangers [where] I set up shop, and began my downwardly-mobile descent . . ." – to be interviewed by another unctuous CIA type (who delivers the famous "Terminate . . . with extreme prejudice" line) before receiving his own secret assignment that, like this one, will also be subverted by an encounter with moral nothingness and end in a blaze of napalm:

The chaos! "The horror, the horror." The same conflagration of faith-eroding poison that had washed through society in the latter half of the 20th century, throwing all of our lives into the wretched mire of purposelessness, making us absurd, faceless, soulless mannequins tumbling through a terrifying abyss . . . this same poison now pumped through my veins, eating me away from the inside." (p. 12)

The "faceless, soulless mannequins" are the interchangeably baby-faced young actors in *The Departed*, instructed by older men like Sheen and Jack Nicholson that: "Frank Costello [Nicholson]: I was your age they would say we can become cops, or criminals. Today, what I'm saying to you is this: when you're facing a loaded gun, what's the difference?"

Or as Nowicki says: "One can fall both ways – gravity often reverses from generation to generation." (p. 15)

Billy Costigan [Di Caprio]: Families are always rising or falling in America, am I right?]

Oliver Queenan [Sheen]: Who said that?

Billy Costigan: Hawthorne.

Dignam [Mark Wahlberg]: What's the matter, smartass, you don't know any fuckin' Shakespeare?

Cop, or criminal? Nowicki's narrator chooses a third, more traditional path:

> I decide I'm going to be a priest! The lovely sense of calm that accompanies this thought. I have a CALLING, instead of just a FALLING. . . . Now that I've declared my calling, in fact, I feel more lonely, more isolated, more doubtfully dubious than I'd ever felt previously . . . (p. 15)

The interview between Sheen and Di Caprio essentially conflates the two sequences in *Under the Nihil*, Sheen tells him he'll "never be a cop" but offers him the chance to "serve and protect" in the role of a rat; Nowicki's hero is told he'll never be a priest: "'Not "no," but "not yet,"' he said. Oh, but he was wrong! It *was* no; the profoundest of nos, to every possible question!" (pp. 2–3).
But he can help win the "War on Terrah" by becoming a lab rat.

> I COULD'VE been a priest, and been happy. I COULD'VE said the Mass reverently, could have composed and delivered worthwhile sermons, could have lived simply, could have counseled people who were in pain or faced difficult straits. Yet they drummed me out. I didn't make the cut; I was deemed defective. (pp. 24–5)

And we know from Oliver Stone's *JFK* what happens when spoiled priests meet up with CIA agents and start living in filthy apartments filled with lab rats:

David Ferrie: All I wanted in the world . . . was to be a Catholic priest. Live in a monastery. Pray. Serve God. I had . . . one terrible fucking weakness. And they defrocked me! Then I started to lose everything.

But what if your vocation really is something else? Perhaps he really does need to become a criminal after all. Maybe this is a blessing in disguise:

They wanted me to snort and snivel and jump through their hoops, to prove myself worthy of their post-Vatican II norms, and I failed their examination, so it was off to the scrap heap for me . . . (p. 25)

Frank Costello: Church wants you on your place. Kneel, stand, kneel, stand. If you go for that sort of thing, I don't know what to do for you. A man makes his own way. No one gives it to you. You have to take it. "Non serviam."

Maybe, like Sheen in *Apocalypse Now*, you need not a career but one more mission. And if you're bad enough, maybe you'll get it.

Yes, I was "saved," but not really. I came "back," but only partly. I hadn't hit bottom, because in spite of everything I *still* found myself hoping against hope for hope. Still a poseur: not a hardcore bone in my brittle frame, my spirit still pitifully seeking its Savior, aching to fill its God-shaped hole with something, anything, unable to reconcile my God-hole to the Void that is, in fact, the very essence of God . . .

The fools who treated me, of course, mistook my relapse for a recovery. It's the typical response of the world to one who almost escapes its clutches, only to be pulled right back into its infernal orbit, as I was. (p. 29)

Under the Nihil is relatively short book, and you can sense that perhaps the middle section, devoted to the narrator's one Nihil-powered adventure, the seduction and humiliation of an older woman and her younger daughter, is only a sample of what could have been, like a Grail romance, or a picaresque novel, or most closely one of those overlong "great books" of the 50s, an *Augie March* or *Sot-Weed Factor* or *Recognitions*, an indefinitely multiplied, ramshackle series of grotesque, literally nihilistic "anti-adventures" in which the stupid, unhip world is one-upped by the anti-hero. Perhaps Nowicki thought one would be enough to make the point, and decided to spare his reader such a numbing and depressing trudge. (Even when Terry Southern did something similar in *The Magic Christian* or *Candy*, he kept it short and did it with humor, albeit of the then-fashionable "black" sort, and it still left a bad taste in the mouth.)

Having acquired a certain notoriety by describing Nowicki, in reviewing his last book, as "the Aldous Huxley of the Alternative Right," I may dare to go further by suggesting that this is his *Brave New World*, with our narrator as The Savage, whose confrontation with a world run by pharmaceutical manipulation—Soma rather than Nihil—ends in an equally futile public suicide. His final rant could have come equally well from The Savage's interview with the World Controller:

> Freedom, you say? Freedom from *what*? Freedom to do . . . *what*?
>
> Freedom to drop their venerable old traditions, which gave their lives a sense of meaning and their deaths a sense of closure? Freedom to jettison their connection with the ancient, and embrace un-shackled materialism? Freedom to degrade themselves, debase themselves, corrupt themselves, turn themselves into animals, into something *worse* than animals? Freedom to elevate their loins over their brains; to make sure their sons become pimps and your daughters whores; to condemn their progeny to Hell forever? (p. 100)

While The Savage has to stage his suicide at a mere lighthouse, Nowicki's narrator has the Statute of Liberty to play with. Still, I find the final scenario—

I hope to light a fire in the big, stony Whore's head, a blaze that will light up the sky over Manhattan Island. I hope to turn many a head, provoke the posting of many a YouTube video, inspire a headline or two. (p. 101)

—a bit of a letdown, in comparison with passage at the beginning:

I have always been falling, falling, falling, but only lately have I had the opportunity to reject and utterly *erase* all of the faux-scenery in my sight that ever led me to assume the existence of a ground under my feet. I am now a burning, falling man, hurtling through a heartless void, but falling is no different from flying when there's nothing substantial beneath you. To be aware that one is sinking forever may be a disconcerting feeling at first, but it soon becomes a pleasant, even a blissful condition. To float into eternal nothingness is to be truly free. (p. 9)

It's a really remarkable image, recalling, perhaps, one more cinematic analogue: the bravura opening of Scorsese's *Casino* (and recently reprised by the opening of *Mad Men*): Robert De Niro as Ace Rothstein, falling endlessly through a blaze of light composed of the flames of a car bomb, Las Vegas neon and Hellfire.

Nowicki's "hero" presumably dies, but the world goes on without him (quick, name one of the 9/11 terrorists) while Rothstein improbably survives—his kind always land on their feet— but it is a living death; everything he loves, from his wife to Vegas itself, having died already.

For Nowicki, as for the producers of *Mad Men*, this is probably the best we can hope for. At this stage of the Kali Yuga there aren't even any tigers to ride; perhaps we can convince ourselves that our falling is really flying after all.

Counter-Currents/*North American New Right*
January 23, 2011

INDEX

ABOUT THE AUTHOR

James J. O'Meara was born in Detroit, educated in Canada, and now lives in an abandoned glove factory in America's Rust Belt. From atop this crumbling remnant of America's industrial might, he broods with morose delectation over the inevitable reappearance of the hordes of White youth known to history as the *Männerbünde*, or Wild Boys. His periodic bulletins on their activities appear on his blog, Where the Wild Boys Are at http://jamesjomeara.blogspot.com/. He is the author of *The Homo and the Negro: Masculinist Meditations on Politics and Popular Culture*, ed. Greg Johnson (San Francisco: Counter-Currents, 2012) and *A Review of James Neill's "The Origins and Role of Same-Sex Relations in Human Societies"* (Amazon.com: Kindle Editions, 2013). His articles and review have also been published by Counter-Currents/*North American New Right*, *Alexandria*, *FringeWare Review*, *Aristokratia*, and *Judaic Book News*.